The Gospel in
Galatians

Living like God is for sale?

Contributors

Carlos Astorga, Th.M.
Rhome van Dyck, Th.M.
S. Jonathan Murphy, Ph.D.
Vanessa van Dyck, M.Ed., M.A.[BS]

field Notes

a journal of exploration and discovery

SacraScript

The Gospel in Galatians:
Living like God is for sale?

Field Notes
Copyright © 2012 Sacra Script Ministries

Published by:
Sacra Script Ministries
2001 West Plano Parkway, Suite 1010, Plano, TX 75075
www.SacraScript.org

Printed in the United States of America

0612.1

For comments, corrections or suggestions, email us at
comments@SacraScript.org

Find us on Facebook at www.facebook.com/SacraScriptMinistries
or Twitter at www.twitter.com/sacrascript

The Purpose of Sacra Script

In the book of Acts chapter 8, Philip was prompted by the Holy Spirit to catch up with an Ethiopian eunuch reading from Isaiah 53 in his chariot. Philip asked the eunuch if he understood what he was reading. The eunuch replied, "How could I unless someone explains it to me?" The experience of the eunuch is common to most people. Just like Philip, Sacra Script's goal is to explain Scripture in light of the Lord Jesus Christ.

The Sacra Script creative team includes gifted pastor-teachers and biblical educators. We seek to explain the Bible within the context in which it was written and help you learn the necessary skills for application. We have also designed exercises and study questions to help you remember and respond to what you have learned so that your Bible study does not end at information but transformation. We have carefully included many different tools to help you understand God's Word. These *Field Notes* include detailed written explanations, outlines, word studies, pictures, notes, illustrations, maps, and timelines in order to capture the meaning of the text in its ancient context. As a result, this book is part guide, part atlas, part Bible dictionary, part history, and part student workbook.

Whether you have never opened the Bible or are seasoned in the faith, these *Field Notes* provide integrated learning of the Bible. Our resources also include an *Expedition Guide* for pastors, teachers, and facilitators which utilize additional notes, references, and teaching aids. Video and audio versions designed to better engage visual and auditory learners are also available. Lastly, a digital version guides the student through the biblical text online or through a variety of media technologies.

At Sacra Script our prayer is that through the study of God's Word and the aid of the Holy Spirit you would come to comprehend and apply the Bible. God gave us his word so that we can understand his will. He wants us to be informed about, and involved in, his plan for the ages. This plan for the ages is a gospel plan; it is good news. The gospel is that eternal life with God is made available by God. It is offered only through the Son of God, Jesus Christ, whose death and resurrection alone satisfies God's wrath toward sin. You can receive God's forgiveness and be assured of eternal life by trusting in Jesus Christ. This is good news. This is the gospel, and all of Scripture points to it.

for more information visit
www.SacraScript.org

This book is a testimony to God's faithfulness
working through his people. Without our team
of supporters giving to the work of the Lord,
this book would not have been written.
May God use these words to build and edify his Church
for the glory of our LORD and Savior Jesus Christ.

Table of Contents

I. How does this book work?

II. Survey the Land

III. Excavate the Site

IV. Analyze the Find

V. Toolbox

How does this book work?

Field Notes

Keys to your Field Notes

Welcome to your *Field Notes* on Galatians. You are about to embark on a journey of discovery. Your destination is first century A.D. Christianity in the regions of Galatia. In order to be ready for your exploration of this book, we highly recommend you spend a few minutes understanding the way your *Field Notes* work. This book serves as a guide to the ancient biblical text as well as a journal for your discoveries along the way. Let's get started.

Studying the Bible

Studying the Bible is much like heading off into an unknown land to dig around the ruins of an ancient civilization. You need to know where to dig, what you are discovering, and what is important about what you find. This book will guide you on a journey of ancient discovery: the discovery of the meaning of the biblical text.

This Bible study follows the metaphor of an expedition, or a quest for biblical and theological discovery. Your *Field Notes* contain three specific parts which correspond to the three steps used in an ancient dig. Each step will help you in the process of understanding and applying God's Word to your soul. Each *Field Study* begins with learning the content and meaning of the text, followed by a section called *Discoveries,* which includes discussion questions, exercises, and activities to apply the text to your life. Let's begin by understanding the three steps.

Step one: Survey the land

The first step to making a discovery is a comprehensive survey of the land, noting everything that is around. In your *Field Notes*, the site is the biblical book we will study. This inspection helps us to better understand the characteristics of the terrain. With regard to the Bible, our survey helps us see the function of a book as part of the grand

A Field Study

Your *Field Notes* are divided into individual field studies. Each *Field Study* is designed to take a minimum of 30 minutes. The content of the *Field Study* takes at least 15 minutes, and the remainder is for *Discoveries* including discussion questions, exercises, and activities. Every *Field Study* contains over an hour's worth of questions and activities. They are designed for you to pick and choose the ones that are most helpful for you or your group.

story of Scripture. We see all the general aspects that provide us the information we need to appreciate the significance of the text once we start our excavation.

Our survey requires the right tools: a compass to know in what direction we are going and a map to understand the lay of the land. Our biblical survey will explore issues related to the historical background of the book, date of composition, author, and intended audience. We will also learn the significance of the book in the Bible, its literary style, and the necessary information for a detailed understanding. Essentially, we will learn all we can to understand what the original audience already knew when they received the writing. This way, as we read the biblical text, we will be closer to thinking the same thoughts as the original audience, and therefore have the same understanding they did. This guides us in correct interpretation.

Step two: Excavate the site

Once we have surveyed the general details of our site, that is, of the book of the Bible we are studying, we proceed with a series of excavations of the land. This will mean hard work with the pick and shovel and sometimes delicate work with a brush or cloth. We will divide the book into units of thought generally composed of a few verses and in some cases, a few paragraphs that make up a single *Field Study*. We will dig into the details of the biblical text in order to unearth its treasures.

We will use specific tools to discover the truth and significance of each passage. In most cases, the following elements will be the tools of our trade:

- **A structural analysis chart of the text.** This tool will help us ask and answer the question, *how is the text arranged?* We will focus on how the author structured the biblical text under the inspiration of the Holy Spirit. The arrangement of the unit we are studying is fundamental to discover the author's thought and purpose. It will help us to discern patterns, contrasts, emphases, progressions, conflicts, and arguments.

- **An explanation of what the passage says.** Here we will ask several different questions pertaining to our particular text. We will begin by asking, *what are the key terms?* We will examine key terms and phrases, identifying those elements in the passage which contribute most significantly to its meaning and message. We will then consider the question, *what is the explanation?*

Discoveries

Each *Field Study* ends with several pages of *Discoveries*. These are questions and exercises to help you remember and apply what you have learned from the biblical text. *Discoveries* have been designed to meet all learning styles. We learn by seeing, by hearing, and by doing. There are questions to discuss, exercises to write down, correlation between various biblical texts to make, and activities to do. They are provided to create the most effective learning experience for you.

Within this section, we may ask a question like, *what about the culture?* where we will consider cultural issues that enlighten us on the original audience of the text. If necessary we will ask, *what about the geography?* or *what about the history?* The Christian faith is a historical faith and therefore bound to time and space. Images, ideas, and cultural practices are all bound to a geo-location which reveal to us the richness of the treasure that lies beneath the dirt.

- **A historical contextual summary of the significance of the text.** After using all of these tools, we are finally ready to take the treasures we discovered and summarize them. In this section, we answer the question, *what is God saying?* Our response will present a brief summary of our findings and conclusions. Many times, this section will also provide us with other biblical examples that further help our understanding and reinforce the lessons we have learned.

- **A summary of the practical implications of the discoveries of our excavation.** We finish every excavation answering the question, *what does God want?* The purpose of these *Field Notes* is to encourage explorers to grow in their faith and live by it. Such faith is not alive unless the treasures we excavate become realities in our daily lives. We will provide for you some of the major principles discovered, along with particular suggestions for practical application. These suggestions are aids which will help you explore additional implications that may apply more significantly to your particular life story.

Step three: Analyze the find

Once you have completed digging through the biblical text, it is time to put down your tools and analyze what you have found. The Bible is God's revelation to humanity and is one grand story of his love for us. It is important that we analyze each book of the Bible in light of the rest of Scripture. Here is what you need to consider:

- **The place of this book within the biblical story.** Here we answer the question, *what does this book of the Bible contribute to the entire story of Scripture?* God wants us to learn about his nature and his character, and each book of the Bible contributes to this understanding. This is why all of God's Word is valuable. It reveals the gracious nature of him who pursues us.

This is the sidebar containing optional information to compliment and explain content from the main section.

This is the title bar showing the title, key theme, and the *Field Study* number.

The biblical text is always shown on an ancient scroll.

Timeline showing key events.

Note the use of pictures, maps, illustrations, and tables.

This is the main section of the page and contains all of the essential information.

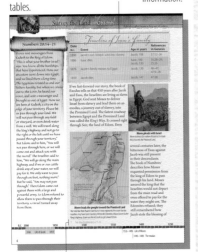

Footnotes are always used for biblical references.

- **The culmination of the story.** Finally, we answer the question, *how does the story end?* This helps us to understand each book of the Bible in light of the grand narrative.

- **The relationship of this book to Christ.** The pinnacle of God's Word is the coming of his Son Jesus, who saves people from their sin. This is the gospel, the good news of Scripture. Our question here is, *how does this book point to Christ?*

Understanding the design

Our *Field Notes* have been purposefully designed to enable you the explorer, to learn and apply more effectively the lessons of each passage you excavate. We strongly encourage you to invest some time in understanding the functionality of the design. This will greatly help your study and will make it more rewarding and enjoyable.

When using these *Field Notes*, please keep in mind the following principles:

- The notes are designed to provide as much relevant information as possible in an efficient way. You may not be able to study everything in one sitting, but you can know there is a wealth of information available for you in a single place. Come back to the study as often as you like and learn something new.

- Feel free to focus your attention in any of the different sections of the page and/or the sections of *Field Notes* as a whole. Everyone learns differently. Learn and apply that which best suits your learning style and your particular needs and interests, but challenge yourself to try something new.

- The main column of each page provides you with the essential content of the lesson. If you have limited time, we encourage you to focus your attention there. The items in the side margins are complementary to the main text and can be skipped if the material is already known.

- Blank spaces are provided in the margins. Use them to record your thoughts, observations, and questions. Make your own notes from the field.

The art of active learning

There are several things that you can do to help yourself learn new material. This is especially true with the Bible, so we have outlined five basic steps to help you engage in the learning process.

1. **Come prepared.** Begin by asking God for wisdom, humility, and dependence on the Holy Spirit to guide you into all truth. Pray, "*Open my eyes that I might see the wonderful things in your law*" from Psalm 119:18. Read with a pen or pencil in hand for marking the text or taking notes. Read aloud at times. This will help you engage your eyes, ears, and voice in the reading process.

2. **Preview the text.** Regardless of what you are going to read, quickly previewing the text will prepare your mind for what you are going to encounter. Look for a basic outline of the thought, the structure, and the key terms and concepts.

3. **Mark the text.** Use intentional, deliberate markings that fit your learning style. This will help you engage your mind in what you are reading and activate your memory. Here are some suggestions:
   - Identify **lists of related ideas** or topics. Itemize the list in the margin. Galatians 5:16–17 is a good example of a listing text.
   - Mark **key words and phrases.** The questions you ask from the text will guide you to key words or phrases. Repetition and contrast also point out key elements of the text.
   - Identify **relationships.** Mark logical relationships like *therefore*, *so that*, or *in order to*. Mark temporal relationships such as *before*, *after*, *the next day*, or *immediately*. Notate contrasts like *but* or *however*, and correlations like *if-then* or *either-or*. Also highlight conjunctions such as *and* or *or* as well as purpose statements like *for this reason*.

4. **Make notes.** Constantly summarize your ideas, write questions, repeat key words, use colors and symbols, and note references. Use your pen or pencil as a pointer so you will not lose your place. Find as many answers as possible to the six basic questions that unlock the content and meaning of a text: who, what, when, where, why, and how. Describe your thoughts completely, but be brief.

5. **Summarize, paraphrase, or outline the text.** Write a paragraph, sentence, or phrase to summarize what you have read in your own words. Reread the passage, paying attention to your markings and notes in the text so you will remember what you have read.

Colors and Symbols

Use a consistent color and/or symbol code that works for you.

- **Color parts of speech**—Use colors for nouns, pronouns, verbs and prepositions.
- **Color themes**—Use colors for key themes like God, faith, love or sin.
- **Color relationships**—Use colors for temporal or logical words like before, therefore, so that, or if-then.
- **Use Symbols**—Mark important concepts or characters with icons:
  - God – triangle
  - Love – heart
  - Jesus – cross
  - Repentance – U-turn
  - Law – tablets
- **Use arrows**—indicate logical or temporal relationships.

Mix colors and symbols as needed but keep it simple and consistent.

Asking Questions

Who—is talking, is being spoken to, is acting, is obeying, is disobeying, is thinking, and is feeling?
What—is happening, is the lesson, must you avoid or imitate, is being said, is not said, did the person do, does the subject feel or think?
When—did this happen, will this happen?
Where—did it happen, is it happening, will it happen?
Why—did things happen, was something said or not said, was an action taken or avoided?
How—did things happen, will they happen, is the teaching illustrated, are conflicts caused or resolved?

Old Testament Scrolls

LAW

Genesis · Exodus · Leviticus · Numbers · Deuteronomy

HISTORY

Joshua · Judges · Ruth · First Samuel · Second Samuel · First Kings · Second Kings · First Chronicles · Second Chronicles · Ezra · Nehemiah · Esther

POETRY

Job · Psalms · Proverbs · Ecclesiastes · Song of Solomon

MAJOR PROPHETS

Isaiah · Jeremiah · Lamentations · Ezekiel · Daniel

MINOR PROPHETS

Hosea · Joel · Amos · Obadiah · Jonah · Micah · Nahum · Habakkuk · Zephaniah · Haggai · Zechariah · Malachi

New Testament Scrolls

GOSPELS

Matthew · Mark · Luke · John

HISTORY

Acts

PAUL'S LETTERS

Romans · 1 & 2 Corinthians · Galatians · Ephesians · Philippians · Colossians · 1 & 2 Thessalonians · 1 & 2 Timothy · Titus · Philemon

GENERAL LETTERS

Hebrews · James · 1 & 2 Peter · 1, 2 & 3 John · Jude

PROPHECY

Revelation

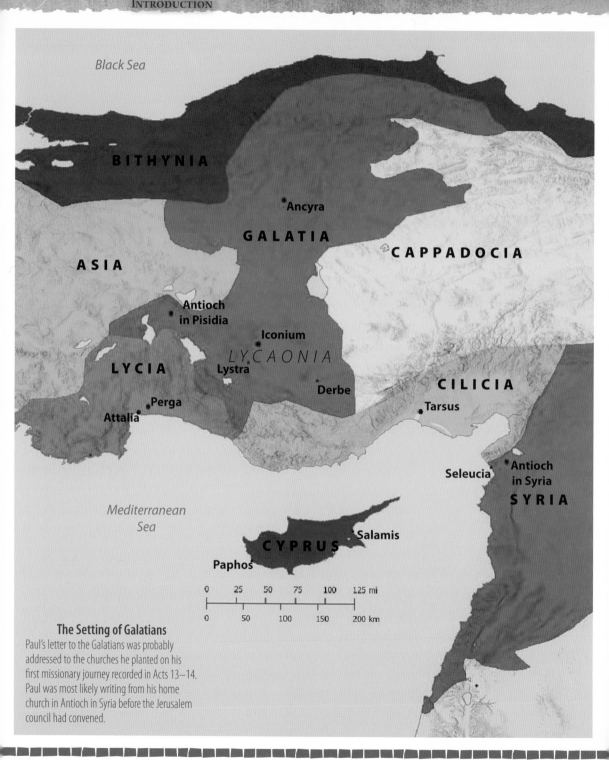

Black Sea

BITHYNIA

•Ancyra

GALATIA

CAPPADOCIA

ASIA

•Antioch
in Pisidia

Iconium

LYCAONIA

LYCIA   •Lystra

•Derbe

CILICIA

•Perga

•Tarsus

Attalia

Mediterranean
Sea

Seleucia• •Antioch
in Syria

SYRIA

CYPRUS   •Salamis

Paphos

| 0 | 25 | 50 | 75 | 100 | 125 mi |
| 0 | 50 | 100 | 150 | 200 km |

The Setting of Galatians
Paul's letter to the Galatians was probably
addressed to the churches he planted on his
first missionary journey recorded in Acts 13–14.
Paul was most likely writing from his home
church in Antioch in Syria before the Jerusalem
council had convened.

Survey the Land
Galatians

Corrupting the gospel is an age-old tendency

Introduction
FIELD STUDY 1

Why should we study Galatians?

The human heart longs for salvation. Though we are good at numbing this desire with comfortable housing, prestigious jobs, and pleasurable distractions, in our most honest moments we are certain that things are not right. Life is not as it should be. This has always been mankind's dilemma. The history of humanity is one on bended knees and outstretched arms; we've been busy trying to invoke, appease, and satisfy whoever and whatever we deem as god.

The Christian message offers truth and hope to the human despair. The gospel of Jesus Christ is the good news that eternal life with the only true God is available. God's good news is an offer of eternal life with him. It comes by his grace through faith in Jesus Christ as a gift to be received. However, it's only available on his terms. God alone determines how he will be pleased. Only then is his holiness upheld.

Yet, another dilemma remains and plagues Christianity across the globe. Why are Christians prone to live as if God's gift of salvation is insufficient? Why do we act as if we must purchase his ongoing love? Why do we drift into living the Christian life as though acceptance before God can be earned? We affirm that salvation comes from him alone, but our daily walk suggests his gift is incomplete until we step in. We think he needs us to finish the job. Sadly, too many Christians live as though God can be bought with actions—it's as though he is

Jean-Léon Gérôme, 1865

Mankind Calling Out
There have been many religions that have promoted various ways to various gods.

Mankind Longing for Salvation
All people from all civilizations desire eternality.

Claude Renault, 2006

1

continually for sale. The Christian *must live* responsibly and morally because God *desires* this lifestyle. Going to church, taking communion, and tithing are God-honoring Christian practices, but not if we think they earn us favor before him. Living the Christian life as if God can be satisfied by a combination of faith in Jesus plus good works signals an ignorance or rejection of the gospel of Jesus Christ.

This is an old problem, which the letter of Galatians dealt with a long time ago. The gospel according to God had been under attack among the churches of Galatia, that is, *among Christians*. It is the same today. Too many believers live life as though Christ's work on the cross is not enough. We accept the gospel of God's grace, yet mix it with our own *merits*. However, God will not accept this and Galatians makes it very clear. We long for God but despite our repeated attempts, he cannot, and need not be bought, bribed, or earned.

The book of Galatians clearly defines God's gospel terms. In doing so, we are offered much needed guidance on how to live the Christian life. Let's now explore this work together. We will not only learn what the gospel *is* but also how to live it out as God intended.

What is the background to our story?

It is essential for us to do a brief study of the history of humanity and its tendency to add to the gospel. This will highlight for us how ancient this dilemma is and it will set us up for understanding its manifestation in Galatians.

Adam and Eve
The first human beings, Adam and Eve, instantly knew they were separated from God due to their sin. Ashamed by their nakedness, they tried to fix the situation themselves.

Mankind's longing for salvation has always been matched by attempts to attain it on our own. Our efforts at self-salvation run deep, as early as the account of our first ancestors Adam and Eve in Genesis 3. When the first man and woman sinned, they instantly became aware of their condition and tried to cover their shame by stitching a few leaves together. Moreover, their son Cain was no different. He thought he could satisfy God with a basket of fruit despite the condition of his heart.

James Tissot, 1902

Genesis 3:7

Then the eyes of both of them were opened, and they knew they were naked; so they sowed fig leaves together and made coverings for themselves.

Genesis 4:3–5

When it was time, Cain brought an offering to the LORD of the fruit of the ground. But Abel brought of the firstborn of his flock. And the LORD looked with favor on Abel and his offering but with Cain and his offering he did not look with favor. So Cain became very angry and his face was downcast.

The greatest example of this self-saving mindset was sustained for centuries by God's chosen people, Israel. They lived as if they alone, among the nations, deserved God even though he called and rescued them from bondage by his grace.[1] God granted them the law, the feasts, and the sacrificial system but these were gifts that were to remind Israel to live by faith in him. They wrongly used these as though by them they earned a right to God.[2] It was a mindset that assumed God's salvation could be earned, impressed, and satisfied by man's own efforts or good deeds. God had reached out by grace to save a powerless humanity. However, the Israelites came to believe that through their religious efforts they had the power to buy life with God. It appeared as if God rewarded man's lifestyle with salvation. God did expect Sabbath

Cain and Abel

The account of Cain and Abel in Genesis 4 exposes the condition of Cain's heart toward God as the underlying reason for God's rejection of his offering. God called Cain to turn from his impending sin but Cain rebelled and murdered his own brother.

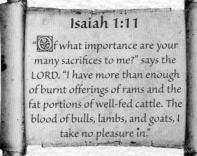

Isaiah 1:11

"Of what importance are your many sacrifices to me?" says the LORD. "I have more than enough of burnt offerings of rams and the fat portions of well-fed cattle. The blood of bulls, lambs, and goats, I take no pleasure in."

observance, circumcision, and obedience to the law in Israel but only as expressions of a heart of faith in anticipation of the Messiah.

Hebrews 10:1, 4, 11

The law is but a shadow of the good things to come but not the reality itself, and therefore is completely unable, by the same sacrifices offered up continually, year after year, to make perfect those who draw near to worship.

For the blood of bulls and goats cannot take away sins.

And every priest stands daily ministering, repeatedly offering the same sacrifices, which can never take away sins.

In the New Testament, the Gospels also testify to man's longing for deliverance as well as his tendency toward self-salvation. Jesus walked

High Priest Offering a Sacrifice

The religious ceremonies and practices of Israel, like the sacrificial system, were intended to be God-sanctioned ways through which the people could express their faith in God.

The Badges of Judaism

The badges of Judaism were circumcision, Sabbath observance, and purity laws. Gentiles who desired a share in God had to become Jews. They were to embrace these badges. They were to do something to earn a right to God.

1. Deuteronomy 7:1–11
2. Romans 9:1–5, 30–33

| 1250 | 1100 | 950 | 800 | 650 | 500 | B.C. |

Saul becomes king 1050

David becomes king 1010

Solomon becomes king 971

930 The kingdom divides

722 Northern kingdom falls to Assyria

Southern kingdom falls to Babylon and the temple is destroyed 586

3

What Makes a Good Jew?

Jesus' attack on how Judaism used the law generated much antagonism against him. Sabbath observance, for example, was one that kept emerging. Jesus often healed on the Sabbath to intentionally provoke a response. It gave him the opportunity to correct the misunderstanding (see Mark 2:23–3:6). The Sermon on the Mount in Matthew 5–7 also contrasts Jesus' interpretation of God's law with what was offered by the Judaism of the first century.

in a Jewish world that understood that only a religious lifestyle would satisfy God. It was believed that perfect obedience to the law made one a good Jew—one who could hold his head high before God. Non-Jews or *Gentiles* could be right before God as well, but only by becoming Jews!

Simeon in the Temple
Even at the time when the sacrificial system was still in operation, we find in the Temple, men such as Simeon who understood that living under the law was not their final hope. These few godly men anticipated the consummation of God's promises in the coming Messiah. See Luke 2:22–35.

Rembrandt van Rijn, 1631

Luke 2:29–31
Now Lord, according to your word let your servant depart in peace, for my eyes have seen your salvation that you have prepared in the presence of all peoples...

Who wrote this book?

The apostle Paul wrote the letter of Galatians. The authorship of the letter is so well established that it is often used by scholars as a gauge to determine whether other epistles are from Paul.

The apostle played a significant role in the early church. God used him like no other man in the spread of the gospel to gentile lands as God stated in Acts 1:8. He was also the divine instrument chosen to interpret and explain all that was previously promised by God in Scripture and the way it was fulfilled in Jesus Christ.

Paul Writing His Epistles
Many scholars believe that Paul wrote the letter to the Galatian churches from his home church at Antioch in Syria.

Valentin de Boulogne, 16th century

Acts 1:8
But you will receive power when the Holy Spirit has come upon you, and you shall be my witnesses in Jerusalem, and in all Judea and Samaria, and to the end of the earth.

Paul was first introduced in the Bible as Saul. He was a Jew born in the gentile city of Tarsus; a Pharisee trained by the best teacher, Gamaliel, and a man unmatched regarding his zeal and devotion to the Jewish faith. In God's sovereign providence however, Christ called him when on route to persecute the church in the city of Damascus. From that point on, he devoted his life to Christ with even greater zeal and passion. The law-abiding Pharisee was reborn and eventually became known as the apostle Paul. His life is a perfect example of the message he sought to communicate in the letter to the Galatians.

B.C.	1	A.D.	10	20	30	40	50

5? Birth of Jesus

4–6? Birth of Paul

John the Baptist begins his ministry 28–29?

Jesus begins his ministry 28–30?

Jesus is crucified and resurrected 30–33?

33–34? Paul encounters Christ on Damascus road

Paul writes Galatians 48?

46–47? First Miss Journey t

Antioch on the Orontes

Today the ancient city of Antioch of Syria is the modern Turkish city of Antakya. At the time of Paul, Antioch rivaled Alexandria in Egypt in importance. The church flourished there and Antioch became known as the cradle of Christianity.

What was going on at the time?

The Christian church sprung from Jewish roots in the first century. Once Christ came, Christianity emerged as the natural offspring of a Jewish faith awaiting his arrival. As the gospel of Jesus Christ spread from Jerusalem to the ends of the earth, the church transitioned from a predominantly Jewish to a Jewish-Gentile constituency just as God had desired. It was a period of excitement and some confusion as a baby church learned about life with God within the framework of a new age.

Acts 13–14 record the account of Paul's first missionary journey with Barnabas. They traveled throughout Cyprus and into the southern areas of Asia Minor in modern day Turkey. Visiting town after town, they preached the gospel and planted churches.

Upon return to their home church in Antioch, Paul received news that other teachers had visited these churches after him. They confused the Gentile believers with a different message. These false teachers proclaimed a gospel with Jewish conditions attached—after all, Christianity had Jewish roots. The law had played a major role in the

The Church at Antioch

The church of Antioch was founded by Christians who left Jerusalem due to the persecutions by Saul following the death of Stephen (Acts 11:19). It soon became the hub of Gentile Christianity and eventually surpassed the church in Jerusalem as the leading church in the first century. This growth was fueled by the multitude of Gentile conversions, the fall of Jerusalem to the Romans in A.D. 66–70, and the missionary passion of this church.

A False Gospel

For a portrait of the type of gospel the false preachers proclaimed in Galatia consider the following Galatian passages:

- On circumcision (2:3; 5:2, 3; 6:12, 13)
- On life according to Jewish customs and calendars (2:14; 4:10)
- On observing the law (2:16; 3:2, 5, 10, 11; 5:4)

Discrediting Paul

A common way of promoting a point was to damage the credibility of the opposing party. It is called an *ad hominem* attack—an attempt to shame a person to discredit his or her message. Many political campaigns use this strategy today. In light of Paul's counter argument in Galatians 1–2, the false teachers were clearly attacking Paul in this way.

| 50 | 60 | 70 | 80 | 90 | 100 A.D. |

| 49? Jerusalem Council | 60–62? Paul arrives in Rome under house arrest | 70 Temple is destroyed | | John writes Revelation 95–96? | |
| 50–52? Second Missionary Journey by Paul | 64 Fire in Rome | 79 | Pompeii and Herculaneum are destroyed by Vesuvius eruption | |

5

Todd Bolen, www.BiblePlaces.com

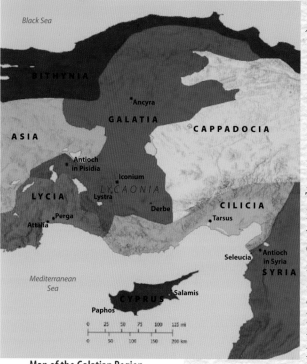

Map of the Galatian Region

On this map, Galatia is the large Roman province encapsulating many different people groups. The *Southern Galatian Theory* suggests that cities like Antioch, Lystra, Iconium, and Derbe, in the southern province of Roman Galatia, are the recipients of the letter. The *North Galatian Theory* proposes the letter is written to an ethnic group, the Galatians, in the northern part of this map but we do not have any biblical references mentioning any northern cities.

history of God's dealings with man so far. These *Judaizers* argued salvation was incomplete if one did not embrace the Jewish lifestyle. They taught that faith in Jesus was essential, but only in partnership with adherence to the law—particularly circumcision. These Judaizers would even quote the Hebrew Scriptures to support their position. To advance their point, Paul's character and credibility was undermined. These false teachers claimed Paul left the Galatians only partly evangelized! Their strategy was effective. The Galatian believers were rapidly deserting Paul and his gospel. This false teaching set human works on equal footing with God's work in Jesus Christ on the cross. It was a subtle deviation from the true gospel coated in biblical language; a contemporary expression within the church of that age-old tendency for man to try to save himself. Even in the early days of the church, the tendency toward self-salvation quickly emerged. Paul knew this was insulting to God and dangerous for man.

Who was the audience?

The letter of Galatians is written to a group of churches located in Galatia. The most important thing to note is that the letter is written to Christians. The identity of the Galatians however, is a disputed issue. The problem is that the term *Galatia* or *Galatian* was used in two distinct ways in ancient society. At times, it was used in the ethnic sense, referring to a specific people group living in a very specific region in northern Asia Minor. This ancient Celtic Kingdom had been under Roman rule since Pompey had captured it in the mid-first century B.C. On other occasions, *Galatia* was used in a political sense by the Romans, referring to a much larger political province and all peoples within it. This province of *Galatia* included southern regions of Asia Minor, which was home to many different people groups.

If the term Galatians is being used in the ethnic sense, then the letter was written at some point after Paul's second missionary journey to allow for his visit to this specific region. This is after Acts 16:6 or Acts 18:23, but is not recorded in detail in the book of Acts. In this case, the writing would be after the Jerusalem Council's decision in

A.D.   40   42   44   46   48   50

Paul's First Missionary Journey   46–47?

Jerusalem Council   49?

Paul writes Galatians
(South Galatian Theory)   48?

Ruins of the Church of St. Paul at Pisidian Antioch

In Acts 13 Paul and Barnabas first arrive at Antioch in Pisidia to preach the gospel. Today, there are remains of a church building there, built several centuries after Paul's arrival, but demonstrating the lasting impact of Christ's message. According to the South Galatian theory, this would have been a church that Galatians was written to.

Acts 15. This is called the *North Galatian Theory*.

On the other hand, if Galatians is used in the political sense of the Roman province, the letter could have been written immediately after Paul's first missionary journey to the Galatian cities recorded and detailed in Acts 13–14. This is known as the *South Galatian Theory*. In this case, the letter was written *before* the Jerusalem Council recorded in Acts 15 and would explain why Paul never mentions it.

Good arguments are made for either option and the matter is not settled. Our study follows the *South Galatian Theory* particularly because of the decision made at the Jerusalem Council in Acts 15. There the church leadership unanimously declared and disseminated the same position Paul advances in the letter of Galatians. It is hard to believe Paul would not appeal to the Council's decision when his letter deals with the very same issue. It certainly would have helped settle the matter.

When did this happen?

The date of the writing of Galatians is clearly based on the location of these churches. If we follow the *North Galatian theory*, this would imply a date sometime around A.D. 53–57. On the other hand, if

| 50 | 52 | 54 | 56 | 58 | 60 A.D. |

53–57? Paul writes Galatians
(North Galatian Theory)

Ancient Letters

Ancient letters followed an established format. These are some of the major features they included:

1. Introduction:
   The introduction named the writer and recipient. It contained a greeting and either a word of thanksgiving, or a prayer of thanksgiving.

2. Main body:
   The main body of the letter dealt with the issue that caused the letter to be written.

3. Conclusion:
   The conclusion expressed final greetings, perhaps a description of how the letter was written—with the assistance of a scribe or not—and a benediction.

The Sacrifice of Lystra

In the Galatian town of Lystra, Paul healed a man who was lame from birth (Acts 14:8–18). The people thought that Paul and Barnabas were gods and wanted to offer sacrifices to them but they tore their clothes in protest stating that they were merely men and it was the Creator God who was the source of power.

Raphael, 1515

Galatians was addressed to the Roman province of Galatia, it would have been written around A.D. 48. The latter seems most likely since it appears from the letter that the Jerusalem council, which occurred around A.D. 49, had not yet convened.

How should we read this type of book?

There are three additional issues you need to be aware of before opening the book of Galatians. Understanding these matters will equip you to dig through this ancient yet timeless document. Consider them tools that will help you frame your thinking in areas that allow you to appreciate what God is declaring in this letter.

First, the book of Galatians is a letter. Ancient letters like ours today had set features. Letters are *situational*; they deal with specific issues that arise in a particular context. Galatians is no different. In it we see only half of a conversation and must build an understanding of the undisclosed other half. We will do this in our study as we go through it. Letters are also very *personal*. They are filled with emotion. Paul wrote knowing that Galatian congregations would listen to the letter as it was publicly read. It is *emotionally packed*. Paul does not shy away from confronting these churches with truth![1] Therefore, read the letter as a passionate, personal letter from God to your situation. The problem it addresses remains relevant today.

Second, you need to understand the broader Christian teaching concerning salvation. Salvation is a broad term which when opened up reveals three aspects: justification, sanctification, and glorification. Understanding these concepts will not only help you stay on track with Paul, it will also help you understand your own Christian walk.

Justification is *being declared righteous*. The instant someone believes in Jesus Christ that individual is justified before God. He is declared saved and set free from the penalty of sin. Justification is the past tense of salvation—that point in time when you first believed.

Sanctification is *the process of being made righteous*. As a justified sinner grows by faith in Christ-likeness throughout life, he or she becomes more

1. Galatians 3:1; 4:19

Paul's First Missionary Journey 46–47?

Jerusalem Council 49?

Paul writes Galatians
(South Galatian Theory) 48?

and more holy. That is, the Spirit of God makes that individual more like Jesus. In this way, the one declared saved is being saved by learning to live free from the power of sin. This is the present tense of salvation—the Christian life.

Glorification is what occurs *when one becomes perfectly righteous*. It will occur when the believer

Ruins of Lystra

Here are a few stone remains of a structure from the ancient city of Lystra. Little more than an archeological mound of dirt or *tel* is left on the site where Paul and Barnabas shared the gospel and were stoned, as recorded in Acts 14.

stands before God in heaven and is actually made holy. The one declared saved who was being saved is now experiencing the culmination of salvation—a sinless life with God. The believer is free from the presence of sin. This is the future tense of salvation.

It is crucial that you understand these categories. Central to the letter of Galatians are the justification and sanctification aspects of salvation. They are part of the outline of the book.

Third, it is important you understand what legalism is and how it relates to Christianity. Legalism is living according to certain standards of conduct in an attempt to gain God's favor. Israel's faith was not intended to be legalistic but it became so in practice as the Jews misused the law. According to the Jewish interpretation of the Mosaic Law, what one did or did not do, determined one's standing before God. This mindset entered the church from the start. Galatians is testimony to it. Christian legalism arises when believers live life as though what they do and don't do in some way earns them favor before God. In God's plan of salvation, good works are not to be used as a currency to buy rights to him. Galatians is addressing this specific issue—legalism. Paul will address legalism by demonstrating that both justification and sanctification function through faith. Make sure you read this letter with this in mind.

50   52   54   56   58   60   A.D.

53–57?   Paul writes Galatians *(North Galatian Theory)*

Basic Outline of Galatians

Chapters 1–2:
    Defense of Paul's Authority

Chapters 3–4:
    Justification: How one
    becomes a Christian

Chapters 5–6:
    Sanctification: How one lives
    as a Christian

Why did God give us this message?

So, why does God want us to explore this letter? It was a letter written by Paul to a particular group of churches long ago. While Paul had no knowledge of us, God does. He wrote Galatians. How he addressed the Galatian problem through Paul's letter, is how he addresses the same issue today. The Galatian problem is a Christian problem. Your heart is inclined toward living as if God's salvation needs to be supplemented with your own good works. It shows that same old tendency toward self-salvation that is so offensive to God. Galatians is crucially important to you. With this in mind, here are a few areas of application to think about before going deeper in this letter. Take some time to answer them personally.

How do you understand the gospel of Jesus Christ?

Think about this question. How have I understood the gospel? Misunderstanding it is a dangerous mistake. Resting on anything other than the true terms of salvation offered by God is to live with false hope. Eternity is at stake! What is the true gospel? Have I believed a counterfeit? Am I ignoring God or even supplementing his provision with my own terms? These are important questions for you to wrestle with. How you have understood the gospel affects the manner in which you live it out. Our study in Galatians will help you.

What role do good works play in your life?

You are a believer—a Christian—just like the Galatians. So, what drives your Christian lifestyle? Why do you dress up, go to church, and tithe when the offering plate passes by? Why do you serve in Christian ministry? What role do godly, Christian practices like baptism, communion, and tithing play in your life? Why do you do the Christian things you do? Is there any sense in which they make you feel like you deserve God—like you are earning a right to him? Living by a list of do's and don'ts as if this achieves holiness is not God's will for your life. There are many things he wants you to do or avoid, but only on his terms. There is such a thing as a Christian lifestyle but how is this lived? We will deal with this in our study. For now, think about whether you are in bondage to a lifestyle that you assume impresses God—as though you're buying life with him. It's easy and subtle to live like that. Are there traces of legalism in your life?

Discoveries

Now that you have completed the survey of the background to the book of Galatians, it's time to put down your tools and see what you have discovered. This section is designed to help you wrestle with the implications of the text and embed the newly learned information in your mind. Find the questions that suit your group best.

Connecting with the community

These are discussion questions to help you understand the significance of what you have learned. Do not merely think of them as questions for you as an individual but rather think of them in light of your family, your community, your nation, and your church.

1. Why is it important to understand all of the background to Galatians before reading the actual text?

2. After reading this introductory *Field Study*, what is the most important reason why we should study this New Testament letter?

3. The *Field Notes* on Galatians are subtitled, "Living like God is for sale?" What does this mean? How did the Galatians live in such a way? How do Christians live in such a way today?

4. In the introduction to Galatians, there were several biblical examples presented of the human tendency to "self-save." Which of these examples do you find more enlightening? Are any of these common in your community? Do you recognize any particular tendencies to self-salvation in your own life?

5. Consider your own life. What has been your personal perception regarding eternal salvation and the means to attain it throughout the different stages of your life? If your family members are believers, would they say the same thing about you or themselves?

6. What has been your understanding of the gospel so far? How do you think your church understands the gospel given how the church functions? Are there any activities that run the risk of being turned into legalistic religious acts?

Notes, Observations & Questions

7. Discuss the meaning of the three terms related to the doctrine of salvation: justification, sanctification, and glorification. How are they related to each other?

8. How is the gospel related to the necessity of good works in the life of the Christian?

9. On a scale of 1 to 10, with 1 representing a little and 10 representing a lot, rate your own knowledge of the book of Galatians. At the end of *Field Study 13*, you will have another opportunity to evaluate your knowledge in light of what you have learned.

    1   2   3   4   5   6   7   8   9   10

a little   a lot

Probing deeper

These exercises are for your continued study of some of the secondary issues in Galatians. They may require you to look at other passages to trace themes that run throughout the rest of Scripture.

1. Explain the relationship between the books of Acts and Galatians. Why is it helpful to refer to Acts when beginning a study of Galatians?

2. Who was considered a "good Jew" in the times of the New Testament? How is this perception related to the issues addressed in the book of Galatians?

3. Who was Paul the apostle? Read some of his background in Acts 7:54–9:31. How does his personal experience before knowing Christ make him an ideal person to address the issues that were causing trouble in the churches of Galatia?

Bringing the story to life

Learning biblical geography helps us to understand the context of the Bible. Locate each of the following features on the map and label them. See the map on page xiv at the beginning of your *Field Notes* for help.

- **Countries and Regions**: Bithynia, Asia, Lycia, Galatia, Lycaonia, Cappadocia, Cilicia, Syria, and Cyprus.
- **Cities**: Myra, Attalia, Perga, Antioch in Pisidia, Lystra, Iconium, Ancyra, Derbe, Paphos, Salamis, Tarsus, Seleucia, and Antioch in Syria.
- **Water**: Black Sea, Mediterranean Sea.

Notes, Observations & Questions

Memorizing the key

The key phrase to memorize for the introduction to Galatians is:

Corrupting the gospel is an age-old tendency

Part of learning the Bible is remembering what the Bible is about and where to find things. Memorizing the key phrases will help you to better understand and apply the key points of each book.

Observation journaling

This section will prepare you for *Field Study* 2. You will read through the first section of the book of Galatians. We have included three types of exercises: some for before you read, some for while you are reading and some for after you have completed the reading.

Before you read

Discuss and fill in the chart below with what you already know about Paul's letter to the Galatians. This exercise will help you learn and remember as you encounter new information. You will fill in the new information after you have read the text.

Reading knowledge chart

	What I already know	What I have learned
What is the problem in the Galatian churches?		
What is Paul saying about the problem?		

While you are reading

On the following page, we have laid out the biblical text with wide margins so you can mark the text with questions, key terms, notes, and structures. We have removed all of the verse markings so you can read it without distractions and have laid out the text with spacing to help you see how the lines are related. Review the guidelines on *The art of active learning* section, page xi at the beginning of your *Field Notes* for some suggestions on reading, learning, and marking the text effectively.

Galatians 1:1–10

Paul, an apostle— not sent from men nor through the agency of man, but through Jesus Christ and God the Father, who raised him from the dead— and all the brothers who are with me,

To the churches in Galatia:

Grace and peace to you from God our Father and the Lord Jesus Christ, who gave himself for our sins to rescue us from this present evil age, according to the will of our God and Father, to whom be glory forever and ever! Amen.

I am astonished that you are so quickly deserting the one who called you by the grace of Christ, for a different gospel— not that there really is another gospel, but there are some who trouble you, and want to distort the gospel of Christ. But even if we or an angel from heaven should preach a gospel contrary to the one we preached to you, let him be accursed! As we have said before, so now I say again: If anyone is preaching to you a gospel contrary to what you received, let him be accursed! Am I now trying to gain the approval of men, or of God? Or am I trying to please men? If I were still trying to please men, I would not be a slave of Christ.

Notes, Observations & Questions

Summarize the text here

After you have read

1. Go back to your *reading knowledge chart* on page 14 and fill in anything that you have learned while reading through this first section of Galatians. Compare it with what you already knew to see what the text has revealed so far.

2. Journaling is another way to help us learn. You will remember more if you respond to what you have read by writing. Therefore, write out Galatians 1:1–10 from the previous page or from your own Bible into a journal word for word. Then journal your thoughts on what the good news is and why it is good?

3. Now read Galatians 1:1–10 in your own Bible. Continue to reread it each day until you get to *Field Study 2*. This will reinforce the learning of Scripture and help you in retention.

Pray

As we learn the Word of God, it is essential that we communicate with him through prayer. First, consider writing out a prayer, psalm, or poem to God about trying to earn God's favor. Do you see a similar struggle in your own life, community, nation, or church? Respond to him through a carefully thought through prayer that you will write out and pray each day this week. Consider the prayer below as a sample. Try doing this with a family member or small group to make it a corporate prayer:

Dear Heavenly Father,

I come before you today with gratitude for the opportunity to begin this journey of exploration. Father, I ask that in your grace you would open my eyes to discover the significance of this book for my life. Even now, I recognize that there are things in my life that need to be changed by the teaching of this book. Father I ask you that you would clarify any areas where I tend to seek my own salvation and seek your approval based on my behavior. Father, let your Holy Spirit show me the glorious blessing and joy of the gospel. Help me find my joy and acceptance before you only in the merits and work of your Son my Savior Jesus Christ. Father I ask you that as a result of this study I might grasp more fully the glory of the gospel and that as a result I might be bolder in proclaiming your good news to those around me. Thank you for the good news of life that is available in the Lord Jesus Christ in whose name I come before you, Amen.

Galatians 1:1–10

FIELD STUDY 2

How is the text arranged?

We now begin our exploration of the text of Galatians in order to discover its contribution to the overall message of the Bible. Our first step is to examine how Paul addresses the Galatian problem in the first ten verses of his letter. He makes his point through a progressive argument. Consider the first section. Read the biblical text several times using different translations if possible. Then read it with the aid of the interpretive guide below. Try to understand the tone in Paul's words. A stern attitude emerges from the very beginning. Try to detect it. The structure can be outlined as follows:

Arranging the Text

Arranging the text in this outline visually helps one appreciate the progress in Paul's reasoning. The indented outline shows how each phrase in this passage relates to one another.

Galatians 1:1—10

Section	Bible Text
Introduction (1:1–5)	
Author	¹ Paul,

Calling and source of authority	an apostle—
	    not sent from men nor through the agency of man,
	    but through Jesus Christ and God the Father,
	        who raised him from the dead—

Supporters	² and all the brothers who are with me,
Recipients	To the churches in Galatia:
Greeting and blessing	³ Grace and peace to you

Previewing the gospel	from God our Father and the Lord Jesus Christ,
	    ⁴ who gave himself for our sins
	        to rescue us from this present evil age,
	            according to the will of our God and Father,

The doxology	⁵ to whom be glory forever and ever! Amen.

Paul's Team

Paul mentions *"the brothers who are with me"* to let the churches in Galatia know that he was not alone in what he proclaimed to them in the letter. It seems that Paul at the very least would have his missionary companion Barnabas in mind as well as his sending church in Antioch. From what he writes in chapter two of this letter, he might even be suggesting that the church in Jerusalem supported him as well. This phrase adds to the argument that both God and godly leaders supported Paul despite what other teachers said. However, these supporters were not co-authors.

Galatians 1:1—10

Section	Bible Text
Cause for the Letter (1:6–10)	
The Galatian problem: - Deserting the true gospel - Embracing a false gospel	⁶ I am astonished that 　　you are so quickly deserting the one 　　who called you by the grace of Christ, 　　for a different gospel— 　　　⁷ not that there really is another gospel, 　　　　but there are some who trouble you, 　　　　and want to distort the gospel of Christ.
Consequence of advancing an alternative gospel	⁸ But even if we or an angel from heaven should preach a gospel contrary to the one we preached to you, let him be accursed!
Consequence repeated	⁹ As we have said before, so now I say again: If anyone is preaching to you a gospel contrary to what you received, let him be accursed!
Motivation for Paul's service including this letter	¹⁰ Am I now trying to gain the approval of men, or of God? 　　Or am I trying to please men? If I were still trying to please men, 　　I would not be a slave of Christ.

Doxology

In the Bible a *doxology* is a brief, well-known formula that expresses praise to God. You can find doxologies in passages such as Exodus 15:18, Matthew 6:13, Romans 16:27 and many others. In verse 5, the apostle offers this doxology after describing the gracious work of the Father accomplished through Jesus Christ, described in verse 4.

Notice what emerges from this outline of the text. We see that Galatians 1:1–10 contains two major movements.

The first movement is, at first glance, a standard introductory greeting. (1– However, we will soon find out that a closer inspection reveals much more. For now, we can see that the typical elements of a first century Greek letter are all found here: the author and recipients are noted, a short greeting or blessing is present, and a doxology is offered to God.

The second movement reveals the occasion of the letter. Paul's (6– purpose in sending this epistle to the churches of Galatia was a defense of the true gospel. The gospel of Christ that the apostle proclaimed had been replaced by a counterfeit gospel after his departure from the region. False teachers followed in Paul's wake promoting an alternative understanding of the good news of Jesus Christ among the newly planted churches. This corrupt alternative spread quickly and the consequence of its advance was severe.

B.C. 2000	1850	1700	1550	1400	1250

2091 God calls Abraham?　　　　　　　　　　　　　　Receiving the Law on Mount Sinai? 1446

　　　1925 God calls Abraham?　　　　　　　　　　　　　　Receiving the Law on Mount Sinai? 1260

Galatians 1:1–10 shows that the gospel of Jesus Christ was under attack. The tragic irony was that the assault took place from within the ranks of the church.

What is this passage saying?

What are some key terms and phrases?

From the beginning of the epistle, Paul introduces ideas, which he will elaborate on later in the letter. These concepts are crucial to the meaning of the text and the significance of its message. The following table contains some of these key words or phrases. They are significant for Galatians and illuminate our understanding of God and the gospel.

Meaning of Key Terms

Key word or phrase	Meaning and significance
Apostle (1:1)	Apostle literally means, "one sent away with orders, a delegate." Many people erroneously think of it as a synonym of disciple. The term as used here in Galatians, has a restricted meaning. The restricted meaning of *apostle* is reserved only for the select group of men who were with Jesus from the beginning of his ministry and were eyewitnesses to his resurrection and ascension as recorded in Acts 1:15–26. The twelve apostles were men set apart by the Holy Spirit from among many disciples of Jesus for this specific and unique role. Paul was added to this group and right from the very beginning of his letter to the Galatians, he defends his apostleship in this technical sense. The epistle begins, "Paul, an apostle." That is emphatic. His apostleship was questioned by false teachers to discredit the authority of his teaching of the gospel. However, like the twelve, he also witnessed the resurrected Lord and was appointed personally by Jesus with a specific mission recorded in Acts 9. In a general sense, all believers are also *apostles* in that we are followers of Jesus with specific orders to proclaim and represent him. We are not however, apostles in the restricted sense that the Twelve mentioned in Acts 1 and Paul were. This role was a foundational one, unique to a particular era of the church, a role no longer necessary according to Ephesians 2:19–20.
Lord Jesus Christ (1:3)	The three-fold reference to God's Son as the "Lord Jesus Christ" is packed with significance. The early church correctly understood this phrase as a title declaring the *Lord* Jesus to be of exalted rank. *Jesus*, meaning *the Lord saves*, reminds us of his role as God's vehicle of salvation. The title *Christ* affirms that he alone is the anticipated Messiah who was to come and fulfill God's promised word. "Lord Jesus Christ" is not just a name. This is a title declaring his identity and commission.

The Twelve Apostles

After the death of Judas, the church thought that it was necessary to name a replacement disciple who could be "counted with the eleven" according to Acts 1:15–26. The new member of the group had to be an eyewitness to Jesus' ministry and resurrection. Matthias was chosen for this role as Judas' replacement. Later, Paul was called as an additional apostle to the Gentiles.

1250	1100	950	800	650	500 B.C.

Saul becomes king 1050
David becomes king 1010
Solomon becomes king 971
930 The kingdom divides
722 Northern kingdom falls to Assyria
Southern kingdom falls to Babylon and the temple is destroyed 586

Ancient Letters

There are many examples of ancient letters that show the common elements included in first century letter writing. Below is a letter from a son writing to his mother about a shameful situation, begging her forgiveness. One can feel the remorse in his tone. Personal letters can evoke strong emotions and, just like in Galatians, readers can detect in them the mood of the author. Note how the format is the same as the letter to the Galatians. It includes the name of the author, recipient, and greeting. However, this letter has an expression of prayer which is conspicuously absent from Galatians.

Letter of a Prodigal Son

ANTONI[U]S LONGUS
TO NILOUS HIS MOTHER

MANY GREETINGS.

CONTINUALLY I PRAY FOR
YOUR HEALTH. SUPPLICATION
ON YOUR BEHALF I DIRECT
EACH DAY TO THE LORD SERAPIS
[HIS GOD]...

BUT I WAS ASHAMED TO COME
TO KARANIS, BECAUSE I AM
GOING ABOUT IN RAGS. I WRITE
YOU THAT I AM NAKED. I
BESEECH YOU, MOTHER, BE
RECONCILED TO ME. BUT I
KNOW WHAT I HAVE BROUGHT
UPON MYSELF. PUNISHED I
HAVE BEEN EVERY WAY. I
KNOW I HAVE SINNED.

(Milligan, Selections from the Greek Papyri, No. 37, Cambridge University Press.)

Meaning of Key Terms

Key word or phrase	Meaning and significance
Astonished at rapid deserting (1:6)	The word *astonished* was commonly used to initiate a rebuke. It has a critical connotation in this context. The word *deserting* initiates an increasingly severe tone perceived in the letter, especially when added to Paul's description of these churches. The imagery of desertion evokes a political traitor or military deserter, both of which were punishable by death! Paul was mystified by their turning from the true gospel to another.

What about the culture?

In ancient letter writing, introductions contained standard elements such as the name of the writer, the recipients, and a personal greeting. This is much like standards of writing formal and informal letters today. Paul generally followed the established forms although at certain times he deviated from them. One common characteristic in his introductions was to include an expression of thanksgiving to God for his recipients. All of Paul's letters contain this element of gratitude, except for one: Galatians. This is significant to the meaning of the letter since it reveals how Paul felt about the situation, adding a serious tone to his words. Why was Paul unhappy with the Galatians?

What is the explanation?

One cannot glide past the first few verses in this letter as though their only purpose was to satisfy ancient letter-writing protocol. Paul's initial words indicate who wrote the letter and to whom it is addressed.[1] A greeting and a blessing are also provided.[2] However, there is much more to this introduction than its recipients anticipated.

Paul immediately claims the authority to be heard   (1– and obeyed. The text begins with this emphasis. Paul asserts his authority as an apostle, a messenger of God. This was not an issue of pride; his goal is not to promote himself. Paul recognizes that discrediting his role as an apostle of Jesus Christ renders the credibility of his message suspect. His gospel was being attacked among the churches in

1. Galatians 1:1, 2
2. Galatians 1:3–5

B.C.	1	A.D.	10	20	30	40	50

5? Birth of Jesus

John the Baptist begins his ministry 28–29?

33–34? Paul encounters Christ on Damascus road

46–47? First Miss Journey

5? Birth of Paul

Jesus begins his ministry 28–30?

Paul writes Galatians 48?

Jesus is crucified and resurrected 30–33?

Galatia. False teachers belittled his position as an apostle. Therefore, Paul *pulls rank*, so to speak. He wants them to understand two things from the start. First, Paul wants the Galatians to remember the source of his authority. His calling and message did not come from man, but from a direct appointment by God. Second, Paul was not alone in his understanding of Christ's gospel. The teaching Paul declares is the same word of God also proclaimed by other believers. The broader church supported Paul and his message.

5) Paul uses his personal greeting of *grace and peace*, to present a summary of his gospel message. In doing so, he foreshadows the direction of the letter and at the same time deals the first blow to those who discredited him. In the course of the letter, they would hear the true message of the gospel repeatedly rephrased in different terms. In Galatians 1:3–4 the gospel is expressed as receiving God's undeserved kindness or *grace* that brings his blessing of *peace*. God desires to offer this blessing in Jesus Christ. He is the one who takes our sins upon himself and delivers us from evil. The gospel is about receiving the gift of grace and peace God provides for us in Jesus. It means that Jesus is the substitution for our sin. Deliverance from evil is only available through Christ. As you can see, the gospel is all about what God, not man, does for us through Jesus, and therefore is all about the glory of God not men!

The Galatians had received the true gospel of God through Paul, a genuine apostle of God. God wanted them to receive it based on his work in Jesus. The gospel is entirely from God. Only he deserves all the praise. Why then, were the Galatians in need of such stern correction? What had happened? Why had they corrupted the gospel by adding works to it? Before we judge them too harshly, it is very important for us to remember that just like the Galatians in the first century; we also are prone to corrupt the true gospel after receiving it.

The Plains of Pisidian Antioch

This is what Paul and Barnabas would have seen as they entered the Roman province of Galatia at Pisidian Antioch.

Todd Bolen, www.BiblePlaces.com

| 50 | 60 | 70 | 80 | 90 | 100 A.D. |

49? Jerusalem Council

50–52? Second Missionary Journey by Paul

60–62? Paul arrives in Rome under house arrest

64 Fire in Rome

70 Temple is destroyed

79 Pompeii and Herculaneum are destroyed by Vesuvius eruption

John writes Revelation 95–96?

Public reading of Scripture

In the ancient world the majority of people were illiterate. It was also very rare to actually own a scroll or parchment on any topic! It is for this reason that in Jewish synagogues and in the early church the Scriptures were publicly read out to those gathered. This was also the case with Galatians. It was written primarily for the ear not the eye. Paul's opponents would no doubt have heard Paul's counter arguments directed toward them while in the presence of the entire church. There is much value in reading Galatians out loud or listening to it being read by someone else since this was Paul's intention.

Repetition

In ancient literature, a common way of expressing emphasis in writing was the use of repetition. In Galatians 1:8–9, the same affirmation was repeated twice. In Galatians 1:6, Paul basically calls the Galatians traitors. Here he uses an even stronger word for the false teachers and anyone joining them proclaiming and believing a false doctrine. Paul uses the word *anathema* twice. This word was used to describe something or someone that was set apart to receive the final judgment of the wrath of God. According to Paul, to distort the gospel as these false teachers were doing was worthy of God's eternal condemnation. The repetition of the term for emphasis is almost as if the apostle was screaming.

In these beginning verses, Paul exposes the problem of the Galatian (6- churches: They were enchanted by a counterfeit gospel. He was stunned by how quickly the believers embraced a different version of the gospel he preached to them. Paul had just been with them! How could this have happened so quickly? It was not just the speed of their desertion that was staggering, but that it would even occur in the first place. Who would abandon receiving God's peace as a gift through Jesus Christ? God had showered the Galatians with grace. They had received his peace. Their sins had been dealt with and they had been delivered from their slavery. Why would they desert all of these blessings by saying goodbye to the gospel according to God and welcoming a fake, non-gospel? Paul was astonished that this would happen. Troublemakers, who were not even worth naming, had entered the church and confused young believers with an alternative message. Their deceptive gospel had succeeded through slight and subtle adjustments dressed in biblical language. Therein was the problem. The counterfeit looked like the real thing.

In these verses, Paul gives a warning to the false teachers who (8- presented a fake gospel. Note that the letter to the Galatians was read publicly. This means that those causing such confusion among the churches no doubt heard Paul's repeated warning towards those advancing a non-gospel. All present for the reading of the letter heard the pronouncement and knew who the guilty parties were. In order to stress the severity of the situation, Paul offers a *hypothetical* situation. Even if an apostle like Paul or an angel from God were to change the gospel message from what the Galatians had received initially, then that individual was to be set aside for God's cursing. This hypothetical situation served as a warning to others. Paul does not say he or an angel would ever change the gospel message, but he emphasizes that no one is under authority to change God's true gospel. Paul's repetition of his point seeks to emphasize the severity of the situation and its eternal consequences.

To adjust God's plan and terms of salvation, however slightly, is an attack against God's truthfulness. The Galatians had to understand the full implications of what they were flirting with. The dangers of a counterfeit gospel reach not only those who spread it but also to everyone who embraces it. Those who receive it are not truly receiving God's gift of salvation and therefore remain alienated from him even though they have been falsely assured of their salvation.

In verse 10, Paul employs a series of rhetorical questions that made (10 clear what accusations were leveled against him by the proponents of the false gospel among the Galatians. In order to discredit Paul, those individuals not only denied Paul's apostleship but also accused him of being a people-pleaser. Paul was accused of preaching a *cheap* or *easy-to-believe* gospel so that he would be popular. However, this was false. As the letter unfolds, Paul will show the relationship between his gospel and the type of life it produces. All he declares at this point

Where else is this taught in Scripture?

God's people, be they Old Testament saints or members of the early church, continually struggled to maintain the purity of what they believed. From the outset of time, Genesis informs us that Adam and Eve misrepresented God's Word and acted erroneously because of it. In Genesis 3:3, we see that Eve added to God's prohibition. God never said they could not touch the tree of the knowledge of good and evil. Eve's distortion of what God did say contributed to her rebellion against him for now he seemed overly harsh to her. The nation of Israel also distorted God's Word when they turned the meaning and purpose of the Mosaic Law into that which God never intended. Adding their laws to God's law in order to protect it turned God's gracious provision of guidance for life in fellowship with him into a terrifying lifestyle of do's and don'ts. The God of grace came to resemble an unforgiving and ruthless being. In the New Testament, the Jerusalem Council recorded in Acts 15 addresses the same problem that emerges in Galatians 1:1–10 albeit in an official manner. Clearly, this tendency to distorting God's Word transcended the region of Galatia. The leaders of the church addressed the issue from a slightly different perspective than Paul in Galatians but the underlying issues and conclusion remained the same. In addressing the question of whether Gentile Christians needed to become Jewish Christians to complete their salvation, the leaders convened at the Council and led by James the Just, the half-brother of Jesus, passed comment on the core of the gospel. Salvation is by God's grace through faith in Jesus Christ alone. The situation and response of the leaders of the church in Acts 15 is a perfect example paralleling that of the letter of Galatians. It is easy to hear man's voice over God's and yet think it is God who speaks. We must be continually careful to understand what God declares, not what we want him to say.

James the Just

James, the half-brother of Jesus, became a Christian after the death and resurrection of Jesus. He soon became the leading figure in the early church in Jerusalem as is clear from the account of the Jerusalem Council recorded in Acts. He also wrote the New Testament book of James.

Acts 15:1–2

Now some men came down from Judea and began to teach the brothers, "Unless you are circumcised according to the custom of Moses, you cannot be saved." When Paul and Barnabas had great dissension and debate with them, Paul and Barnabas and some others were appointed to go up to Jerusalem to see the apostles and elders about this issue.

23

Pleasing God

Paul's all-encompassing desire and commitment to please God is amply evident throughout the New Testament. Consider the following passages:

- 1 Thessalonians 2:4
- 2 Corinthians 5:9
- Philippians 3:7–17
- Acts 20:24

in the letter is that *people-pleasers* do not hurl curses at others! Paul's motivation in proclaiming, and now defending, the gospel was to please God. He no longer lived his life according to his own merit.

What is God saying?
What is God Saying in Galatians?

After excavating the ground of Galatians 1:1–10, we are now ready to summarize its meaning and significance. A serious problem had emerged in the Galatian churches and needed stern attention. It concerned a corruption of God's good news in Jesus Christ. This

Where else does this happen in history?

Throughout church history, there has always been a temptation to modify the gospel so that it includes the possibility of pleasing God and seeking salvation through our own ability and good works. Historically, a critical point in this discussion occurred in the Early Middle Ages because of the controversy between Augustine and Pelagius over the doctrine of original sin. Augustine affirmed that, because of the fall and the consequent depravity of man seen in Genesis 3 and Romans 5:12, mankind is absolutely incapable of producing righteous works that could lead him to salvation. The monk Pelagius contested this teaching affirming the inner goodness of mankind and his natural ability to respond with obedience to the commandments of God. As time passed, the Church condemned Pelagianism and affirmed the doctrine of original sin as described by Augustine. However, the Roman church eventually affirmed, although incorrectly, that through the grace of baptism, man's ability to respond to God in faith and obedience was partially restored. The Council of Orange in A.D. 529 declares in its concluding statement:

Augustine of Hippo
Augustine was a 4–5th century A.D. philosopher and theologian. His works greatly influenced Christianity's understanding of several key doctrines.

Philippe de Champaigne: 1645–1660

We also believe that after grace has been received through baptism, all baptized persons have the ability and responsibility, if they desire to labor faithfully, to perform with the aid and cooperation of Christ what is of essential importance in regard to the salvation of their soul... We also believe and confess to our benefit that in every good work it is not we who take the initiative and are then assisted through the mercy of God, but God himself first inspires in us both faith in him and love for him without any previous good works of our own that deserve reward, so that we may both faithfully seek the sacrament of baptism, and after baptism be able by his help to do what is pleasing to him.

From this point, it was easy to descend to a complete doctrine of salvation by works. The purity of the gospel has always been and will always be at risk.

corruption spread rapidly because its proponents belittled the one who initially proclaimed the gospel to the Galatians—Paul. To embrace this counterfeit gospel was to act like a spiritual traitor and bring God's judgment. In spite of these attacks, Paul did not back off his message. The good news of Christ was under attack.

Of course, these verses declare what God reiterates elsewhere. Jesus himself affirmed that he came on a rescue mission to seek and save the lost.[1] Moreover, he declared that life with God is only available through him.[2] There is no room for anything else but Christ. False teaching has and will always plague the church.[3] Christians need to stand strong like Paul against it.[4]

Iconium

Ancient Iconium is now modern day Konya in Turkey. Iconium was one of the Galatian cities that Paul and Barnabas visited on their First Missionary journey mentioned in Acts 13 and 14.

His work and invitation to mankind cannot be altered in any way, no matter how subtle. Troublemakers must be held accountable for their actions. Guarding the truth is essential, especially the truth of Jesus Christ. Preserving the purity of the gospel is still a problem in the church today. You may be aware of it in your church or in a person you know. Whether this is the case or not, digging through the letter of Galatians will bless you as you hear all over again God's offer of life through Jesus Christ.

What does God want?

God desires to change us so that we may become all that he made us to be. So, what does he want to do through Galatians 1:1–10? Let us examine a few general ideas to wrestle with in light of our findings in this study. Much more could be said of course, but these are a good starting point. They will reemerge in different forms as our dig

1. Mark 10:45
2. John 14:6
3. Colossians 2:8; 1 Timothy 4:1; 2 Timothy 3:5; 4:3
4. 2 Timothy 1:14

through Galatians continues. The *Discoveries* section will explore these and others further.

The Gospel is about *receiving* what God offers in Jesus

God made a commitment to deliver mankind from its bondage to sin as only he could. The good news is that by God's grace through faith in Jesus Christ, we can receive the offer of peace with God. For this reason, only he deserves the praise. At this point, it is important to grasp what Paul previewed at the beginning of the letter. God invites you to receive his deliverance from the grip and penalty of sin only through the Lord Jesus Christ. Any attempts to self-save or co-save, however slight, are a distortion of the terms of God's offer.

Subtle changes to the gospel amount to desertion

It is easy to distort God's gospel with our own version. This is particularly the case when we blend what God says in one place and what we think he is saying elsewhere. The change may be so slight and coated with Bible language that it is barely recognizable even by you. God knows in who or what you put your trust. If your trust is not exclusively in what he has done through Christ, then a counterfeit gospel has emerged. Any change is offensive to him and dangerous to us. It amounts to desertion. Proclaiming a false gospel has clear, eternal consequences. This calls for a heart check! It is a good habit to ask yourself continually, why you do what you do. Why do you go to church, read your Bible, or tithe?

There are a few other things to bear in mind. They are important but secondary to the main thrust of Galatians 1:1–10. Note some of Paul's responses to the personal attack against him. He modeled practical advice for us in specific situations. We see that others brought up his past to belittle his current work for Jesus. Likewise, *some people will remind you of your past to discredit your present*. This will be the case particularly if they are jealous or have a personal agenda to advance. Do not let this happen. Our next *Field Study* will explore Paul's response to these attacks. At this point though, we learn to stand firm through his example. We are not to let others belittle our work for the Lord because God has forgiven our past. Paul's example in this text also *teaches us to let go of living our lives to please people*. Our goal in life must be to please God and God alone. There is nothing wrong with wanting to please others, but people-pleasing cannot be the driving motive of our activity. Servants of Christ must live to serve Christ!

Discoveries

Now that you have completed your first excavation into the rich soil of Galatians, it is time to consider what you have learned. Choose the questions that are most helpful to you or your group.

Connecting with the community

These group questions are designed to help you apply what God wants from you. When applicable, think of these questions not only as an individual but also in terms of your family, your community, your nation, and your church.

1. In this *Field Study*, it was mentioned several times that the Galatian error was to seek a modified "gospel" tweaked according to their personal preference. How is this idea contrary to the true gospel of God?

2. Read carefully Galatians 1:6. Why is this verse important to the introduction to the letter and to the message of the entire book?

3. One of the most dangerous ways of destroying the truth of the gospel is by mixing it or diluting it. You can simply add a small detail or remove a little piece from it. It still looks pretty much the same but it has actually been subtly destroyed. What are some ways in which Christians today tweak the gospel in seemingly insignificant ways?

4. *Apostolic succession* is the idea that the original apostles passed on their authority through a line of bishops. What is the technical definition of an apostle? Think about the implications. What does it suggest in regards to the idea of *apostolic succession*? Where does ultimate authority reside today?

5. Congregations often attack their leaders unjustly seeking to force them to modify their teachings to doctrines pleasing to the people rather than God. What can we learn from Paul's response in this text regarding how to respond to false accusations and pressure to change the teaching of Scripture?

Notes, Observations & Questions

6. Why is Paul's statement of the Galatians' doctrine in Galatians 1:8–9 so severe? What does that mean for the subtle changes that some people make to the gospel today?

7. Why do you think it is not possible to serve God while trying to please people? How would you know if you are trying to please man while seeking to serve God? How can you identify this attitude/intention in your own heart or that of others around you? What are the attitudes or actions that characterize a people-pleaser? Can a people-pleaser be a good servant of Christ? Why or why not?

8. In Galatians 1:6, Paul calls the Galatian attitude "deserting the gospel." Review the notes about the significance of the word *deserting* and discuss with your group the significance of this word in order to understand the severity of this sin.

9. Have you ever met any troublemakers in the church? How do they cause trouble? Would there be any issue more serious than distorting the gospel? Do you think churches today consider changes to the gospel to be a trouble? How conscious are churches of potential challenges to their gospel message?

Probing deeper

These exercises are for your continued study of our Galatians passage by addressing some of the secondary issues in the text. They may require you to look at other passages beyond the text of Galatians and need to be thought of in terms of yourself, your family, your community, your nation, and your church.

1. Read the introduction to three other epistles by Paul in Ephesians 1:1–3, Philippians 1:1–6, and Colossians 1:1–8. Can you see the difference when you compare them to the introduction of Galatians? Why is this difference important?

2. Read Colossians 2. How was the church in Colossae struggling due to false teachers? How were these false teachers changing the gospel? In what sense was the situation in Colossae similar to the one in Galatia?

3. In Galatians 1:7–8, Paul thought it possible for man to abandon the true gospel and begin preaching a modified version of it that corrupted its message. In Scripture, we have the example of Demas, a collaborator with Paul in Colossians 4:14 and Philemon 24, who at some point abandoned the faith. If you were at a church where the pastor or leader suddenly changed his views on the gospel and started preaching a human doctrine or merely used the pulpit to please his congregation for personal benefit, what would you do? What would your reaction would be? Would you fight for the gospel?

Bringing the story to life

Paul uses a brief doxology at the beginning of his letter to the Galatians to state that the gospel is the work of God and that God alone is worthy of all glory. Doxologies affirm something that God has done or will do and then they ascribe attributes to God, which account for these actions. In Galatians 1:4 Paul speaks of the action of God:

who gave himself for our sins
to rescue us from this present evil age,
according to the will of our God and Father,

He then ascribes God's attribute or reason for his actions in verse 5. In this case, it is for God's glory:

to whom be glory forever and ever! Amen.

Look for doxologies in Psalm 41, 72, 89, 106, and 150. Try to find five clear examples of doxologies from hymns or praise songs that you are familiar with. Identify both the action of God and the attribute that accomplishes the action. Once you have found all of examples of doxologies, write one of your own. Be sure to include an action of God and then the corresponding attribute that makes the action possible. Share it with someone as a testimony to who God is and what he has done.

Memorizing the key

Commit to memory the key phrase for Galatians 1:1–10, which is:

Tampering with the gospel offends God

Part of learning the Bible is remembering what the Bible is about and where to find things. Memorizing the key phrases will help you to better understand and apply the key points of each book.

Excavate the Site   Galatians 1:1–10
FIELD STUDY 2
Tampering with the gospel offends God

Notes, Observations & Questions

Observation journaling

This section will prepare you for *Field Study 3*. You will read Galatians 1:11–24. We have included three types of exercises: some for before you read, some for while you are reading, and some for after you have completed the reading.

Before you read

What are three questions that you would like to know from the first ten verses of Galatians? Review Galatians 1:1–10 and write down questions that you hope Paul will explain or expand upon later in the letter. Your questions may include who, what, where, when, why or how. By writing questions, you prepare to engage with what you are about to read.

Question #1:

Question #2:

Question #3:

While you are reading

On the following page, we have laid out the biblical text with wide margins so you can mark the text with questions, key terms, notes, and structures. We have removed all of the verse markings so you can read it without distractions and have laid out the text with spacing to help you see how the lines are related. Review the guidelines on *The art of active learning* section, page xi at the beginning of your *Field Notes* for some suggestions on reading, learning, and marking the text effectively.

Galatians 1:11–24

I want you to know, brothers, that the gospel that was preached by me is not something that man made up. For I did not receive it from any man, nor was I taught it; but I received it by revelation of Jesus Christ. For you have heard of my former life in Judaism, how savagely I persecuted the church of God and tried to destroy it. I was advancing in Judaism beyond many of my contemporaries my own age among my countrymen, and was extremely zealous for the traditions of my fathers.

But when God, who had set me apart from birth and called me by his grace, was pleased to reveal his Son in me so that I might preach him among the Gentiles, I did not immediately consult with anyone, nor did I go up to Jerusalem to those who were apostles before me, but I right away went into Arabia and later returned to Damascus. Then after three years, I went up to Jerusalem to visit Cephas and stayed with him fifteen days. But I saw none of the other apostles except James, the Lord's brother.

I assure you before God that in what I am writing you, I am not lying. Then I went to Syria and Cilicia. And I was personally unknown to the churches of Judea that are in Christ. They were only hearing, "He who formerly persecuted us is now preaching the faith he once tried to destroy." And they glorified God because of me.

Notes, Observations & Questions

Summarize the text here

After you have read

1. Go back and look at the questions you wrote down from the *before you read* exercise. Did the text answer any of your questions?

2. Write out Galatians 1:11–24 from the previous page or your own Bible into a journal word for word. This practice will help you to remember and understand what you have just read. This week, journal your thoughts as you consider what it means to tamper with the gospel and its impact relating to your own family, community, nation, and church.

3. Now read Galatians 1:11–24 in your own Bible. Continue to reread it each day until you get to *Field Study 3*. This will reinforce the learning of Scripture and help you to better retain its message.

Pray

As we learn the Word of God, it is essential that we communicate with him through prayer. Commit to praying throughout the week alone or with others, asking God to help you identify areas in your life that distort his truth. Also, ask him to forgive you for doing so. Write your own prayer or use this as a sample prayer:

Dear Heavenly Father,

I thank you today for speaking truth into my life. Thank you for men like Paul who stood boldly for your truth. Thank you for exposing the tendencies of my heart and helping me see how offensive they can be to you. Please help me recognize if I have been tampering with your gospel, however slightly, thinking I can craft a better version of my own. I now see how subtle and severe this offense can be. I confess that I've distorted the intent behind some of the great practices and disciplines of the Christian faith. I know I often do the godly things I do because I think that through them I earn you. Father, help me examine my own heart and forgive me where I have failed you. I ask that the Holy Spirit will move not just in my heart but also in the hearts of believers in my church and across my nation so that we would turn to you and live, as you desire. Please also remove from our midst those who trouble us with falsehood. Thank you for treating me so patiently. Thank you for treating my church—your church—so graciously. Thank you, for inviting us to receive your offer of life through the Lord Jesus Christ. In him we pray, Amen.

Excavate the Site

Only God has the power to change lives

Galatians 1:11–24

FIELD STUDY 3

How is the text arranged?

We have learned that the gospel of God proclaimed by Paul was under attack and an alternative was spreading. As we dig into this section of the letter, a recurrent pattern begins that will continue into Galatians 2. Paul defends the truthfulness of his gospel by a series of arguments rooted in his unique personal experience. In this section of the letter, Paul defends his credibility by sourcing his gospel in God himself. God authorized his message. Paul's gospel is God's gospel. Let's examine how his defense unfolds. In your Bible, read Galatians 1:11–24 several times and try to identify the progression of his argument. After you finished your reading, look at the following outline.

Galatians 1:11–24

Section	Bible Text
The Legitimacy of Paul's Gospel	
Not man-made	¹¹ I want you to know, brothers, that the gospel that was preached by me is not something that man made up.
Received from Jesus Christ	¹² For I did not receive it from any man, nor was I taught it; but I received it by revelation of Jesus Christ.
Evidence One: A life changed by divine power	
Paul's Past: Paul was a zealous advocate of Jewish traditions	¹³ For you have heard of my former life in Judaism, how savagely I persecuted the church of God and tried to destroy it. ¹⁴ I was advancing in Judaism beyond many of my contemporaries my own age among my countrymen, and was extremely zealous for the traditions of my fathers.

Galatians 1:11–24

Section	Bible Text
Turning point: Paul was called by God's grace to know Jesus	[15] But when God, who had set me apart from birth and called me by his grace, was pleased [16] to reveal his Son in me so that I might preach him among the Gentiles,
Paul's Present: Paul becomes a zealous advocate of faith in Jesus because of God's commissioning not man's	I did not immediately consult with anyone, [17] nor did I go up to Jerusalem to those who were apostles before me, but I right away went into Arabia and later returned to Damascus. [18] Then after three years, I went up to Jerusalem to visit Cephas and stayed with him fifteen days. [19] But I saw none of the other apostles except James, the Lord's brother. [20] I assure you before God that in what I am writing you, I am not lying. [21] Then I went to Syria and Cilicia. [22] And I was personally unknown to the churches of Judea that are in Christ. [23] They were only hearing, "He who formerly persecuted us is now preaching the faith he once tried to destroy." [24] And they glorified God because of me.

As the outline shows, the structure of Galatians 1:11–24 contains two major movements: *the legitimacy of Paul's gospel* and *a life changed by divine power.*

In the first movement, Paul makes a statement that will become the basis of his defense throughout chapters 1 and 2. He declares that his gospel finds its authority in a single source: Jesus Christ.

The next movement contains the first formal piece of evidence Paul provides in defense of his statement in verses 11–12. This is the first proof in a long series that will continue until the end of chapter 2. In this proof, Paul presents an account of his own personal testimony. He recounts his experience before and after encountering Jesus on the road to Damascus. The progression from his past to present situation gives structure to his thoughts. The turning point of Paul's life is clearly his encounter with Jesus Christ.[1]

Paul's Testimony

You can find detailed descriptions of Paul's conversion and ministry in several passages of the New Testament. As a book, 2 Corinthians is in itself a defense of his ministry. Consider the following passages:
- Acts 9:1–20
- Acts 22:1–24
- Acts 26:1–28
- 2 Corinthians 11:16–33
- Philippians 3:3–14

1.   Acts 9:1–31

2091 God calls Abraham?

1925 God calls Abraham?

Receiving the Law on Mount Sinai? 1446

Receiving the Law on Mount Sinai? 1260

What is this passage saying?
What are some key terms and phrases?

Now let's dig a little deeper into the text. The following table presents a few key terms and phrases useful to our understanding of Galatians 1:11–24. Study them and seek to grasp their significance to this section.

Meaning of Key Terms

Key word or phrase	Meaning and significance
A revelation of Jesus Christ (1:12)	There are two valid ways to understand this phrase. More precisely, the English preposition "of" means one of two things. If the original Greek phrase is classified as an *objective genitive* then it means a revelation *about* Jesus Christ. The implication is that God the Father revealed Jesus to Paul. This is what is meant in verse 16 when the idea reemerges. If, however, the phrase is a *subjective genitive* then it was a revelation *from* Jesus Christ. Either option is valid. Both maintain the source of Paul's gospel as divine, so in that sense, nothing is at stake. Even if this was a revelation about Jesus, by the Father, not from Jesus, we know Paul did directly encounter Jesus in his life. Interestingly, this is also the phrase that begins the book of Revelation which provides the title of the book, the "revelation or unveiling *of* Jesus Christ."
Set apart from before birth (1:15)	Paul's use of this phrase in reference to his life is a window into the sovereign workings of God. God knew Paul before Paul knew him. God providentially guided his life even before his conversion. It is the same with us. God knew you before you ever knew or received him!
Active verbs (1:15, 16)	In the biblical text, it is always important to observe the *voice* of the verbs. The voice tells us if the verb is active or passive. When the voice is active, the subject is doing the action of the verb. When the passive voice is used, the subject is receiving the action of the verb. Paul *was set apart*, or *called* by God, and the Son *was* revealed to him. These are active verbs and God is the subject. Paul is passively receiving the action of God and affirming that God alone is doing the work.
They glorified God (1:5, 24)	Galatians 1:11–24 ends with God being glorified. Paul's conversion and proclamation of the gospel exalted God even among believers who didn't know the apostle personally. It is important to emphasize who receives the glory. The true gospel working in one's life brings glory to God, not man.

What does "of" mean in verse 12?

about **Jesus Christ** / objective genitive	= God revealed Jesus to Paul
or	
from **Jesus Christ** / subjective genitive	= Jesus revealed the gospel to Paul

---

What about the culture?

In verse 14, Paul classifies his former lifestyle as one *in Judaism.*[2] He

1250	1100	950	800	650	500 B.C.

Saul becomes king 1050

David becomes king 1010

Solomon becomes king 971

930 The kingdom divides

722 Northern kingdom falls to Assyria

Southern kingdom falls to Babylon and the temple is destroyed 586

Irony?

Paul's comment about believers who did not know him may contain some irony. Those who didn't know him personally glorified God because of his life and ministry. Sadly, those like the Galatians who had known first-hand the impact of Paul's service to Christ, were seeking to destroy him.

Ancient Sources

In addition to the Bible, we can learn much about the practices of Judaism in the Greek and Roman period from many ancient documents such as the works of Philo, Flavius Josephus, the Apocrypha, and other later Jewish writings like the Mishnah.

Pharisees

The Pharisees were a popular sect of Judaism. They were extremely influential among the common Jews of the first century. The name is rooted in the concept of holiness or *being set apart* which was their goal—holiness before God. They were a conservative party who were zealous for the traditions of Israel. Their goal was to enforce and apply God's law, both written and oral, in the context of everyday life. They also practiced a strict observance of Jewish ceremonies and for this reason were deemed the role models of godliness.

also refers to it as *the traditions of my fathers.*[1] It is important for us to explore this topic a little deeper. The practices of Judaism were uniform for the most part. There were common denominators such as ethnicity expressed in circumcision, claims on a history with God, and the Scriptures/Law. However, just as Protestantism today is varied, so Judaism was diverse in certain aspects. There were several Jewish schools of thought: Pharisees, Sadducees, Zealots, Essenes, and other minor groups. Each practiced Judaism a bit differently. Paul was a Pharisee.[2]

Pharisees were passionate about guarding, interpreting, and applying God's law and its practices. Both the laws written in the Scriptures and also those passed down orally through their fathers. They were zealous about Israel's relationship with God, and the nation's responsibility before him. Israel's history of disobedience to God and the resulting exile fueled their zeal. They were adamant about not repeating the same mistakes, so they decided to protect God's law by making their own laws. They got lost in the *how* and the *what* of the religious laws they practiced, and in the process, they missed *why* they followed them. Their efforts to enforce godliness looked godly but actually were not. Christianity, with its emphasis on grace and faith, was a threat to this type of *performance based* Judaism even though it was consistent with God's plan as expressed throughout the Old Testament Scriptures. Paul felt this threat before knowing Jesus since a life in Judaism "according to the traditions of my fathers," was one steeped in the rules, regulations, and religious practices of Israel in an attempt to satisfy God.

What is the explanation?

We are now ready to work our way through the text in detail. First, we will carefully study the meaning of some textual elements that will help us understand the significance of this section. Later we will also look at some cultural issues that illuminate the operation of the first century world.

The legitimacy of Paul's gospel: In these verses, Paul makes a clear (11– and emphatic statement to the Galatian believers. It serves as the introduction for the idea that he will defend in this section. Paul gives them his main point at the beginning so he can be clear. The Galatians were not to doubt his authority given the source of it.

It is interesting to observe that, during Paul's defense of his authority,

1. Galatians 1:14
2. Philippians 3:5; Acts 23:6

secondary issues emerge. For example, we have a small glimpse of one of the attacks that was presented against the apostle. It is as if his opponents were saying, "You really don't know Paul do you?" The fact that Paul referred to the Galatians as *brothers* is evidence that these potential deserters were believers. Later in the letter, we will see that Paul was convinced of their faith. In light of these issues, the main point Paul emphatically makes is presented in a dual manner, through both negative and positive statements. First, Paul denies his gospel was of human origin. He negates this three times:

1. It was not *man-made* (verse 11)
2. It was not *man given* (verse 12)
3. It was not *man taught* (verse 12)

Secondly, he affirms he received the gospel as a divine revelation. The authority of Paul's message laid in its source—God. Can you see how Paul subtly reaffirmed the source of the gospel as we saw in *Field Study 2*? The gospel is all about receiving from God through Jesus Christ.

Evidence One: The Power to change a life: Paul provides several pieces of personal evidence to prove to the Galatians the authority of the true gospel they initially believed. We will study the first piece of evidence here and the rest in *Field Studies 4* and *5*. This means that Galatians 1:11–12 is defended beyond the first chapter. Paul's line of reasoning moves from what he was to what he has become emphasizing how the change occurred.

4) **Paul's past:** The Galatians knew who Paul used to be. Whether they heard this directly from him or as a defamation of his character as part of his opponents' strategy, is not known. Either way, the Galatians knew Paul was once steeped in Judaism. He was a role model of a system of Jewish rules and traditions. He was top of the class—a rising star. He fanatically lived to please God by his lifestyle of adhering to the laws and practices of the Pharisees.[3] He expressed his zeal with a violence that could only be described as a Jewish version of Islamic jihad.[4] Therefore, Paul had every right to talk about living life to earn God according to the laws and traditions of Israel—the very thing the Galatians were adding to their faith in Jesus. He had once lived thinking he could satisfy God. He modeled this religious system better than anyone else did. People may have used Paul's past against him, but Paul used it to highlight the grace of God's intervention. Look carefully at the way the logical argument develops.

3. Philippians 3:3–7
4. Acts 9:1–2

Brothers

Believers in the early church used the term *brothers* as a gender inclusive term to refer to each other. It is a beautiful way of reminding one another of the close bond that exists between believers because of our relationship to Jesus Christ. We are children of God! Yet it is more than a designation. It is also a call for believers to treat each other in a loving manner as it is fitting of members in the family of God. Many Christians, including entire broad movements like *The Brethren*, still use this word today to refer to one another.

Receive

The word *receive* is clearly important to the apostle's defense of the gospel. It was the source of Paul's gospel that was questioned and his opponents must have argued that he got it from another man. Paul responded that the Galatians *received* (verse 9) what he *received* (verse 12) from God. The word itself implies passivity. The recipient simply accepts what is given. The choice of this word insists Paul did not alter what came from God. This same emphasis is also clear in 1 Corinthians 15:1–4.

1250	1100	950	800	650	500 B.C.

Saul becomes king 1050
David becomes king 1010
Solomon becomes king 971
930 The kingdom divides
Southern kingdom exile to Babylon 605
Third wave of Babylon exile 586
722 Northern kingdom exiled to Assyria
597 Second wave of Babylon exile
37

RÉSUMÉ
SAUL OF TARSUS
CURRENT HOMETOWN: ANTIOCH

BACKGROUND
Ethnically Jewish with Roman citizenship
Born around A.D. 5 in intellectual hub of Tarsus
    in modern day, south central Turkey
Zealous Jew of Pharisaic strand: circumcised
    on 8th day, Benjamite tribal ancestry,
Pharisee and son of a Pharisee,
    blameless before the law.

EDUCATION
Early Education in Tarsus
Higher Education: Pharisaic training in Jerusalem
    under Gamaliel

EMPLOYMENT
Teacher and enforcer of God's Law
Tent-maker by training

EXPERIENCE
Entrusted by the Jewish Ruling Council in Jerusalem to
supervise the stoning of Stephen, a Christian, for blasphemy.

Apostle of the Jewish Ruling Council in Jerusalem entrusted
with persecuting and removing Christians from Jerusalem
and beyond including women and children.

Murderer of Christians.

REFERENCES
Dr Luke in Acts 7:58; 8:1; 9:1–2; 21:39; 2:3; 23:6; 26:4

Saul of Tarsus
Saul of Tarsus was undoubtedly a zealous Jew
opposed to Christianity. His conversion is clearly one
of the most striking and crucial turning points in the
history of the church.

Gamaliel was a leading figure in first century
Judaism. He was a renowned expert and teacher
of Jewish law, of the Pharisaic variety between A.D.
22–55. He is mentioned in Acts 5:34–39 calling for
calm and discretion in the treatment of Christians.
This stands in contrast to his most famous disciple,
Saul of Tarsus. Christian tradition claims Gamaliel
became a Christian, but Judaism denies it. Was his
former disciple influential in this?

Turning point: So what happened to Paul? (15
What caused the turnaround in his life?
Simply put, God graciously intervened as
he had planned to do all along.[1] Paul did
not deserve it. His religious lifestyle could
not earn the right to know God and satisfy
him. Paul's encounter with Christ and his
commissioning to the Gentiles originated
with God. He obeyed God's call to proclaim
the gospel to Gentiles like the Galatians.
Therefore, Paul's time in Galatia was not
accidental. Such a radical turnaround
in lifestyle could only occur by the
intervention of the power of God's sovereign
grace through Jesus. A person, not a system,
changes lives. God changed Paul and then
sent him to the Galatian Gentiles.

Paul's Present: Paul ends this first (16
piece of evidence by outlining his travel
itinerary since his encounter with Jesus.
This highlights the authority of his gospel
through his own experience. Note the point
he makes. Paul transitioned from his past
life to his present life without interruption
(though for purposes of discussion we
divided verse 16). Paul's reasoning can be
paraphrased to flow as follows from the
beginning of verse 16:

*"When God called and commissioned me that
was enough. I did not need any man—not even
the apostles in Jerusalem—to sanction what God already approved.
And so I traveled here and there as his representative and even
churches that did not know me praised God for they recognized his
work through me."*

Paul essentially restates what we read in verses 1–2. He was a
representative of God, appointed by God and not man, yet was
supported by the broader Christian church. Have a look at Paul's
travels through Arabia, Damascus, up briefly to Jerusalem, to Syria,
and Cilicia. He traveled long distances showing his devotion to God's
call on his life. There was a sense in which Paul's belittlers were right.

1. See also Jeremiah 1:5; Isaiah 49:1–6

B.C.	1	A.D.		10		20		30		40		50

5? Birth of Jesus

5? Birth of Paul

John the Baptist begins his ministry 28–29?

Jesus begins his ministry 28–30?

Jesus is crucified and resurrected 30–33?

33–34? Paul encounters Christ on Damascus road

Paul writes Galatians 48?

46–47? First Miss Journey b

He was independent of the Jerusalem leadership and the Judean churches although he knew some members. However, this did not mean he was independent from God. The zealous advocate of a religion that tried to earn God became a passionate proclaimer of a relationship with God by grace through faith in Jesus. The Galatian churches could get a character reference even from churches who did not know Paul personally. These churches recognized and responded to the authority of his gospel of faith. The work of God results in praise to God.

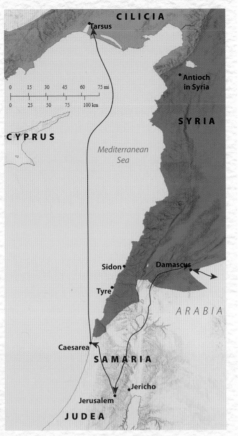

Therefore, Paul's past antagonism to Jesus was no reason to doubt his present proclamation of the gospel. Rather, it was the opposite. God transformed Paul and saved him from trying to earn his salvation. Now he lived by faith in Jesus alone. His personal testimony proved God's direct intervention in his life.

What is God saying?

Paul's credibility was undermined to discredit his gospel message. It appears his opponents believed Paul's gospel was diluted and tailor-made for Gentile audiences. They even seemed to accuse him of being a liar.[2] To these accusations, Paul answered by firmly anchoring his gospel in God. This study provides us with his first piece of evidence to prove this truth. Paul received Jesus by God's gracious intervention. Only this encounter with a person, not a system, could change someone like him from persecutor to proclaimer of faith in Christ. Because God called him directly, he was not inferior to other apostles. The gospel the Galatians received from him was the one he received directly from God.

2. Galatians 1:20

From Saul to Paul

The apostle Paul was formerly known as Saul. We do not know for sure the reason for the change. Some suggest the name Paul means *little* and so the change either reflects his physical stature or his humility upon conversion to Jesus Christ. Others suggest that Paul is simply a Latin or Roman version of the Hebrew Saul. Interestingly, the shift in name occurs during the first missionary journey when he is in Cyprus evangelizing a man also called Paul—*Sergius Paulus* in Acts 13:9. Shifting to a more Gentile name perhaps signals Paul's determination to become all things to all men for the sake of the gospel.

Saul's Early Travels

Saul first encountered Jesus on the way from Jerusalem to Damascus. Galatians 1:17 states that Paul then went into Arabia for a time before returning to Damascus and then Jerusalem. After learning of a threat on his life, Paul journeyed from Jerusalem to Caesarea and then on to his home town of Tarsus.

Travel in the first century

In the times of Jesus and Paul, travel was rarely done for leisure. Given the terrain, it was difficult, expensive, dangerous, and slow. Even though the Romans had built many roads, they were unsafe and unattractive. This partly was due to the common presence of robbers. See 2 Corinthians 11:26.

50	60	70	80	90	100 A.D.

49? Jerusalem Council

50–52? Second Missionary Journey by Paul

60–62? Paul arrives in Rome under house arrest

64 Fire in Rome

70 Temple is destroyed

79 Pompeii and Herculaneum are destroyed by Vesuvius eruption

John writes Revelation 95–96?

The Scriptures present the power of God himself as the agent of life-change on many occasions. Jacob, for example, only changed from lying and cheating when he wrestled personally with God.[1] Moses also changed from trying to deliver Israel on his own strength to actually accomplishing this many years later but only when he personally encountered God.[2] A believer in Jesus is one changed by the power of God. As believers we are channels of change in society around us only if we live according to the power of God not in the power of our religious customs and practices.

Where else is this taught in Scripture?

In the Old Testament, one of the most powerful examples of God's gracious power to transform the lives of wicked sinners is Manasseh king of Judah. Manasseh became king at age twelve and reigned fifty-five years in Jerusalem:

King Manasseh

The Kingdom of Israel had already succumbed to Assyria. Manasseh pleaded before the Lord in humility to be rescued from this evil empire.

> He did evil in the eyes of the LORD, according to the abominable practices of the nations whom the LORD drove out before the Israelites. For he rebuilt the high places that his father Hezekiah had destroyed; he also erected altars for the Baals and made Asherah poles, and worshipped all the host of heaven and served them. He built altars in the temple of the LORD of which the LORD had said, "In Jerusalem shall my name be forever."
>
> But Manasseh misled Judah and the inhabitants of Jerusalem so that they sinned more than the nations whom the LORD had destroyed before the Israelites.

2 Chronicles 33:2–4, 9

The nation of Judah never had a king more wicked than Manasseh. Disciplined by God, he was taken captive by the king of Assyria and found himself in anguish. After a lifetime of wickedness, a single heart-felt prayer was sufficient to find God's gracious forgiveness and restoration. God's grace forgave him and changed him into a new man:

> In his distress he called on the favor of the LORD his God and humbled himself greatly before the God of his fathers. When he prayed to him, the LORD was moved by his entreaty and heard his plea and brought him back to Jerusalem to his kingdom. Then Manasseh knew that the LORD is God.
>
> After this, he built the outer wall for the city of David west of the Gihon in the valley to the entrance of the Fish gate and encircling the Ophel, making it much higher. He also took away the foreign gods and the idol from the temple of the LORD and all the altars he had built on the hill of the temple of the LORD and in Jerusalem; he threw them outside the city. He also restored the altar of the LORD and sacrificed peace offerings and thank offerings, and told Judah to serve the LORD, the God of Israel.

1. Genesis 32:22–32
2. Exodus 3:1–22

Where else does this happen in history?

Charles Simeon

Charles Simeon was an English pastor who lived from 1759 to 1836.

Paul's sufferings should not be foreign to any Christian with a passion to serve the Lord. One of the great examples of faithfulness in the midst of opposition is found in the life of Pastor Charles Simeon towards the end of the 18th century in England. When the vicar of Trinity Church in Cambridge died in 1782, Charles Simeon was named as the new vicar by the bishop. The parishioners were not happy with the appointment and from the very beginning, they vehemently opposed Simeon. As part of their rebellion, the congregation refused to let him be the Sunday evening lecturer, and for five years they assigned the lecture to Mr. Hammond, the man who they wanted as their vicar. When he left, instead of letting their pastor of five years do the lecture, they assigned it to another independent man for seven more years! At last, in 1794, Simeon was the chosen lecturer. Imagine serving for 12 years in a church so unhappy with your leadership that they would not let you preach on Sunday evenings!

In addition to being forbidden to preach in the evening service, the members of the church also locked the pew doors on Sunday mornings. The pewholders refused to come and refused to let others sit in their personal pews. Simeon set up seats in the aisles and nooks and corners at his own expense. But the church wardens took them out and threw them in the churchyard. When he tried to visit people in their homes, hardly anyone would open the door to him. This situation lasted at least ten years. In spite of all the attacks against him, he persisted in the ministry of the Word and prayer and gradually overcame the opposition.

After he had been there 30 years, new opponents arose that sought to remove him from ministry for almost five years! Once again, Simeon remained faithful to his calling. It is said that towards the end of his ministry, Simeon was asked one afternoon by his friend, Joseph Gurney, how he had resisted persecution and conquered all the great prejudice against him in his forty-nine year ministry. He said to Gurney, "My dear brother, we must not mind a little suffering for Christ's sake."

What does God want?

What should we do in response to our study of Scripture in Galatians 1:11–24? What are some of the major issues God wants us to think through and live out? We will provide a few for you. Consider how these truths can be specifically lived out in your life.

God, not a religious system, changes you

Paul made it very clear in Galatians 1:11–24 and elsewhere that you can live a religious life and still be deemed a persecutor of God.[3] Though Paul lived much of his life trying to satisfy God before his encounter with Christ, his approach was wrong and ill motivated. His

3.　Philippians 3:5; Acts 9:1–5

The Trinity

The Christian doctrine of the Trinity teaches that the one true God exists in three distinct Persons—Father, Son, and Holy Spirit. Each distinct Person of the Godhead has distinct roles in the plan of salvation, but they are all co-equal.

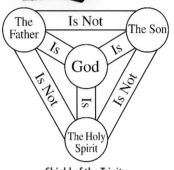

Shield of the Trinity

This shield of the Trinity or *"Scutum Fideo"* as it is known in Latin is a visual way of expressing or symbolizing the person of God in Western Christianity.

Matthew 28:19

Therefore go and make disciples of all nations, baptizing them in the name of the Father and of the Son and of the Holy Spirit...

2 Corinthians 13:14

The grace of the Lord Jesus Christ and the love of God and the fellowship of the Holy Spirit be with you all.

clean-cut, religious living had no power to save him nor gave him any right to a relationship with God. Only the triune God can create a relationship by his grace through faith in Jesus. Paul experienced this and only then was he changed. Therefore, a stance before God that satisfies him is uniquely by his own doing: his work, his power, and a fulfillment of his promised plan. He accomplishes this in Jesus Christ. To add to what he has done is ineffective and takes praise away from God. Think about this for a while. Do you steal God's praise? We must be very careful here for we run the same risk of being accused of what Paul had been accused of in verse 10—easy believism![1] Righteous acts cannot earn God's love but living upright lives is God's will for believers.[2] God expects this of us but only as an overflow of love, gratitude, and loyalty to him because of his work in us.

God changes you to use you in his service

Paul's experience can be ours too. God planned to call Paul to salvation and use him in his pursuit of others through the proclamation of the gospel. Believers are saved to serve. There are many avenues through which to serve God, of course, and he has gifted us and empowered us with his Spirit. Many believers, however, appear to live the Christian life as though they have no responsibility in God's plans. There are many reasons for this—ignorance of God's will, fear, rebellion, and indecision, but none are excusable. Try to serve God this week. Perhaps do what Paul did in our passage here. He shared his testimony. Your life story, with God's gracious intervention through Jesus as its turning point, is a powerful proof of what God can do. Tell others about it!

There are a few other interesting points to consider. First, look at Paul's itinerary following his conversion. He went to Arabia, Damascus, Jerusalem, and Syria and Cilicia. Paul went to Arabia to be alone with God. He had to reexamine all he believed in light of his encounter with Jesus. In Damascus, he returned to the place where he had sought to destroy the church. That must have been hard. Paul put his life at stake returning to Jerusalem from where he was sent out to destroy the church. He had betrayed friends there. In Syria and Cilicia, Paul took the gospel home. Proclaiming the gospel to those closest to us may be hard but that is no excuse. *Paul took his message to difficult places and underwent difficult circumstances.* Secondly, do not let others use your *godless* past against you. Use it to highlight the grace of God's intervention. If you have received God's grace through faith in Jesus Christ, you are a changed person, a new creation. *Don't let your past prevent you from living to praise and serve God in the present.*

1.   See also Romans 6:1–23
2.   Ephesians 2:10

Discoveries

Now that you have completed your second excavation into the ancient riches of God's Word found in Galatians, it's time to sift through your *Discoveries* and see what you have learned. Find the questions that are most helpful for you and your group.

Connecting with the community

These discussion questions will help you apply what God wants from you. Consider each of these questions in terms of yourself, your family, your community, your nation, and your church.

1. In Galatians 1:12, the apostle Paul affirms no one taught him the gospel. Rather, he received it by revelation. Why do you think this is a relevant argument in favor of his authority and message?

2. In what way is the history of Paul's travels after his conversion important to his argument?

3. How did Paul use his opponents' slander against him to defend the truth of the gospel?

4. According to verses 16–24, even though Paul was rejected by his own spiritual children in Galatia, he was actually admired in many other regions of the empire where he had never been present. Why is this situation so common in life and ministry? Do you know any personal examples of this irony?

5. Summarize and discuss the main components of Judaism described in *Field Study 3*.

6. If Judaism was a biblical faith, why did Paul abandon it?

7. Is Christianity a form of Judaism? Why or why not? Create a small table to compare and contrast Christianity and Judaism. How are they similar? How are they different?

8. Do you think it is possible for people to change regarding their innermost character qualities and faults? Why or why not?

9. How have you been changed or transformed by the gospel? Can you share one or two specific ways in which your character has been molded into the character of Christ because of your faith in the truth of the gospel?

10. What is the purpose of God's transformational work in you? Is that purpose currently being fulfilled in your life? If not, why not?

11. Is it possible to serve God without first being transformed by the gospel? How much do we need to change before we can serve? Should we think of this as a process where service follows transformation or do they happen together?

Probing deeper

These exercises are to help you look deeper into some of the secondary issues of our passage and may require reading from the rest of Scripture. Consider each of these questions in terms of yourself, your family, your community, your nation, and your church.

1. The Judaism of the first century that had developed out of the Old Testament was a ritualistic practice that did not follow what God had commanded. Stephen's speech in Acts 7:1–53 presents a selective history of God's works in the Old Testament. In this speech, Stephen gives several examples of what God wanted done versus what the people actually did. Make a chart from Acts 7:1–53 with a column listing what God wanted and a second column listing what the Jews actually did. What does this show about Paul's former life of Judaism?

2. Review the notes of this chapter about passive and active verbs, and then read Galatians 1:15–16 as well as Acts 26:1–32. Was Paul active or passive in his election, conversion, and vocational calling? Why/how is this significant? Does every Christian's election, conversion, and calling happen as Paul's did? Why or why not?

3. Paul's conversion is one of the most dramatic examples in the Bible of the power of God to transform sinners into saints. Moses was a murderer. David was an adulterer and murderer. Paul, when he was still Saul, approved of murder and set out to murder. God can change anyone including you. Can you recall other biblical characters who also demonstrated the transforming power of the Word of God in those who believe?

Notes, Observations & Questions

4. In many contemporary cultures, there are movements and even industries for self-help and motivation. Do you believe that the teaching of this text contradicts the basic assumption of the self-help movement? Can people change themselves in any significant way? If people can really change themselves, can we still affirm that the gospel is necessary? Why or why not?

Bringing the story to life

The apostle Paul was completely transformed by his encounter with Jesus on the road to Damascus. He spent the rest of his life serving the risen Savior who was changing him. We too are being transformed by Christ and are called to serve him.

Come up with a project where you can serve Christ in your church or community. Do not rely on service you are already doing but rather do something as a specific response to Paul's example in Galatians 1:11–24. If possible, make it a group project involving others who are studying Galatians with you or anyone else who would like to take part. Ideas may include:

- Clean up or restoration projects for the church or community
- Visiting or serving those who are sick, disabled or elderly who cannot get out easily
- Volunteering at existing places that already serve the community
- Creating a kids event such as a puppet show or play to teach about Christ's commands to love and serve others
- Any other idea that you can do in service to Christ

Remember, the goal is to serve on Christ's behalf. Ideally the service project will create an opportunity to share the gospel, just as Paul did with the Galatians.

Memorizing the key

Commit to memory the key phrase for Galatians 1:11–24 which is:

> Only God has the power to change lives

Part of learning the Bible is remembering what the Bible is about and where to find things. Memorizing the key phrases will help you to better understand and apply the key points of Galatians and remember each topic the book covers.

Observation journaling

This section will prepare you for *Field Study 4* by reading through the next section of Galatians. We have included three types of exercises: some for before you read, some for while you are reading, and some for after you have completed the reading.

Before you read

In Galatians 2, Paul will continue his travel itinerary after encountering Christ on the road to Damascus. Review Galatians 1:11–24 listing in order the places Paul traveled. Beside each place, list the amount of time Paul spent there if the time is given. This will prepare you for Galatians 2:1–10 where Paul continues to describe the events in his life before traveling to Galatia.

Galatians 1:11–24

Places Paul Traveled
(in chronological order)

Time Spent
(if recorded in the text)

While you are reading

On the following page, we have laid out the biblical text with wide margins so you can mark the text with questions, key terms, notes, and structures. We have removed all of the verse markings so you can read it without distractions and have laid out the text with spacing to help you see how the lines are related. Review the guidelines on *The art of active learning* section, page xi at the beginning of your *Field Notes* for some suggestions on reading, learning, and marking the text effectively.

Galatians 2:1–10

Then after fourteen years I went up again to Jerusalem with Barnabas, taking Titus along too. I went up because of a revelation and set before them the gospel that I preach among the Gentiles. But I did this in private to those who seemed influential, for fear that I was running or had run in vain.

But not even Titus, who was with me, was forced to be circumcised, even though he was a Greek. Now this matter arose because of the false brothers secretly brought in had infiltrated our ranks to spy on our freedom that we have in Christ Jesus and to bring us into slavery. But we did not surrender to them even for a moment, so that the truth of the gospel would remain with you.

As for those who seemed influential—whatever they were makes no difference to me; God shows no partiality—those who seemed influential added nothing to my message. But on the contrary, they saw that I had been entrusted with the gospel to the uncircumcised, just as Peter had been to the circumcised. For God, who was at work through Peter as an apostle to the circumcised, was also at work in my ministry as an apostle to the Gentiles, and James, Cephas and John, who were reputed to be pillars, gave Barnabas and me the right hand of fellowship when they recognized the grace given to me. They agreed that we should go to the Gentiles, and they to the circumcised. All they asked was to continue to remember the poor, the very thing I was eager to do.

Notes, Observations & Questions

Summarize the text here

Notes, Observations & Questions

After you have read

1. Journaling is another way to help us learn. Write out Galatians 2:1–10 from the previous page or your own Bible into a journal word for word. This practice will help you to remember and understand what you have just read. This week, journal your thoughts as you consider the freedom that we have in Jesus Christ and how it affects you, your family, your community, your nation, and your church. Write down what God wants you to do with that freedom and then act accordingly.

2. Now read Galatians 2:1–10 in your own Bible. Continue to reread it each day until you get to *Field Study 4*. This will reinforce the learning of Scripture and help you in retention.

Pray

As we learn the Word of God, it is essential that we communicate with him through prayer. Consider writing a prayer or psalm or poem to God. Writing it out will help you reflect on God's power to transform lives. How has God changed your life? Commit to praying through the week asking God that you, your family, your church, and your nation may be transformed. Try to pray with a friend or family member. Consider this as a sample prayer:

Dear God,

Thank you for faithful servants like Paul whom you used greatly in your service. Help me, and those around me, respect, encourage, and support those whom you have placed over us at home, in church, and our nation. It is so easy to criticize and discredit even good leaders when our personal agendas are not advanced. Lord, I also thank you for personally revealing the message of the gospel. I can stand with confidence in what it declares because it is backed directly by you. I know you will do what you committed to do for your Name's sake. As I meditate on what you teach, it makes so much sense, God, that only you have the power to change a life like mine since you created me. How silly of me to live as if impersonal, even Christian, traditions could change me. What a great joy it is too, Lord, to know that your plan included me long before my birth. You truly are a personal God! Thank you for saving me because of faith in Christ, and not my past performance. I would be doomed otherwise! Help me, Holy Spirit, to figure out how I can serve you today. Grant me a creative mind to look for ways to serve. In the name of the Lord Jesus Christ I pray, Amen.

Excavate the Site
Galatians 2:1–10

The truth of the gospel must never be compromised

Galatians 2:1–10
FIELD STUDY 4

How is the text arranged?

In the previous section of Galatians, Paul made a very clear statement: his gospel is God's gospel.[1] He defended it using his personal encounter with Christ as a starting point, which is Paul's first of three evidences. He was called and set apart by God's grace to know Jesus and proclaim him among the Gentiles. Only God's power could release Paul from slavery to a religious lifestyle so that he could embrace God through faith in Jesus. Therefore, discrediting Paul in order to attack his gospel was a direct challenge to God. While Paul was autonomous from all men, his second proof shows that even the other apostles supported him. They believed Paul's gospel was their gospel, the true gospel from God. Read the biblical text several times and see if you can identify the structure before looking at the one provided:

Galatians 2:1–10

Section	Bible Text
Evidence Two: The Apostles agree with Paul	
A God-initiated situation	¹ Then after fourteen years I went up again to Jerusalem with Barnabas, taking Titus along too. ² I went up because of a revelation and set before them the gospel that I preach among the Gentiles. But I did this in private to those who seemed influential, for fear that I was running or had run in vain.

---

1. Galatians 1:11–12

Galatians 2:1–10

Section	Bible Text
An example proving harmony	[3] But not even Titus, who was with me, was forced to be circumcised, even though he was a Greek. [4] Now this matter arose because of the false brothers secretly brought in had infiltrated our ranks to spy on our freedom that we have in Christ Jesus and to bring us into slavery. [5] But we did not surrender to them even for a moment, so that the truth of the gospel would remain with you.
Official harmony between Paul and other apostles expressed	[6] As for those who seemed influential— whatever they were makes no difference to me; God shows no partiality— those who seemed influential added nothing to my message. [7] But on the contrary, they saw that I had been entrusted with the gospel to the uncircumcised, just as Peter had been to the circumcised. [8] For God, who was at work through Peter as an apostle to the circumcised, was also at work in my ministry as an apostle to the Gentiles, [9] and James, Cephas and John, who were reputed to be pillars, gave Barnabas and me the right hand of fellowship when they recognized the grace given to me. They agreed that we should go to the Gentiles, and they to the circumcised. [10] All they asked was to continue to remember the poor, the very thing I was eager to do.

Let's now briefly analyze the logical structure of the text. There are three major aspects to Paul's evidence to show that the gospel he presented to the Galatian churches originated with God. First he clarifies that his visit to Jerusalem was God's idea. Then he proceeds to show that during his visit, Titus was not forced to be circumcised. Finally the apostle shows that the meeting with the earlier apostles resulted in clear harmony with respect to their gospel proclamation.

B.C. 2000   1850   1700   1550   1400   1250

2091 God calls Abraham?   Receiving the Law on Mount Sinai? 1446

1925 God calls Abraham?   Receiving the Law on Mount Sinai? 1260

What is this passage saying?

What are some key terms and phrases?

In the following table, we present some key terms, phrases, and concepts useful to understanding this passage. They prepare you for grasping the "explanation" section that follows. Take some time to study and understand them.

Meaning of Key Terms

Key word or phrase	Meaning and significance
Was not running or had not run in vain (2:2)	The apostle Paul enjoyed sports, or at least using the sporting imagery of his day (1 Corinthians 9:24–27; 2 Timothy 2:5; 4:7). At first glance, this may read as though Paul had doubts about the accuracy of the gospel he preached; as though he needed the approval of the Jerusalem leadership. The private nature of the meeting added to this impression, but this was not the case. To understand the text this way would undermine the very point Paul has been making in Galatians so far. Paul did not doubt the validity and accuracy of the gospel message he preached. Nevertheless, he did recognize that its advancement was hindered if the Jerusalem leaders did not agree with him. It was not the Jerusalem leadership who had to approve Paul's gospel. God had done that. However, Paul recognized his work for God could not be sabotaged by others—like the false teachers in Galatia—if there was explicit agreement between Paul and the leaders of the Jerusalem church on this very matter.
Reputed influential leaders (2:2–9)	In verse 2, Paul says he presented his gospel message before the *influential leaders* in Jerusalem. In verse 9, these leaders are identified as James, Peter, and John. The way he refers to them could appear at first glance to be belittling—as though they were *reputed* to be influential but really were not (see verses 2, 6, 9). Was Paul actually derogatory toward the other apostles? His contention in this passage was to declare that these men agreed with him, so it does not make sense that he would belittle those he is enlisting as support. Moreover, the fact that he went to them was indicative of his recognition of their God-granted status. For these reasons, it is best to understand what Paul says about them as simply voicing what his opponents were arguing. They seemed to argue that the *real reputable* apostles—not Paul—were to be heard. Paul shows that those *truly reputable* leaders agreed with him. He was not demeaning them. Rather, Paul was using his opponents' argument against them.

Formulating beliefs

There is a process by which Christian beliefs are defined. It is not a practice that invents *new* doctrines, but rather articulates them carefully, precisely, and in a manner consistent with Scripture:

1. The church proclaims the recognized Christian faith through teaching and practice.
2. There is a contemporary challenge to the faith through false or innovative teaching.
3. The church responds with a process of confirmation, clarification, and redefinition of the content of the Christian faith.

This cycle is what has caused church councils like Nicaea to describe carefully what Christians have always believed (Jude 3). Even though Galatians 2 is not an official church council, it is a private precursor to it.

| 1250 | 1100 | 950 | 800 | 650 | 500 B.C. |

Saul becomes king 1050

David becomes king 1010

Solomon becomes king 971

930 The kingdom divides

722 Northern kingdom falls to Assyria

Southern kingdom falls to Babylon and the temple is destroyed 586

51

Modern Christian Cults

To this day, the Christian church has always experienced the threat of false teachers who seek to corrupt the sound doctrine of the gospel. How can we identify a cult or a sect? The following list includes common characteristics of cultic groups:

1. **Denial of the Trinity**. Most cultic groups begin their slippery slope towards heresy by modifying the doctrine of God.

2. **Exclusivism**. Most sects consider themselves to be the only preservers of the true faith. All other groups are marked as false.

3. **Distortion of the Bible**. They affirm to believe in the Bible but in reality they twist the meaning of Scripture to fit their purposes and man-made beliefs.

4. **Redefinition of Christian terms**. Sects tend to use Christian words but change their meanings creating doctrines diametrically opposed to orthodox Christian beliefs.

5. **Denial of the true gospel**. Most sects deny that man can be saved simply by believing in the gospel and trusting in the work of Christ.

6. **Additional sources of authority**. Most cultic groups also have other documents or figures that serve as authoritative in proclaiming the content of their faith. Scripture is only one of their sacred sources of faith and practice.

Meaning of Key Terms

Key word or phrase	Meaning and significance
False brothers "secretly brought in" and "slipped in to spy" (2:4)	Note how the Jerusalem attack on both Paul and his gospel message occurred. It was introduced *secretly* through individuals who perpetuated it. While they looked like believers, they were in fact *false brothers*. The phrase means *to sneak in, enter by stealth*, or *creep in*. It was a subtle infiltration without much notice. Therein was the danger. Add to this the mention of the intent *to spy*. As you can see, there was a period during this time when danger lurked unnoticed, unvoiced, and yet was still active. Evidence was gathered to use against people while they were not aware. Falsehood is not always instantly recognized. Whether Paul wanted the Galatians to see a parallel between his situation in Jerusalem and their own is impossible to know for sure, though it seems likely. Then, and now, that type of individual is *a false brother*. The subtle manner in which false teaching slips in among us should be enough to warn us to be on the alert.
Truth of the Gospel (2:5)	Up to this point, the apostle Paul has referred to his gospel message in several ways. He has called it *the gospel of Christ* in verse 7, *not man's gospel* in verse 11, *the faith he once tried to destroy* in Galatians 1:23, and *the gospel I proclaim among the Gentiles* in Galatians 2:2. Here in Galatians 2:5 he finally describes it as *the truth of the gospel*. As the letter unfolds, Paul clearly presents what his gospel is. For now, it is important to remember two things. First, Paul's gospel is the true gospel. Second, Paul's gospel is God's gospel; it is the gospel according to what God proclaimed through Paul. Keep reading the epistle with these phrases in mind and see if you can discover the essential elements of the *truth of the gospel* as the apostle Paul presents it.
A gospel to the uncircumcised and to the circumcised? (2:7)	It is important to understand the distinction made here concerning the two ways in which Jews classified all of humanity. From their perspective, the *uncircumcised* were the Gentiles, that is, all who were not Jews. The *circumcised* were the Jews. God did not approve of two different gospels among the apostles. Peter's call to take the gospel to the Jews and Paul's call to take it to the Gentiles involved proclaiming the same gospel. The Spirit of God worked through both men as shown in verse 8. To explore this issue further, take time to read 1 Corinthians 15:1–11.

What about the culture?

A key component of the corrupt gospel spreading among the Galatians was the practice of circumcision. Given this, it's hard to understand why the Galatian desertion was so rapid! It is important

B.C. 1 A.D.   10   20   30   40   50

5? Birth of Jesus   Paul encounters Christ on Damascus road 33–34?   First Missionary Journey 46–47?

          4–6? Birth of Paul   Paul writes Galatians   48?

52   Paul's private meeting in Jerusalem 45–46?

to pause and explore this issue since it was such a big problem in the early church. Even though circumcision is not a problem today, the underlying reason behind it still plagues the church although expressed in different ways.

Male circumcision in Israel was the act of cutting off a male's foreskin as an external sign of inclusion in the community of God's people in accordance with the Abrahamic Covenant.[1] God gave circumcision to Abraham and his descendants. A God-honoring Jew was circumcised while an uncircumcised Jew was spiritually and physically cut off from God's people. Any non-Jew desiring to entrust himself to Israel's God was able to do so, but needed to be circumcised. Therefore, circumcision was a key component for covenantal fellowship in Israel in the Old Testament. Those that sought to enforce it in the church in the first century pointed to such passages. The underlying reason they embraced it however was a misunderstanding of the role of this rite in the Old Testament. It was also the result of ignorance regarding the implications of what God had done through the advent, death, and resurrection of Jesus. A new community—the church—was now born. Christianity is not ethnically defined as Israel was. Membership in the church is not membership in Israel. Therefore, a Gentile did not need to become a Jew to become a Christian. To do so would be to act as if Jesus had not yet come. Paul was not against circumcision as a matter of principle[2] since he circumcised Timothy after the Jerusalem Council.[3] However, he was adamantly opposed to it as an essential component of the gospel.

What is the explanation?

–2) *A God-initiated Situation:* Fourteen years passed before Paul returned to Jerusalem. This gave church officials more than enough time to oppose Paul if they had disagreed with him. The Galatians' rapid abandonment of Paul's gospel is clearly contrasted to the ongoing acceptance of it by the Jerusalem leaders. Paul had brought two companions with him to the meeting, Barnabas and Titus. This was

Male Circumcision

This is an Egyptian drawing of a tomb or wall painting from the necropolis or burial ground at Saqqara in Egypt. There is an accompanying inscription that reads, "the ointment is to make it acceptable," and "hold him so that he does not fall." It is the oldest known illustration of circumcision.

Ancient circumcision

The Egyptians practiced circumcision as far back as the Sixth Dynasty (2345–2181 B.C.). In the fifth century B.C. the Greek writer Herodotus, known as the *father of history*, stated that the Egyptians practiced circumcision for cleanliness and passed on the practice to other nations. Some have speculated that the Egyptians may have used circumcision as a rite of passage from childhood to adulthood.

1. Genesis 17
2. Galatians 5:6; 6:15
3. Acts 16

50   60   70   80   90   100 A.D.

49? Jerusalem Council | 60–62? Paul arrives in Rome under house arrest | 70 Temple is destroyed | John writes Revelation 95–96?
50–52? Second Missionary Journey by Paul | 64 Fire in Rome | 79 Pompeii and Herculaneum are destroyed by Vesuvius eruption

53

Timothy's circumcision

Timothy was half-Jewish and accompanied Paul to the Jewish synagogues. Paul thought that it was just easier to have Timothy circumcised than to lose a hearing in front of Jews. He needed to proclaim the gospel and circumcision was not essential to it.

Paul's return to Jerusalem

Acts records five visits by Paul to Jerusalem. Which visit in Acts corresponds to this reference in Galatians 2:1? The most likely options are either the visit recorded in Acts 11:27–30 or the Jerusalem Council visit of Acts 15. The purpose of the Jerusalem Council was to publicly and officially settle how a Gentile was saved. If it had already convened, Paul would have appealed to it in this letter to the Galatians to settle these matters. However, he didn't refer to the Council because most likely, it hadn't occurred yet. This means that Paul wrote Galatians before his visit to Jerusalem in Acts 15. It seems that Galatians 2:1 corresponds to Acts 11:27–30.

important and strategic. It shows that Paul's visit was not summoned by the Jerusalem leaders. It's not as if Paul was in trouble! God initiated the encounter through a revelation. God ensured that Paul and the other apostles discussed this very matter privately foreseeing it as a growing problem in the church. Jerusalem remained a hostile city to Judaism's most prominent deserter. It was also sensible to discuss important matters freely in the company of mature believers.

It is crucial to understand that Paul is not low on confidence concerning the gospel he preached. He did not look for the apostles' approval. God knew the proclamation of his gospel would meet obstacles from within the church if there was no explicit agreement by the church leadership on the issue. Paul also felt the weight of the practical hurdles he faced if the view of the apostles in Jerusalem did not agree with his; it could render his ministry fruitless. This private meeting was a great opportunity for him to discuss a matter that later became public in the Jerusalem Council. At this point, Paul wanted to let the Galatians know that God had called this meeting. He set the agenda.

Paul shows the harmony between the gospel he preached and that which the apostles advanced in two ways. The first is implicit. He provides the example of Titus and the absence of a corrective reaction by the apostles.[1] The second is explicit. The apostles outwardly express their solidarity with Paul in verses 6–10. Notice how thorough Paul is in his argument. He was a trained debater!

The Example of Titus: Since the gospel concerns all people, Titus was the perfect test case regarding the inclusion of circumcision as a necessary element of the gospel. Titus was not a Jew but rather a Greek believer who was present at this meeting. This provided a clear opportunity for the Jerusalem leaders to enforce circumcision on Titus if they believed it to be an essential part of the gospel. Paul implies the apostles were aware that Titus was uncircumcised.

(3–

Kyiv Caves Monastery, Kyiv, Ukraine, 12th century unknown monk.

Titus

Titus was a uncircumcised Gentile coworker with Paul. He eventually pastored the church on the island of Crete after Paul helped to establish it.

1. Galatians 2:3–5

B.C. 1 A.D. 10 20 30 40 50

5? Birth of Jesus   Paul encounters Christ on Damascus road 33–34?   First Missionary Journey 46–47?

4–6? Birth of Paul   Paul writes Galatians 48?

54   Paul's private meeting in Jerusalem 45–46?

He made it clear that this issue came up through false brothers with foul motives similar to the ones the Galatians were embracing. These people spied on believers' legitimate freedom in Christ. This is the implication Paul makes by mentioning Titus. But clearly, James, Peter, and John did not believe that circumcision was essential to the gospel. The apostles stood firm with Paul because they also believed that deserting one's freedom in light of Christ's deliverance, was to return to a state of slavery.

0) *Clear Harmony:* Paul seeks to leave no doubt in the minds of the Galatians regarding the agreement that the apostles in Jerusalem had with him. If the example of Titus was not enough, Paul also explicitly declares that the Jerusalem leadership was in harmony with him concerning the gospel. This is so crucial to his counter-argument, that he explicitly affirms their equality before God. Even though the other apostles knew Jesus while he was on earth, there was no reason to appeal to them and dismiss Paul's authority. Moreover, in expressing their agreement with Paul and Barnabas by shaking hands with them, the apostles affirmed their unity with both the message and the messenger—the very thing under attack in Galatia! There were no additions, alterations, or corrections. Quite the opposite, Paul's calling by God was the same as Peter's. This alone should have undermined the belittling of Paul and his message. God was at work through both men. Different target audiences did not mean different gospels. The other apostles added nothing to Paul's authority. Their only request for Paul was to remember the poor, which was exactly what he was doing. The recipients of the true gospel reached out to others with practical compassion. Paul was both in agreement with them, and independent from them.

What is God saying?

Galatians 2:1–10 adds new evidence to Paul's basic contention: His gospel is God's gospel. Moreover, his gospel was actually the official teaching of the Church. No external religious act—no matter how prevalent and divinely endorsed in the Old Testament, can

Barnabas Caring for the Poor
Barnabas was a Jew from Cyprus who accompanied Paul on his first missionary journey recorded in Acts 13–14. He is known for his gifts of service and encouragement.

Paolo Veronese, 1566

Barnabas & Titus

Paul's companions on this trip included Barnabas, a Jew, and Titus, an uncircumcised Greek. Taking Titus into Jerusalem was both a risk and an immediate invitation to dissension. This however, was by divine design and had the purpose of establishing the unity of faith and message between the apostles in Jerusalem, and Paul, the apostle to the Gentiles. Thus, in the meeting with the apostles, there were representatives of both the Gentile and the Jewish parties. The response of the leaders of Jerusalem served as evidence of the *quality* and *purity* of Paul's gospel.

Pillars

It appears the early church and even Paul viewed the apostles as pillars. Paul, for example, understood God's people to be God's temple with the main supporting columns being God's appointed leaders:
- 1 Corinthians 3:16–17
- 2 Corinthians 6:16
- Ephesians 2:21
- Revelation 3:12

There are also Jewish writings written after the New Testament that use *pillar* language to refer to Abraham and Moses as supporting the world such as *Exodus Rabbah*, the Midrash to Exodus 2:13 and 3:4. Paul is giving these apostles the honor due them.

50   60   70   80   90   100   A.D.

49? Jerusalem Council

50–52? Second Missionary Journey by Paul

60–62? Paul arrives in Rome under house arrest

64 Fire in Rome

70 Temple is destroyed

79 Pompeii and Herculaneum are destroyed by Vesuvius eruption

John writes Revelation 95–96?

55

Gospel and Compassion

The ministry of Paul demonstrates that an inevitable outcome of the gospel is compassion. Consider the following passages:
- 1 Corinthians 16:1–4
- 2 Corinthians 8:1–9:15
- Romans 15:25–28

The apostle constantly modeled for us the practical aspects of his ministry of proclamation. The visit to Jerusalem recorded in Galatians 2 was partly for the purpose of famine relief. See Acts 11:27–30.

or should be imposed as a requirement for one seeking to please God. The Old Testament teachings recognized this with the issue of circumcision itself. Jeremiah affirmed that circumcision of the flesh was to be an expression of God's work in the heart.[1] The external act was meaningless without the internal change. This is the same as with the practice of giving. Jesus points out how ridiculous it is to tithe and yet ignore what God wants from within you.[2] He is only satisfied in Christ and those that seek God must approach him by faith in Christ.

The Galatians had to realize that this problem was not new. It had already popped up through sneaky false teachers in Jerusalem itself long before the Galatians came to know Christ.[3] Paul fought them then and he would fight them again. God blessed the Jews with his Son. This meant that to enjoy God, one does not have to become a Jew; rather, he or she has to become a Christian.

Where else is this taught in Scripture?

The Apostle Paul

Paul sought to be all things to all people so that some might be saved.

In the book of Acts, chapter 21, we find the record of Paul's return to Jerusalem several years after the letter of Galatians was written. He met with the leadership of the church there and reported on God's work among the Gentiles. Those present rejoiced at the news but also feared how some Jewish Christians would react. This suggests that the agreement between Paul and the leaders as recorded in Galatians 2:1–10, or even Acts 15, did not remove the desire of some in the church to compel Gentiles toward circumcision. Such compulsion to force others to live the Christian life according to man-made standards is hard to remove. In Acts 21, Paul accepted the request of the Jerusalem leaders and sought to pacify Jewish believers. He attended the Jewish purification rites of four men. This was not a battle to fight. At times, we must be patient with the weaker believers and pray they grow in Christ as Paul declares it in 1 Corinthians 9:20–21.

When they heard this, they praised God. Then they said to him, "You see, brother, how many thousands of Jews there are who have believed, and they are all zealous for the law, and they have been told about you, that you are teaching all the Jews that are among the Gentiles to forsake Moses, telling them not to circumcise their children or follow other Jewish customs. What should we do? They will no doubt hear that you have come. Therefore, do what we tell you: We have four men who have taken a vow, take them and purify yourself along with them and pay their expenses..."

1. Jeremiah 4:4
2. Matthew 23:23
3. Galatians 2:4–5

Where else does this happen in history?

Baptism, like circumcision, has been one of many doctrines that believers have mistakenly added to the essential content of the gospel throughout the ages. As early as the second century A.D., the church began to consider water baptism as a necessary exercise for salvation and the forgiveness of sins. The historical and theological reasons for this misconception are very interesting. Both circumcision and baptism are considered by many as a sacrament or *a sign of an invisible grace*. All people as physical beings are *sacramental*, in that we try to express invisible realities by participating in special rituals that include the use of signs or symbols. For example, the promises of marriage are sealed or *signified* by the wedding ring. The ring is a physical, visible sign that serves as a constant reminder of the invisible promises of marriage. Similarly, in Scripture, the people of God also expressed their belief on the benefits of God's promises by participating in a visible ritual. The external act, be it circumcision or baptism, becomes the visible sign of a blessing that is otherwise invisibly received by faith. In the case of baptism, the early church often practiced the ceremony immediately after the profession of faith of the new believer. Consider Acts 2:37–41 and 7:26–40. In time, the non-baptized Christian was a rarity. Water baptism was soon believed to be the sacrament that removed the guilt and condemnation of original sin. For this reason, the church instituted the practice of infant baptism. The idea was and is to protect the baby from damnation by baptizing him or her only a few days after being born. This idea eventually led to controversy. Pelagius thought that infant baptism was unnecessary since the idea of original sin was false and there was no need for a rite that removed an imaginary guilt. Augustine countered with the clear Biblical teaching of original sin. To this day, some church traditions include baptism as a necessary element for salvation. But just as with circumcision, even though baptism is a Christian ordinance instituted by the Lord himself, when it is added as a necessary element of the gospel, it becomes an ungodly practice.

Augustine of Hippo
Augustine (A.D. 354–A.D. 430) demonstrated that the Bible taught that all people inherit guilt from Adam's original sin.

Pelagius
Pelagius (A.D. 354– A.D. 420/440) denied that people inherit any sin from Adam.

What does God want?

Now that we have explored this portion of Scripture, we are ready to think through how we can live out the implications of God's Word. Remember that Paul continues to argue the same points. They are so important that two of the six chapters of Galatians are devoted to them. Here are a few important ideas that emerge from our study. Please consider them and be intentional about customizing their application to your own situation.

We are united in what we believe yet diverse in how we proclaim it.
Paul and the Jerusalem leadership believed the same gospel. They
stood firm and united against any corruption of God's truth. They
also embraced the different roles they had in advancing the good
news. Their message was the same, but the method and context was
different. Unity and diversity are not necessarily opposed. God unites
very different people in Christ and empowers them to represent him
in many ways. We will do well to learn this lesson. The church today,
just like then, has problems. More often than not, the problems we
face are of our own making. They do not concern points of truth but
preferences in practice. Paul teaches us to be bold in the defense of the
truth of the gospel but to respect the role of others in Christ's service.
The one truth can also be proclaimed in different manners today. Like
Paul, James, Peter, and John, we proclaim the one gospel but embrace
the varying roles, gifts, and ministries of others in its proclamation.

Watch out for false teaching creeps in subtly.
The Galatians were not the first or last to flirt with a distortion of
God's message. Paul clearly opposed the Galatian problem before
them and after. Approaching God with a legalistic attitude or trying
to appease him with our efforts is still rampant today. The danger is
often subtle. If false teaching came in the front door—say as Hinduism
or Buddhism—most would object immediately. However, this
type of false teaching sneaks in the back door. It enters clothed in
biblical language since it is practiced in other parts of Scripture. For
example, practices which in and of themselves are good—like church
attendance and prayer—can be a sugar-coating for a self-righteous
heart. Legalism looks spiritual yet is slightly off. But slightly off is fully
off! There were no problems with the Jewish practices in themselves;
there was no problem with circumcision. The problem was to believe
that this was the way to earn or satisfy God. Ignoring the changes
brought about by Christ is a dangerous yet easy thing to do. Therefore,
a warning flows out of this passage. False teaching creeps in subtly.
It calls for another heart check. So ask yourself again, why do you
practice your faith the way that you do?

Discoveries

Now you have completed your third excavation into the text of Galatians. It is again time to stop digging and carefully examine what we have learned and what difference it can make in our lives. Pick the questions that will be most helpful for you or your community.

Connecting with the community

Here are some discussion questions to help you better understand the main purpose of the text. Do not merely reflect on them as an individual but rather think of each question, when applicable, in terms of your family, your community, your nation, and your church.

1. According to Galatians 2:1–2, why did Paul finally decide to visit the apostles in Jerusalem?

2. Paul knew that there were false brothers infiltrated in the congregation when he visited Jerusalem. Why was circumcision so important to these false brothers? What was the real issue behind the practice of the rite?

3. Was the gospel of Paul the same as the gospel of Peter, James, and John? Why or why not?

4. According to Galatians 2:10, Paul was eager to "remember the poor." How is compassion related to the work of the gospel in the heart of the believer? How compassionate toward the poor are believers in your community?

5. Why was it important to meet with the leaders of Jerusalem in private? What can we learn from the God-revealed way of dealing with this issue? Are you willing to submit to the private decisions of God-appointed leaders? Why or why not?

6. Was Paul against circumcision? What was the function of this rite in Judaism? Did Paul forbid the circumcision of believers? Would it have been tragic to enforce Titus to be circumcised? Why or why not?

Notes, Observations & Questions

7. Is the fear Paul expresses in Galatians 2:2 an indication of uncertainty about the truthfulness of his gospel? Defend your answer from the content of the letter we have studied so far.

8. In what way was the inclusion of Titus in the trip to Jerusalem another confirmation of the truthfulness of Paul's gospel?

9. Is it important to consider the cultural context in which the gospel is proclaimed, or should we ignore any cultural nuances when fulfilling the great commission? How does acknowledging cultural differences help promote the gospel?

10. False teaching enters the church subtly. Many times, it even includes biblical language and principles. How can you safeguard your faith and that of your congregation from falling prey to false teachers as the Galatians did?

11. Are there any teachings in your Christian community that appear to contradict the gospel? Is the gospel being tweaked in any way? Are there any works or rituals being added as a necessary part of the gospel in your community?

Probing deeper

These exercises take you deeper into some of the secondary issues of our passage. They require additional reading from other key passages that will supplement your understanding from Galatians. Consider how each question relates to yourself, your family, your community, your nation, and your church.

1. Read Romans 9:1–5. How does this text also testify to Paul's compassion? How does it show the inadequacy of Judaism as a way to attain righteousness?

2. We observe in Galatians 2:1–10 that Paul and Peter proclaimed the same gospel. Their audience however was vastly different in their culture and traditions. Consider Paul's words in 1 Corinthians 9:19–23. Can you identify different cultures present in your community? How would the proclamation of the gospel be different in each of these cultures?

Notes, Observations & Questions

3. How can you communicate the gospel in different cultural contexts without compromising the purity of the gospel? Read Acts 17:16–34. What can we learn about how Paul presented the gospel on Mars Hill in a culturally relevant way?

Bringing the story to life

Paul reminds us in Galatians 2:1–10 that there is only one gospel but that it needs to be communicated in a way that resonates with our audience. Come up with a way to present the gospel message to a specific cultural group within your community. This will work best with a small group. Begin by identifying a cultural group that you can engage. Consider some of the following questions as you prepare to present the gospel to them:

- Do they speak another language?
- What are some of their cultural traditions that affect how they would receive the gospel?
- What religion does that culture practice or has practiced in the past?

Once you have gained an understanding of the cultural group, come up with a way of presenting the gospel in a way that engages their mindset. Remember that the gospel message does not change but the method or context may be unique to the cultural group you are working with. Your presentation may be written, oral or any other way you come up with to communicate the gospel clearly.

Pray for an opportunity to engage a person or group from that culture. Learn all you can about their culture. Commit to loving them and praying for them. Ask the Lord to bless your efforts and present the gospel message. Were they receptive? Did it make sense to them? Is there something you can do differently? Continue to love and pray for those you had opportunity to share with.

Memorizing the key

Commit to memory the key phrase for this *Field Study*. The key phrase for Galatians 2:1–10 is:

> The truth of the gospel must never be compromised

Part of learning the Bible is remembering what the Bible is about and where to find things. Memorizing the key phrases will help you to better understand and apply the key points of Galatians and remember each topic in the book.

Observation journaling

This section will prepare you for *Field Study 5* by reading through the next section of Galatians. We have included three types of exercises: some for before you read, some for while you are reading and some for after you have completed the reading.

Before you read

Review the key terms from *Field Studies 2* through 4 to insure you remember all of them. This will help you to follow the message that God is communicating through Paul's letter to the Galatian churches.

The key terms:

- From *Field Study 2* are on page 19–20.

- From *Field Study 3* are on page 35.

- From *Field Study 4* are on page 51–52.

Which key terms and definitions have been particularly helpful in understanding the message of Galatians? Why?

While you are reading

On the following page, we have laid out the biblical text with wide margins so you can mark the text with questions, key terms, notes, and structures. We have removed all of the verse markings so you can read it without distractions and have laid out the text with spacing to help you see how the lines are related. Review the guidelines on *The art of active learning* section, page xi at the beginning of your *Field Notes* for some suggestions on reading, learning, and marking the text effectively.

Galatians 2:11–21

But when Peter came to Antioch, I opposed him to his face, because he stood condemned. For before certain men came from James, he was eating with the Gentiles. But when they arrived, he drew back and separated himself from the Gentiles, fearing those who belonged to the circumcision group. The rest of the Jews joined him in his hypocrisy, so that even Barnabas was led astray by their hypocrisy. But when I saw that their conduct was not in line with the truth of the gospel, I said to Peter in front of them all, "If you being a Jew, live like a Gentile and not like a Jew, how can you force Gentiles to live like Jews?"

We are Jews by birth and not Gentile sinners; yet we know that no one is justified by works of the law, but through faith in Jesus Christ. So we also have believed in Christ Jesus that we may be justified by faith in Christ and not by works of the law, because by works of the law no one will be justified. But if, while seeking to be justified in Christ, we too were found to be sinners, does that mean that Christ promotes sin? Absolutely not! For if I rebuild what I destroyed, I prove myself to be a lawbreaker. For through the law I died to the law so that I might live to God. I have been crucified with Christ and it is no longer I who live, but Christ who lives in me. The life I live in the body, I live by faith in the Son of God, who loved me and gave himself for me. I do not set aside the grace of God, for if righteousness comes through the law, Christ died for nothing!

Notes, Observations & Questions

Summarize the text here

After you have read

1. Journaling is another way to help us learn. You will remember more if you read a passage and then do something with it such as writing it down. Therefore, write out Galatians 2:11–21 from the previous page or from your own Bible into a journal word for word. This practice will help you to remember and understand what you have just read. Consider journaling your thoughts on the gospel. What is the good news and why is it good?

2. Now read Galatians 2:11–21 in your own Bible. Continue to reread it each day until you start *Field Study 5*. This will reinforce the learning of Scripture and help you in retention.

Pray

As we learn the Word of God, it is essential that we communicate with him through prayer. First, consider writing a prayer, psalm, or poem to God. What would God have you pray in order to guard yourself and others from a corrupted gospel? Pray for your church, your nation, your community, your family and yourself. Try to pray with a friend or family member or even in a small group. Consider this sample prayer:

Father,

I thank you, Lord, for expanding my understanding of how you work in the world. I realize that unity and diversity are not opposites. Believers of different ages and places can represent the one gospel in many ways. Help me not restrict how others represent the gospel in my neighborhood so that they conform to my preferences. Help me encourage and support the many different ministries in my church that seek to declare the one message. Father, help me to stand with other believers against the subtle intrusions of false teachings into my family and church life. It enters so shrewdly. I desire to understand your Word so that I can detect when it is misused. Answer my prayer, Father, for I raise my voice to you based solely on the power of the Holy Spirit working in me because of my standing before you in Jesus Christ, Amen.

Galatians 2:11–21

FIELD STUDY 5

How is the text arranged?

This *Field Study* closes out the first major section in Galatians. The gospel of Jesus Christ proclaimed by Paul was under attack. The tragedy was that the attack was from within the church; *believers* were corrupting the gospel. This moved Paul to defend his authority in order to defend his message. This study explores a third piece of evidence or a third proof from Paul that ends chapter 2 with a summary presentation of the essence of the gospel. Read and meditate on the text for a few moments in order to recognize its basic outline and argument. Remember to make use of the guide provided. The passage presents the following logical structure:

Galatians 2:11–21

Section	Bible Text
Evidence Three: Paul's authority to correct the apostle Peter	
Conflict	¹¹ But when Peter came to Antioch, I opposed him to his face, because he stood condemned.
Cause	¹² For before certain men came from James, he was eating with the Gentiles. But when they arrived, he drew back and separated himself from the Gentiles, fearing those who belonged to the circumcision group. ¹³ The rest of the Jews joined him in his hypocrisy, so that even Barnabas was led astray by their hypocrisy.

The Names of Peter

The apostle Peter is also referred to in the Bible as both Simon and Cephas. Simon seems to be Peter's given name, but he was renamed Cephas by Jesus in Matthew 16:18. Cephas is the Aramaic equivalent of the Greek word for Peter meaning *rock*. See John 1:35–42; Matthew 4:18; Mark 1:16; Luke 5:1–11; 6:13 and Mark 3:16.

Galatians 2:11–21

Section	Bible Text
Corrective Confrontation	¹⁴ But when I saw that their conduct was not in line with the truth of the gospel, I said to Peter in front of them all, "If you being a Jew, live like a Gentile and not like a Jew, how can you force Gentiles to live like Jews?"

Concluding summary that presents the gospel

Section	Bible Text
Justification by faith in Jesus not works	¹⁵ We are Jews by birth and not Gentile sinners; ¹⁶ yet we know that no one is justified by works of the law, but through faith in Jesus Christ. So we also have believed in Christ Jesus that we may be justified by faith in Christ and not by works of the law, because by works of the law no one will be justified.
Answer to an objection	¹⁷ But if, while seeking to be justified in Christ, we too were found to be sinners, does that mean that Christ promotes sin? Absolutely not! ¹⁸ For if I rebuild what I destroyed, I prove myself to be a lawbreaker. ¹⁹ For through the law I died to the law so that I might live to God. ²⁰ I have been crucified with Christ and it is no longer I who live, but Christ who lives in me. The life I live in the body, I live by faith in the Son of God, who loved me and gave himself for me. ²¹ I do not set aside the grace of God, for if righteousness comes through the law, Christ died for nothing!

Ad hominem

The Latin phrase *ad hominem* is short for *argumentum ad hominem*. It means "to the man" or "to the person." This type of argument is an attempt to negate the truth of a claim by pointing out a negative characteristic or belief of the person supporting it. It is considered a logical fallacy.

As you can see from our structural outline of the passage, there are two major movements in this section: in verses 11–14, we have a third proof from Paul's personal experience. The second movement is a summary presentation of the gospel in verses 15–21, which concludes the first two chapters of Galatians.

Evidence three: Paul continues to defend his authority through an interesting counter-argument to the *ad hominem* type of attack he faced. The attack was to discredit his message. He therefore establishes his credibility and that of his message by telling the Galatians of the time when he rebuked even the great apostle Peter on a similar issue to

(11

the one the Galatians' were entertaining. If he could rebuke Peter, he could rebuke them.

-21) *Conclusion:* The rebuke of Peter leads smoothly in to a summary conclusion of what the gospel is and is not. As Paul closes out the first division of his letter, he declares up front what he will then proceed to explain. The gospel is all about God's gracious provision of Christ. A right standing before God is only possible by faith in God's provision of Jesus, not by works of the law.

What is this passage saying?
What are some key terms and phrases?
We will now examine several terms, phrases, and concepts that occur in this passage. Understanding them will help us grasp the meaning and significance of this section of the letter.

Meaning of Key Terms

Key word or phrase	Meaning and significance
The Circumcision Party (2:12)	The circumcision party was a group within the early church who believed Christians were to continue to embrace the demands of the Mosaic Law; particularly the requirement for circumcision and certain dietary prohibitions. They took offense at believers who did not live according to these laws and practices. This group, or those closely aligned with them, often appear in the events of the early church. It is important to understand that many of them were true believers that were just struggling to understand the role of their Jewish history with God now that they had embraced Christ. Others were not believers. Those causing trouble in the Galatian churches were part of the circumcision party which emerges elsewhere in the New Testament. See for example Acts 11:2; 15:1; 21:17–26; Titus 1:10.
Hypocrisy (2:13)	Paul rightly renders the actions of Peter and of those who followed him as hypocrisy. This word originates in the ancient theatres. It translates literally as *play-acting* and describes what stage actors did. They wore masks, for example, to exhibit the role of a character in the play and in doing so hide who they were in reality. You can see from this how the term came to be used negatively of those who pretend to be or do what they are not. Paul's charge of hypocrisy is tough but true. Peter's behavior violated his own convictions about the gospel.

Ancient Theater Masks

This mosaic from the baths of Decius in Hadrian's villa on Aventine Hill in Rome, pictures second century theatrical masks of tragedy and comedy. It is from these face-masks that the idea of hypocrisy originated.

Antmoose, 2005

1250 · 1100 · 950 · 800 · 650 · 500 B.C.

Saul becomes king 1050
David becomes king 1010
Solomon becomes king 971
930 The kingdom divides
722 Northern kingdom falls to Assyria
Southern kingdom falls to Babylon and the temple is destroyed 586

Importance of Justification

Justification is an aspect of salvation. It is the point in time when a believer first embraces the promises of the gospel. This is a central topic to our passage as well as to the teaching of Galatians 3–4. Be sure to understand it.

Meaning of Key Terms

Key word or phrase	Meaning and significance
Justification (2:16, 17)	*Justification* is a term borrowed from the courts of law where a verbal verdict was pronounced on an accused standing before a judge. This idea is carried into the realm of sinful man, standing before God as judge. To be *justified* is to be *declared righteous* or *declared holy* by God. It is a heavenly verdict pronounced over a sinner. Justification does not mean to be *made* just but to be *declared* just. Paul is convinced one is *declared* just only by faith in Jesus Christ, for Christ alone satisfies God's justice. This is central to his God-given gospel message. Man's good works do not count towards being *declared* just before God. When one trusts in Christ alone, Jesus represents that person before God, who then renders a verdict of *not guilty*. Because of Jesus' sacrifice on the cross, God is able to pronounce such a verdict on those trusting his Son without compromising his divine justice.
Union with Christ (2:20)	The teaching of the believer's union with Christ helps us understand the language of verse 20. Faith in Jesus unites the believer with Christ so closely that Christ's experience becomes that of the individual. The individual shares in the death, burial, and resurrection of Jesus. It is because of this intimate union with Christ that Paul can declare that he "has been crucified with Christ." Paul elaborates this concept elsewhere in passages such as Romans 6:1–6. Take time to read it.

What about the culture?

A few cultural issues will help our understanding of this passage. Let's look now at three of them.

The Love Feast

While the only direct mention of the *love feast* in Scripture is in Jude 1:12, there are several early church writings that discuss it, including Ignatius of Antioch's letter to Smyrna. Unfortunately, as time passed the *love feast* stopped due to abuses of over indulgence. Paul shows us abuse was occurring even in his day.

Believers ate together at the church in Antioch. This was a common practice in the early church often referred to as a *love feast*.[1] Fellowshipping around food was a common custom in Mediterranean cultures at the time. In church gatherings, these practices often lead to partaking of communion together. Though fellowship around food was common in that society, the Christian love feast stood out since in no other context would you see the rich and poor, the free and slaves, men and women, and Jews and Gentiles eating together in a spirit of equality, unity, acceptance, and love. As such, it was a visual testimony to society that believers are equal under God through faith in Jesus Christ. Peter himself regularly enjoyed food fellowship in Antioch.

1.   1 Corinthians 11:20–34

B.C.	1	A.D.		10		20		30		40		50

5?   Birth of Jesus   John the Baptist begins his ministry   28–29?   33–34?   Paul encounters Christ on Damascus road   46–47?   First M. Journe

4–6?   Birth of Paul   Jesus begins his ministry   28–30?

Jesus is crucified and resurrected   30–33?   Paul writes Galatians   48?

What was the big deal with Peter eating with Gentiles? Why the tension? The issue was initially rooted in the dietary prohibitions found in the Law of Moses.[2] God communicated to Israel his desire for them to be set apart or *holy* in the midst of a godless world. The sacrificial system, the seasonal festivities, and the laws guided holy living to maintain fellowship with God. He also granted Israel food prohibitions in order that they remain undefiled and separate for him. In time, Jews protected these food restraints in mixed-cultures by not eating with Gentiles. In mixed company, they couldn't be sure where the food came from or how it was prepared—perhaps it was bought in the market after being sacrificed to an idol. Such prohibitions to engage with Gentiles transcended food and reached into business and travel. In short, Jews who became Christians often struggled not just with what to do with the Law of Moses but with embracing an unrestricted lifestyle with Gentile Christians.

Love Feast Fresco

This fresco or mural painted on a tomb in the catacomb of Saints Marcellinus and Peter in Rome depicts Christians celebrating the Lord's Supper as they ate together.

Catacomb of Saints Marcellinus and Peter, Via Labicana, Rome, Italy

Lastly, we must discuss the historical situation that added to the existing tension between Gentiles and Jews. The ancient Jewish writer Josephus tells us of a surge in Jewish militant nationalism at this time. The Romans came down hard on militant leaders, crucifying two of them. Jews who were perceived to be socializing with Gentiles or adopting aspects of their lifestyle were despised and viewed as traitors. The church's unrestrained Gentile contact was a practical problem for Jewish Christians who feared reprisal. They may also have seen it as an obstacle in the evangelism of Jews.

What is the explanation?

Let's examine in closer detail what Paul is saying in this passage of Scripture.

14) *Third evidence:* Paul now provides the Galatians with a third personal example that validates his authority and that of his gospel message. The setting is the church in Antioch. While there had been harmony between Paul and Peter in Jerusalem concerning the gospel, tension arose between them in Antioch. Paul confronted Peter directly

Jewish Nationalism

"But of the fourth sect of Jewish philosophy, Judas the Galilean was the author. These men agree in all other things with the Pharisaic notions; but they have an inviolable attachment to liberty; and say that God is to be their only Ruler and Lord. They also do not value dying any kind of death, nor indeed do they heed the deaths of their relations and friends, nor can any such fear make them call any man Lord."
(Flavius Josephus and William Whiston, Antiquities of the Jews, 18:23)

Josephus went on to record that this fourth sect desired to lead the Jews in a revolt against the Romans.

2. Leviticus 11

| 50 | 60 | 70 | 80 | 90 | 100 A.D. |

49? Jerusalem Council

50–52? Second Missionary Journey by Paul

60–62? Paul arrives in Rome under house arrest

64 Fire in Rome

70 Temple is destroyed

79 Pompeii and Herculaneum are destroyed by Vesuvius eruption

John writes Revelation 95–96?

69

Primus inter pares

Although the New Testament never gives any formal position of authority to Peter over the rest of the apostles, it is clear from the narratives of the Gospels and Acts that Peter was a natural leader (Acts 1–3). He was frequently mentioned first as in Luke 9:27–28 and was also the apostle with greater initiative to lead the rest of the group (Luke 9:32–33; Matthew 16:13–18). For this reason he has been recognized throughout church history as a *leader among equals* or *the first among equals* which in Latin is expressed with the phrase *primus inter pares*.

because Peter was wrong; his conduct was inconsistent with his belief.[1] We cannot underestimate the shock this would bring to believers in the early church since Peter was considered *primus inter pares*. But Peter was fallible, and in this letter Paul tells us Peter's error.[2] Peter rightly enjoyed eating with Gentile believers in Antioch. He did so regularly, which was consistent with his understanding of the gospel of Jesus Christ. After all, he had already experienced the vision from God presented in Acts 10. God had told him directly that the Old Testament dietary prohibitions had been abolished. Circumcision and dietary laws were irrelevant to the gospel.

It appears that when news of his eating with Gentiles reached Jerusalem, James sent some messengers to Peter to let him know his actions were grieving a particular faction of the church—the *circumcision party*. Out of fear of this group, Peter withdrew from mixed table-fellowship. Presumably, tables were set up for Christian Jews and others for Christian Gentiles, which led other believers, including Barnabas to follow suit. Paul recognized this behavior was born out of hypocrisy. In principle, Peter believed the gospel granted the freedom to enjoy interracial fellowship. But now out of fear of man, Peter changed his behavior and his conduct no longer reflected his belief. He was evidently endorsing primary and secondary status in the body of Christ. Paul publicly and personally called Peter out on this. This was not to embarrass Peter, but to address a growing, public

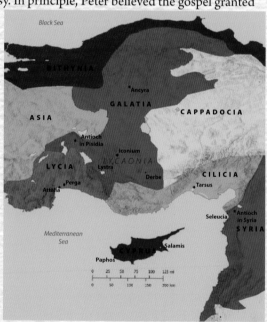

The Church in Antioch

The church in Antioch was on the north side of the Roman Province of Syria. It was in this church that Paul and Barnabas were called by the Spirit to the missionary work in the regions of Asia and Galatia. It is therefore an important church in the history of the expansion of Christianity. The travels of Paul began here. You can read more about it in Acts 13.

Antioch in Syria

Antioch was founded in the fourth century B.C. by Seleucus I Nicator, one of Alexander the Great's generals. It has sometimes been referred to as the "cradle of Christianity" because of the important role it played in the spread of the gospel.

1. Galatians 2:11
2. Galatians 2:12–13

B.C.	1	A.D.	10	20	30	40	50

5? Birth of Jesus

4–6? Birth of Paul

John the Baptist begins his ministry 28–29?

Jesus begins his ministry 28–30?

Jesus is crucified and resurrected 30–33?

33–34? Paul encounters Christ on Damascus road

Paul writes Galatians 48?

46–47? First Miss Journey

problem before it got out of hand. Peter was not walking in step with the truth of the gospel.[3] He had acted as the Galatians were acting now, and in both cases, Paul had the authority to correct such deviation from the essential message of the gospel.

21) *Conclusion:* This section of the letter ends with a summary presentation of what the gospel is in contrast to what it is not. The Galatians got to hear the gospel again! Let us now trace Paul's reasoning carefully in order to understand the complexity of his affirmations.

16) The Galatian churches were adding at least one Jewish work, namely circumcision, as an essential part of salvation. They were deserting the truth for a different gospel, which required a Gentile to become a Jew in order to be a Christian. Paul, therefore, argues from the perspective of those who were both Jews by birth, and Christian—the very state these Galatians wanted to adopt. In verse 15, Paul uses the phrase, "*we of Jewish birth.*" These men like Paul, Peter, and Barnabas were not born as *Gentile sinners.* Paul argues that even these Jewish believers knew that one is declared righteous or *justified* before God only by faith in Jesus Christ. They were not made righteous by practices and adherence to Jewish laws. Paul is so emphatic about the impossibility of justification by works that in these two verses he repeats the truth repeatedly. Three times, he declares one does not satisfy God by *works of the law* and twice he states that it is by *faith* in Jesus. He argues from a shared belief with the apostle Peter. It's as though he is saying, "We who are exactly what you Gentiles desire to be, do not believe it is necessary to become a Jew in order to embrace the gospel." Jews and Gentiles alike satisfy God through *faith in Christ.*[4]

20) Paul is charged with implying that Jesus opposed good works because the gospel was exclusively by faith in Jesus and not works of the law. We see this repeatedly in Paul's other letters. His opponents claimed that he was a promoter of lawless living, an advocate of a lifestyle of sin. There are glimpses of this in Galatians 1:10. But this was definitely not the case. *Faith in Jesus* and *works of the law* are opposed only if competing or collaborating to render a person right before God. Paul counters the charge beginning in verses 17–18. He reasons that it is illogical to return to a manner of living, which was never designed to

Paul rebuking Peter

Given the forward chronological movement Paul employs in Galatians 1–2 when presenting his activities, it appears this event took place after the private meeting in Jerusalem described in Galatians 2:1–10 and Acts 11:27–30. It seems likely the rebuke also occurred before the Jerusalem Council recorded in Acts 15 since Peter speaks there in agreement with Paul on not needing to become a Jew to be a Christian. It is unlikely Peter and Barnabas would have acted as they did after the Jerusalem Council.

What was Peter thinking?

Though wrong for his hypocritical actions, even though it was unintentional hypocrisy, you can't but feel a little sorry for Peter. He probably did not think through the broader implications of his actions and thought he was invoking what Paul elaborates elsewhere as the weaker brother principle: setting aside legitimate rights of conduct in Christ to avoid difficulty for an immature Christian. Peter and Barnabas probably thought they were minimizing tension in the church and problems in the evangelism of Jews. In doing so, they were creating problems about an essential truth of the Christian faith. This was too public an event, and Peter too big a figure, for it to go unnoticed. A Jewish-Gentile class structure was being sanctioned within the church and Paul had to correct it.

3.   Galatians 2:14
4.   Romans 3–5

50   60   70   80   90   100 A.D.

49? Jerusalem Council

60–62? Paul arrives in Rome under house arrest

70 Temple is destroyed

John writes Revelation 95–96?

50–52? Second Missionary Journey by Paul

64   Fire in Rome

79 Pompeii and Herculaneum are destroyed by Vesuvius eruption

71

please God. Even if a Jewish Christian like Paul, reverted back to an attempt to satisfy God through law-keeping, then he would find that under the law he was a failure—a law-breaker. That is what the law reveals in a man living under it. Verse 19 tells us that life under the law accomplished exactly what it was supposed to do—kill any confidence that God could be satisfied this way. The law should lead one to faith in God, not faith in God's law. In doing so, one turned to God, not laws to find life. The introduction of the phrase "death to the law" and "life to God" in verse 19–20 is a perfect platform to describe how faith in Jesus and not laws, allows one to live to God. When we are united to Jesus by faith, we benefit from the only sacrifice that satisfies God's justice—Christ's death!

Paul closes out this short albeit complex presentation of the gospel with a clear statement. To add laws to faith in Jesus in order to satisfy God is to nullify God's gracious way of salvation through Jesus Christ. It renders the death of Jesus pointless. It is to live as though God could be satisfied without the need for Christ!

Where else is this taught in Scripture?

Abraham's Journey to Canaan
By faith, Abraham trusted in God to lead him to this new and unknown land. Abraham believed in God throughout his life and was saved by faith.

Paul devotes considerable attention to salvation by faith alone in Romans 3:21–5:21 which is an expansion of Galatians 2:15–21. Read this section of Romans with the following summary in mind: God justifies an individual by grace through faith in Jesus because only Christ's sacrifice satisfies God's justice and justifies those who turn to him. This removes any ground for boasting in how one lives. Abraham, before the law, and David, during the period of the law, demonstrate this. Only in following their example of justification by faith can a person find abiding peace, future hope, joy despite suffering, assurance of love, and the aversion of God's wrath. Only then does one stand before God under the headship of Christ.

David Playing the Harp
God called David a man after his own heart because of his faith rather than because David kept the law.

Romans 3:28
We consider that a person is justified by faith apart from works of the law.

Romans 3:26
...So that he would be just and the justifier of the one who has faith in Jesus.

What is God saying?

At the start of his argument, Paul declared that his gospel is God's gospel.[1] After presenting three pieces of evidence,[2] he concludes with a brief presentation of that same gospel he had already preached to the Galatians. In this passage, we saw Paul's third evidence, which was his need to oppose Peter in Antioch. This stands out as a huge contrast with the previous piece of evidence where Paul and Peter were presented in harmony in Jerusalem. However, Peter was acting inconsistently with the gospel he believed. In correcting even Peter on an issue of the gospel, Paul makes it clear to the Galatians that his authority and message are not to be disputed. This case of positive rebuke is not unlike Jesus' ongoing training of the disciples in the entire Gospel of Mark. Read, for example, the rebuke of James, John and then the rest of the disciples in Mark 10:35–45 where Jesus teaches them concerning true greatness. No follower of Jesus is above constructive rebuke.

Antinomianism

Antinomianism literally means *against the law*. The most common understanding of this idea is that a believer is under no obligation to live by a moral code because salvation is by grace through faith. This is not what Paul is declaring here though it is what he was accused of advancing. Paul is against the wrongful use of the law but still maintains believers have a responsibility to live a life of good works in light of their faith in God. Paul will address this further in Galatians 5–6.

Where else does this happen in history?

The teaching that justification before God is by faith alone in Christ alone got a hold of the life of a young monk and rising theologian in the early 1500's. His name was Martin Luther. Luther had pursued pleasing God through being a monk and had eventually confessed that he hated God because he could never please him. It wasn't until he began to teach through the book of Romans that Luther found comfort in the message of Romans 1:17. His response was the spark that ignited the Protestant Reformation. For Luther, this truth as expressed by Paul in passages like Galatians 2:15–21 or Romans 1:17 was a gateway to heaven. In them, Luther learned that God is the one who justifies a person. All a person has to do is to receive God's gift by faith. Luther saw that the righteousness of God was a status that sinners could possess by faith. It was not something to be feared. Justification by faith changed Luther's life and transformed the church. Soon, the institutional church lost its grip on people's conscience because Luther and the other reformers helped to recover the biblical teaching of salvation by faith alone in Christ alone. One's standing before God is not based on any merit of their own.

Romans 1:17

For in the gospel a righteousness of God is revealed from faith to faith, just as it is written: 'the righteous will live by faith.'

Lucas Cranach the Elder, 16th century

Luther as an Augustinian Monk

Martin Luther pursued salvation by trying to please God as a monk. He devoted himself to prayer, fasting, going without sleep, whipping himself and other practices of self denial. He later stated that, "if anyone could have earned heaven by the life of a monk, it was I."

1. Galatians 1:11–12
2. Galatians 1:13–24; 2:1–10; 2:11–14

As Paul closes out his three-fold defense, he reiterates his gospel message for the Galatians: Man is justified before God only by faith in Jesus Christ and not by works of the law. This is a theme Paul emphatically presents in many of his writings.[1] It is a truth that runs through Scripture. Paul shows this in Galatians 3–4 where he appeals to other biblical passages.

What does God want?

Now that we have explored in depth this portion of Scripture, we are ready to propose some applications for our Christian walk. Here are some of the important lessons we find in this passage. Think about their implications for your life:

Acceptance before God is only in Jesus so don't render him pointless

Paul reminds us that only Jesus Christ can satisfy God's justice. For this reason, only trusting in his gracious provision of salvation is sufficient. To attempt to earn God, motivated by a combination of *faith in Jesus* and *self-effort* is to ignore what God said and did in Jesus Christ. To offer up your good works in this arena alongside of Jesus is to compete with Jesus. It presumes his work on the cross is insufficient. But we are justified by faith in Jesus, not by living well! This is not to say, however, that believers have the right to live as they please. Remember, trusting in Jesus alone, not *good living* does not mean Jesus endorses *sinful living*. Believers are not licensed to sin. They are responsible for outwardly manifesting the life of Jesus Christ who resides within them. God desires you to live a godly life by faith, a life of love for God. You do not need to earn God's love.

Live aware that your day-to-day activities proclaim the gospel

Peter reminds us that how we live our daily lives makes a statement concerning the gospel. He warns us to be careful. Our conduct must be consistent with our convictions and anything else is hypocrisy. Peter made a mistake. Godly people make mistakes. However, we must strive to make sure our actions, reactions, words, and attitudes are in line with what we believe concerning God and his will for our lives. How we live out our new life in Jesus Christ is important. Don't contradict the gospel by the way you live. Be warned that fear of man is a powerful motivator. Peter made the mistake of modeling a false gospel. We all compromise our faith out of fear of people at times, and compromise can be contagious, leading others astray. Rather, we as individuals and as the body of Christ are to take the right stand because of fear of God. The person, who consistently fears God, consistently lives by faith in Jesus.

1.   Romans 3:28; Ephesians 2:9; Philippians 3:6–8

Discoveries

Notes, Observations & Questions

Now you have completed your fourth excavation into the book of Galatians. It is again time to stop digging and carefully examine what we have learned and what difference it can make in our lives. Pick the questions that will be most helpful for you or your community.

Connecting with the community

Here are some discussion questions to help you better understand the text. Do not merely reflect on them as an individual but rather think of each question, when applicable, in terms of your family, your community, your nation, and your church.

1. In Galatians 2:11–14, Paul describes the attitude of Peter and the other Jews as having "a conduct not in line with the truth of the gospel." Could this attitude be considered a form of "preaching a different gospel" (Galatians 1:8–9)? What does the attitude of Peter teach you regarding the potential that every believer has for corrupting the truth of the gospel?

2. Verses 15–16 are a major peak in the argument of the epistle. What are the doctrinal principles presented by the apostle? Why do you think this is so important to the gospel of God? How is this relevant in your life and the life of your church?

3. In light of the principles of verses 15–16, what is the purpose of verses 17–19? What is the objection Paul foresees that may arise from his teaching?

4. Explain the meaning of verse 20. How can you live your life "in the body" as "by faith in the Son of God?" What does this kind of life look like within the body of believers?

5. According to verse 21, what kind of attitude and belief would imply that "Christ died for nothing?" Do you see this kind of attitude and belief in your church?

6. What purpose does the rebuke of Peter serve in Paul's defense of his gospel message? Meditate carefully for a moment on the

Notes, Observations & Questions

behavior of Peter, Barnabas and the rest of the Jews. If you had been the observer of such conduct, would you have considered it a big issue? Would you have seen their actions as "contrary to the gospel" and dangerous to the local church? Defend your answer.

7. The concept of justification is crucial to the message of verses 15–17. What does justification mean? How is a sinner justified before God?

8. Sometimes, division arises in the church as a result of the most common and seemingly irrelevant things, such as food. This was the case in Galatia. Can you think of any other topics that today tend to cause strife in a congregation even though they are simple and seemingly unrelated to doctrinal issues?

9. What is the basis of your acceptance before God? Have you ever tried to earn God's favor through your actions? Is your acceptance based on any way in your behavior?

10. When you experience failure in your Christian walk, what is your response? What do you think God wants you to do after falling?

Probing deeper

These exercises are to help you look deeper into some of the secondary issues of our passage and may require reading from the rest of Scripture.

1. Read Acts 10. Do you believe the attitude of Peter described in Galatians is in some way connected to his experience in Acts 10? What does this event tell you about the impact leaders can have in the rest of the community?

2. Take some time now to summarize the differences we have explored so far between the gospel preached by Paul and that embraced by the Galatians. What can you learn from these differences? Ask a close friend or mentor if he or she thinks your faith resembles more the gospel of Paul or the gospel of the Galatians. What can you learn from this?

3. Make a list of the most important activities that guide your actions through a typical day. How can you proclaim the gospel in the context where God has placed you?

Notes, Observations & Questions

4. Read Romans 3:28; Ephesians 2:9 and Philippians 3:6–8. What is the role of the law in our salvation? Write out your answer and show it to a Christian friend or family member. See if they agree that you have accurately captured the meaning of these texts.

Bringing the story to life

Paul is adamant in this section of Galatians that we as believers are not justified by the works of the law. In light of this lesson, create a one-page handout or explanation explaining why our self-effort does not please God. Create your handout for a specific individual or group. You can design it to teach children or young adults this concept.

Your one-page handout can be creative in the way you explain the concepts Paul teaches us in Galatians 2:11–21 however, you must include this Galatians reference on the handout. Pictures, timelines, exercises, questions, role-play or any other creative idea can be used to help your students understand this important message.

Take the opportunity to use your one-page handout in a real teaching setting. Make sure you review Paul's message in Galatians 2:11–21, and this *Field Study* carefully before you teach. You may also do this as a group project with several people involved in making the lesson clear and memorable to your students.

The purpose is to carefully and creatively explain to others what Paul is saying. This will help you internalize the message for yourself.

Memorizing the key

Commit to memory the key phrase for this *Field Study*. The key phrase for Galatians 2:11–21 is:

> Justification before God is only by faith in Jesus

Part of learning the Bible is remembering what the Bible is about and where to find things. Memorizing each of the key phrases will help you to better understand and apply the key points of Galatians. Once you have completed the entire study of Galatians, you will be able to recite the main point or purpose of each section of Galatians. These phrases will remind you of the entire argument that Paul makes through the letter.

Notes, Observations & Questions

Observation journaling

This section will prepare you for *Field Study 6* by reading through the next section of Galatians. We have included three types of exercises: some for before you read, some for while you are reading, and some for after you have completed the reading.

Before you read

Review Galatians 2:11–21. In verse 20, Paul states that he has been crucified with Christ. Carefully review verse 20 within the context of Galatians 2:11–21. Write a short paragraph below summarizing what Paul is saying in verse 20. Make sure you draw the meaning from context of the passage.

While you are reading

On the following page, we have laid out the biblical text with wide margins so you can mark the text with questions, key terms, notes, and structures. We have removed all of the verse markings so you can read it without distractions and have laid out the text with spacing to help you see how the lines are related. Review the guidelines on *The art of active learning* section, page xi at the beginning of your *Field Notes* for some suggestions on reading, learning, and marking the text effectively.

Galatians 3:1–14

you foolish Galatians! Who has bewitched you? It was before your very eyes Jesus Christ was publicly portrayed as crucified. The only thing I want to learn from you is this: Did you receive the Spirit by works of the law, or by hearing with faith? Are you so foolish? After beginning with the Spirit, are you now being perfected by the flesh? Have you suffered so much in vain—if indeed it was in vain? Does God give you his Spirit and work miracles among you by your doing works of the law, or by hearing with faith?

Just as Abraham believed God, and it was credited to him as righteousness, understand then that those who believe are sons of Abraham. The Scripture foreseeing that God would justify the Gentiles by faith, preached the gospel beforehand to Abraham saying, "All nations will be blessed in you."

So then, those who have faith are blessed along with Abraham, the man of faith. All who rely on works of the law are under a curse, for it is written, "Cursed is everyone who does not keep on doing everything written in the Book of the Law." Now it is clear that no one is justified before God by the law because, "The righteous will live by faith." But the law is not of faith, rather "The man who does these things will live by them." Christ redeemed us from the curse of the law by becoming a curse for us, for it is written, "Cursed is everyone who hangs on a tree" in order that in Christ Jesus the blessing of Abraham might come to the Gentiles, so that by faith we might receive the promise of the Spirit.

Notes, Observations & Questions

Summarize the text here

After you have read

1. Writing is an important part of learning and remembering what you have read. Write out Galatians 2:11–21 from the previous page or from your own Bible into a journal word for word. This practice will help you to remember and understand what you have just read. Do you have a tendency to think that you can earn God's favor from your good works? Consider journaling your thoughts on how God has saved you and why it is important.

2. Now read Galatians 3:1–14 in your own Bible. Continue to reread it each day until you start *Field Study 6*. This will reinforce the learning of Scripture and help you in retention.

Pray

As we learn the Word of God, it is essential that we communicate with him through prayer. First, consider writing a prayer, psalm, or poem to God. What would God have you pray in light of the work Christ accomplished on the cross? Pray with someone for the effectiveness of the work of Christ in your church, your nation, your community, your family and yourself. Consider this sample prayer as a guideline:

Lord,

What a privilege it is to be able to open your Word and hear you speak into my life. Thank you for the Lord Jesus Christ. Father, I understand that only his life and his sacrifice satisfy your system of justice. He is your gracious provision and so he alone is enough. I stand before you, Father, in Jesus Christ! Forgive me for acting as if his work is incomplete without my help. Help me to live in a manner that honors you. I know trusting in Jesus alone is not permission to live immorally or irresponsibly. I need the help of the Holy Spirit on a daily basis to conduct myself consistent with the truth of your gospel. Help me to yield to him. I do ask you bring mature Christians into my life who can help me when I am wrong. Use me to help others too in my church with a compassionate and caring spirit. I love you, Lord, for who you are and what you have done in the Lord Jesus Christ, Amen.

Galatians 3:1–14

FIELD STUDY 6

How is the text arranged?

This *Field Study* begins a new major segment of the letter of Galatians. In chapters 1–2, Paul defended the authority of the message he proclaimed, proving that his gospel is God's gospel. In chapters 3–4, Paul will now present in detail the gospel he introduced in Galatians 2:15–21. In this new section, we will examine five more pieces of evidence demonstrating that the gospel is about justification by faith alone in Jesus Christ. This study examines the first three proofs. Take some time to meditate prayerfully on the text we will dig through together. Try to identify its basic outline and argument. You should see a structure similar to this:

Galatians 3:1–14

Section	Bible Text
Proof One: The personal experience of the Galatians	[1] *O you foolish Galatians! Who has bewitched you? It was before your very eyes Jesus Christ was publicly portrayed as crucified.* [2] *The only thing I want to learn from you is this: Did you receive the Spirit by works of the law, or by hearing with faith?* [3] *Are you so foolish? After beginning with the Spirit, are you now being perfected by the flesh?* [4] *Have you suffered so much in vain— if indeed it was in vain?* [5] *Does God give you his Spirit and work miracles among you by your doing works of the law, or by hearing with faith?*

Receiving the Spirit

When a person is justified before God, he or she immediately receives the Holy Spirit, which is a sure sign of salvation. However, how can one know that they have received the Spirit? One thing the Spirit produces is assurance that one belongs to the Father. While Paul will address this later in Galatians, he also writes about this in Romans 8:15–16 and 1 Corinthians 12:3.

Galatians 3:1–14

Section	Bible Text

Proof Two: The personal experience of Abraham the father of all Jews	[6] Just as Abraham believed God,
	      and it was credited to him as righteousness,
	 [7] understand then that those who believe
	      are sons of Abraham.
	 [8] The Scripture foreseeing that God
	      would justify the Gentiles by faith,
	      preached the gospel beforehand to Abraham saying,
	      "All nations will be blessed in you."

Proof Three: The testimony of the Scriptural record	[9] So then, those who have faith are blessed
	      along with Abraham, the man of faith.
	 [10] All who rely on works of the law are under a curse,
	      for it is written, "Cursed is everyone
	      who does not keep on doing everything
	      written in the Book of the Law."
	 [11] Now it is clear that no one is justified before God
	      by the law because,
	      "The righteous will live by faith."
	 [12] But the law is not of faith, rather
	      "The man who does these things will live by them."
	 [13] Christ redeemed us from the curse of the law
	      by becoming a curse for us, for it is written,
	      "Cursed is everyone who hangs on a tree"
	 [14] in order that in Christ Jesus
	      the blessing of Abraham might come to the Gentiles,
	      so that by faith we might receive
	      the promise of the Spirit.

As you can see from the outline, Paul offers in this text three pieces of evidence that should convince the Galatians that justification before God is possible only by faith in Jesus Christ. First, he reminds the Galatian believers of their own experience of coming to Christ. Then he proceeds to show that Abraham's experience was similar. He was justified by faith as well. In the final proof we examine in this study, Paul shows us that the Old Testament Scriptures teach an approach to God by faith rather than works of the law. Enjoy exploring and discovering how God, through Paul, verifies the truth of the gospel that justification is by faith alone in Jesus Christ.

B.C. 2000	1850	1700	1550	1400	1250

2091 God calls Abraham?

1925 God calls Abraham?

Receiving the Law on Mount Sinai? 1446

Receiving the Law on Mount Sinai? 1260

What is this passage saying?

What are some key terms and phrases?

We must examine a few terms, phrases, and concepts in the text more closely. This will enhance our understanding of the passage. It would be good for you to read the passage again after examining these issues. Some of these concepts are key truths that permeate other letters of Paul. Investing time now to grasp their significance will help you even beyond this text of Galatians.

Letter of Commendation

...ABOVE ALL I PRAY THAT YOU MAY BE IN HEALTH UNHARMED BY THE EVIL EYE AND FAIRING PROSPEROUSLY

(Milligan, Selections from the Greek Papyri, A Letter of Commendation, No. 14. Cambridge University Press.)

Meaning of Key Terms

Key word or phrase	Meaning and significance
Bewitched (3:1)	The Galatians were acting as though they were "bewitched." This is a word meaning *deceived*, *deluded*, or *to have become the object of black magic*. It is this last meaning that creates the idea of *coming under a spell*, or *bewitched*. In this part of the ancient world, it was believed that a person could fall under some kind of evil influence simply by being looked at with an *evil eye*. Paul invokes this perception here in describing the Galatians' attitude in this manner. He labels their dissent as so irrational that it is as though they are under an evil influence. Calling them *bewitched* is also a direct attack on the troublemakers preaching falsehood.
The reception/ giving of the Spirit (3:2, 3, 5, 14)	The reception or giving of the Holy Spirit in this passage is equated with believing or hearing by faith. Though the Holy Spirit has many ministries, he is clearly involved in justification since his presence in a person's life *in this sense* is proof that the individual is "declared righteous" before God. So Paul uses the language of *receive*, *began*, or *give* the Spirit interchangeably with believing or hearing by faith. They are two sides of the same coin. Salvation as a whole is a work of the Father, Son, *and* Holy Spirit with each person of the Godhead having distinct roles in accomplishing it.
Two opposing ways of approaching God	As you read our passage, note how Paul sets up two contrasting categories for everyone who approaches God. On the one hand, *Spirit, faith, justification, righteousness, gospel, blessing*, and *sonship of Abraham* are related. On the other, *works of the law, law, flesh*, and *curse* are related. Therefore, Paul presents two opposing, non-overlapping options to satisfy God. The first results in the blessing of a right standing before God. The second brings a curse.

The Evil Eye

In some societies today, fear of the *evil eye* is still common. For example, in Spain and México, to give someone the *evil eye* or *mal de ojo* is to give a dirty look with the intention of casting evil out toward someone. In some Turkish regions (formerly Galatia), those with green eyes are believed to posses the power to cast an evil spell with a look.

Two Approaches to God

Justification before God	Cursed by God
Spirit, faith, gospel, justification, blessing, righteousness, sonship of Abraham	Law, works of the law, flesh

1250　　1100　　950　　800　　650　　500　B.C.

Saul becomes king 1050

David becomes king 1010

Solomon becomes king 971

930 The kingdom divides

722 Northern kingdom falls to Assyria

Southern kingdom falls to Babylon and the temple is destroyed 586

83

Meaning of Key Terms

Key word or phrase	Meaning and significance
Curse of the Law (3:10, 13)	Deuteronomy 27:26 describes life under the law, as life under a curse since this is precisely the consequence of breaking it. The Jewish rabbis or teachers divided into differing schools of thought regarding the meaning and the extent of the application of the curse to law breakers. One school argued that the curse fell upon those breaching 51% of the law. Another school proposed the curse fell on those breaking any of it. Paul rightfully highlights an *all or nothing* situation. Any breach of the law incurred the curse, which is alienation from God and his blessings. At this point, Paul desires that we understand that seeking to satisfy God according to our works only leads to law breaking and results in a divine curse. The curses of breaking the law, moreover, were clearly ingrained in the minds of the Jews. Moses called the entire nation to recite the curses and blessings of the law to each other on top of two mountains, Ebal and Gerizim. Paul quotes Deuteronomy 27:26 which is a passage found in that very context.
Redemption (3:13)	The theme of redemption runs throughout Scripture and it is crucial for you to understand it. The roots of the word lie in the realm of business transactions in which a person pays a price to purchase something; often something previously owned. In the ancient world, this included slaves. In the Bible, the concept of redemption is applied to describe the action of God toward people. One can see why it is so suitable. Man, who once belonged to God, is in bondage to sin. God buys man back at a cost. The price paid was the death of Christ himself.

Deuteronomy 27:26

Cursed is the one who does not uphold the words of this law by doing them. Then all the people will say, "Amen!"

Mount Ebal and Mount Gerizim

In the vicinity of ancient Shechem are Mount Gerizim on the southern side and Mount Ebal on the northern side. When Israel entered the land, God wanted six tribes to go up Mount Gerizim and the other six to go up Mount Ebal. The blessings and curses of the Mosaic Covenant would be uttered aloud by the tribes as a vivid reminder to all present of what God expects from his people. As you can see, the mountains function like a natural amphitheater.

Todd Bolen, www.BiblePlace.com

Deuteronomy 27:12–13

When you cross the Jordan, the following tribes must stand to bless the people on Mount Gerizim: Simeon, Levi, Judah, Issachar, Joseph, and Benjamin. And these other tribes shall stand on Mount Ebal to pronounce the curses: Reuben, Gad, Asher, Zebulun, Dan, and Naphtali.

B.C.	1	A.D.	10	20	30	40	50

5? Birth of Jesus

4–6? Birth of Paul

John the Baptist begins his ministry 28–29?

Jesus begins his ministry 28–30?

Jesus is crucified and resurrected 30–33?

33–34? Paul encounters Christ on Damascus road

46–47? First Mis Journey

Paul writes Galatians 48?

What about the culture?

Now that we are well immersed in the book of Galatians, it is helpful to pause and consider Paul's writing style. Paul's rhetoric is very effective because it is so thorough. He exhibits a style of writing in his letters known as *diatribe*. It was a technique of writing or speech that used multiple devices such as rhetorical questioning, or voicing and answering potential objections, whether real or hypothetical to make a point. It was well respected as an educated mode of debate since it established the point and defended the issue from multiple angles.

While Paul's background was Jewish, the diatribe style came from his Greek education. Paul, who was from Tarsus, was a *Hellenistic Jew*. This was a person who was brought up in the Greek culture, outside of the Jewish homeland. Hellenistic Jews were often more zealous about their Jewish heritage because they felt they had to make up for not living in Israel. As you can see, God called a highly trained Greek speaking Jew whom he providentially prepared so that the gospel would move from the Jews to the Gentiles. Paul was an expert in the Jewish Scriptures and in Greek debate and led the charge of the proclamation of the gospel into the Hellenistic Mediterranean world.

What is the explanation?

Let's dig a little deeper into each of the arguments Paul presents in these verses to remind the Galatian believers that justification is by faith in Jesus Christ alone.

5) *Proof One:* Paul begins his series of arguments to the Galatians with an emotionally charged piece of evidence—the Galatians' personal experience. It reads like an outburst, which blends both disappointment and concern for these believers. Paul is torn. He calls them *foolish* twice since they are acting as though they lack understanding. He describes their condition as *bewitched*, as though hypnotized under a spell. He bombards them with rhetorical questions that ridicule what they are toying with in light of their personal experience with God when they first believed. The little interjection "O" that starts it all off, however, frames his words with a tone of concern and deep emotion. Paul feels this problem deep within for he remembers their initial conversion to Jesus Christ. He wants them to remember it as well. Though acting as if they came under *an evil eye*, they must remember that a crucified Jesus Christ was proclaimed before their *eyes*.

Codex Sinaiticus

This is a single page or leaf from one of the oldest copies of the New Testament found in a manuscript called *Codex Sinaiticus*. It was copied in Greek by hand around A.D. 330–360 and rediscovered in Saint Catherine's Monastery at the base of Mount Sinai in 1862. Paul's writing style in Galatians can be analyzed today because of scribes who faithfully copied the Bible in manuscripts like this.

Public Domain

INRI

INRI is a Latin acronym which stands for *Iesus Nazarenus, Rex Iudaeorum*, or in English, *Jesus the Nazarene, King of the Jews*. According to John 19:20 the inscription above Jesus on the cross was written in Aramaic, Latin, and Greek.

Chmee2, 2010

50	60	70	80	90	100 A.D.

49? Jerusalem Council

50–52? Second Missionary Journey by Paul

60–62? Paul arrives in Rome under house arrest

64 Fire in Rome

70 Temple is destroyed

79 Pompeii and Herculaneum are destroyed by Vesuvius eruption

John writes Revelation 95–96?

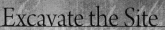

Began and Complete

The words *began* and *complete* are used in ancient Greek cultic worship ceremonies. The first was used for the act of scattering barley on and around the offering at the beginning of the sacrifice. The second was the term used to note the completion of the sacrifice. Paul uses familiar cultic terminology and applies it to Christians whose lives are a sacrifice to God from beginning to end by faith. Note also how here we have that same truth Paul teaches in Philippians 1:6. It is God who begins and completes his work in the life of a believer! He doesn't start it and step aside.

Central to the gospel is what Jesus does at the cross. Remember, to (1– add anything else to his work, is to nullify Christ's sacrifice.[1] Paul's rhetorical questions point to the right answer in the Galatians own experience and aim to *break them out* of their folly. They received the Spirit by believing the gospel by faith and not as a reward for law observance. Now they were acting foolishly in thinking their walk with God would be perfected by their own corrupt efforts. Moreover, their suffering for their faith would be pointless—but it didn't have to be; there was still time to change course. God had provided the Spirit unleashing his power because of their faith, not works. Therefore, in chapters 1 and 2 Paul presented his own personal experience. Now he asks *them* personal questions. They were to realize how illogical their desertion was in light of their own experience. Like Peter who was rebuked for his hypocrisy, their conduct was also inconsistent with their experience of faith with God.

Proof Two: Paul's second piece of evidence comes from Abraham's (6– experience. This is a clever example to prove his point again from another angle. The Galatians are deserting to a *Jewish-flavored* gospel. The troublemakers advancing this error are clearly appealing to the writings of Moses, Israel's great deliverer even though they are misunderstanding his instructions. Therefore, Paul takes them a step further. He appeals to Abraham, the founder and father of all Jews including Moses. Abraham's experience with God was even recorded by Moses. How clever is that?

Abraham and Isaac
God promised Abraham a son through his wife Sarah, and by faith, Abraham believed even though they were much too old to have children. That faith that Abraham exhibited is what Paul appeals to.

Look at how Paul unfolds his argument in favor of justification by faith in Christ alone. Paul quotes what Moses wrote in Genesis 15:6 to declare the basis upon which Abraham was justified by God. He believed or trusted in God. Faith was the basis upon which he received God's promise. Just as faith was the operating principle for satisfying God back then, so it is still in Paul's day and today. God is satisfied in the present as he was in the past. It's just that now we know the details of the content of this faith. Therefore, all who believe as Abraham believed are sons of Abraham in this nonmaterial sense. This was God's plan all along. The conversion of the Gentile Galatians to Jesus Christ by faith was

Anthony van Dyck, 1617

1. Galatians 2:21

| B.C. 2000 | 1850 | 1700 | 1550 | 1400 | 1250 |

2091 God calls Abraham? Receiving the Law on Mount Sinai? 1446

1925 God calls Abraham? Receiving the Law on Mount Sinai? 1260

86

always part of God's plan. Paul shows them this principle from Genesis 12:3 and Genesis 18:18. That is to say, Paul is telling the Galatians that they can be children of Abraham without embracing Judaism. There is no need to be circumcised. It is by faith that one receives the blessing that Abraham, the man of faith, received from God. Neither circumcision nor any other works of the law can make anyone a son of Abraham in a justifying sense. Faith does.

4) *Proof Three:* In the third piece of evidence, Paul argues from the Scriptural record to advance his point. In presenting his argument, it is no accident that three of the four biblical references he uses as support are from the books of the law. Paul is arguing against a law-based gospel, from the law itself. It is also intentional that the only positive reference concerning the manner of satisfying God is from a verse quoted from *outside* the books of the law! Once again, we need to follow his reasoning closely.

According to Deuteronomy 27:26, the law to which the Galatians want to submit, declares a curse on those who do not keep it. Since perfect adherence to the law is essential to satisfy God, he who submits to it is subject to God's curse upon failure. On the other hand, Paul argues from Habakkuk 2:4 that Scripture is clear in declaring that both justification and sanctification are by faith. Seeking to live by the law brings a curse. Seeking to live by faith brings justification. Paul then proceeds to quote from the law once again, citing Leviticus 18:5.

Living under the law to satisfy God is not living a life based on faith. They are mutually exclusive. The Galatians cannot have it both ways; you live under either one or the other.

Moses the Deliverer

Moses was Israel's great deliverer and receiver of God's Law. Judaizers such as those causing trouble in Galatia would have been stunned after learning from Paul that Moses himself proclaimed that Abraham was justified by faith alone.

James Joseph Jacques Tissot, 1896–1902

Leviticus 18:5

So you must keep my decrees and laws; anyone who does so will live by keeping them. I am the LORD.

At this point in verse 13, the apostle reaffirms to the Galatians once again the work of God in and through the gospel of Christ. Christ's death on the cross transfers the curse of the law from guilty men unto him.[2] It is only through Christ's death on the cross that man can be redeemed. It is in this redemption by Christ that the same justification that Abraham experienced, can come to the Gentiles. It is a blessing now guaranteed by receiving the promised Spirit. This blessing is received by faith. In short, the rest of

Purpose of the Law

At this point you should be asking, what then was the purpose of the law? Good question. It means you are tracking with Paul. Remember, his diatribe style? He will get to it in a moment.

2. Deuteronomy 21:23

1250   1100   950   800   650   500 B.C.

Saul becomes king 1050
David becomes king 1010   930 The kingdom divides   722 Northern kingdom falls to Assyria
                                                              Southern kingdom falls to 586
Solomon becomes king 971   Babylon and the temple is destroyed

87

the Bible supports Paul's position. Even those who lived to satisfy God in a justifying sense in the Old Testament, did so by faith. The law tells us justification is not by the law. The prophets tell us it is by faith. The Scriptural record argues against the Galatians' false gospel.

What is God saying?

Like a boxer jabbing at his opponent, Paul repeatedly counters objections to the gospel sustaining his argument. His point is always the same though demonstrated in several different ways. Paul is not seeking to destroy the Galatians; he wants to help them break out of their daze. Through Paul, God declares a single truth three different ways:

Where else is this taught in Scripture?

Sacrificing on the Altar

God established a very specific and elaborate ceremony of sacrifice for the forgiveness of sins. In part, it was to communicate the need for an intermediary, who was represented by the priest.

The sacrificial system in the Old Testament was a visual way of depicting both the need for forgiveness of sin and the expression of faith in God through the death of an animal on the altar in substitution for the believing offeror. For example, in the book of Leviticus chapters 1 to 7, detailed legislation is given concerning the sacrifices of Israel. The sacrifices presented are classified as either "sweet aroma" offerings, which included burnt, grain, and fellowship offerings, or "non-sweet aroma" sacrifices, which were sin and guilt offerings. The first group expressed what results from fellowship between a grateful redeemed Israelite sinner and a holy God. The second group revealed how to restore fellowship between a redeemed Israelite who had sinned and broken fellowship with God. The sacrifices were at the heart of worship. They expressed the unworthiness, powerlessness, and dependence of the offeror as well as God's provision. They were a divinely instituted drama that enacted outwardly inner faith in God for his provision of forgiveness. Faith was at the heart of the sacrificial system because without faith it is impossible to please God (Hebrews 11:6). The sacrifice presented once a year on the *Day of Atonement* presented in Leviticus 16 communicates very clearly the principle of faith in God for the forgiveness of sin through the substitutionary death of an innocent animal. Once a year, the High Priest alone entered into the holiest part of the Tabernacle/Temple after extensive purification rituals. Then, he offered sacrifices on behalf of the nation before God: a bull offering for the priests, a goat offering for the people, and the dispatch of another goat, the scapegoat, into the wilderness representing the sending away of the sins of the people (Leviticus 16:1–34). In all this, the Old Testament Scriptures repeatedly present justification before God as being attained by faith.

Where else does this happen in history?

Sadly, history provides multiple examples of men and women seemingly under the influence of an *evil eye*. They are deceived into thinking they are worshipping and honoring God. In 1978, for example, over 900 individuals who were members of the Peoples Temple committed mass suicide. They were under the evil influence of Reverend Jim Jones. In 1993, nearly 100 people died in Waco, Texas, members of the Branch Davidian religious sect. Its leader at the time was David Koresh, a name chosen by the individual to declare himself a messianic figure as a descendant of both King David, and the Persian king Cyrus, or *Koresh*. This type of delusion happens in many other places around the world. In 1912, Leonardo Alcalá from a small village in Jalisco, México, claimed that he had received the divine power of the

Jim Jones

Jim Jones (1931–1978) was the founder and leader of the Peoples Temple which committed mass suicide in Guyana.

Father, the Son, and the Holy Spirit. He claimed he was converted into a "human radio" of the eternal father and their deities (God Father, God Son, God Holy Spirit, Virgin Mary and Joseph Elijah!). Since then, Alcalá devoted himself to transmit God's universal orders and prophecies of the creator. In 1937 he received a revelation and founded the Reign of the Holy Spirit in Mexico City where he was proclaimed "The God of the Third Age" (Moses, Jesus Christ, and now Leonardo). Although Alcalá died in 1984 his followers still worship him as "El Dios Alcalá" under the leadership of one of his oldest followers. There are many examples of groups like this even today. The temptation the Galatians were undergoing toward a false religious stance is still a problem today.

1. *Your personal experience* in receiving the Spirit testifies that justification is by faith in what God has done and not in what you do.

2. *The experience of Abraham* the patriarch testifies that justification is by faith in what God does, not in what you do.

3. *The Old Testament Scriptures* testify that justification is by faith in what God does, not in what you do.

However, we cannot be too hard on the Galatians for their error. The tendency to be deluded and misunderstand God's workings is common. Paul warns the Corinthian Christians about being deceived also.[1] Peter also warns his Christian readers to be on alert.[2] On the road to Emmaus, Jesus himself stood before some disciples who did not recognize this wonderful truth. They were slow to see and

1.   2 Corinthians 11:3–4
2.   1 Peter 5:8

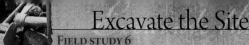

appreciate the workings of God. Jesus did what Paul does right here in Galatians; he uses the Scriptures to explain how God's plan worked out in Christ.[1] Paul and Jesus used the Scriptures. The Bible is still a necessary guard against deception.

What does God want?

There are many important lessons to embrace in light of our dig. Here are a few applicational triggers from the evidence Paul provided. Take time to think through how they apply in your life.

Continue as you began

Paul calls believers to remember their past. It is important you take a few moments this week to answer the questions God asks you in Galatians 3:1–5. It is easy for believers to drift toward wrongly motivated *works* as the Galatians did. Our journey with God began by faith in Christ. In time, things may have gotten murky. Good Christian activities like going to church, tithing, reading the Bible, serving in some capacity, or even taking communion might define you as a Christian, as one upright before God. Yet today you are still only right with God because of faith in him. We need to continue walking by faith in Jesus since that is how we began our life with him. It is of utmost importance we learn to distinguish between our faith in Christ and our responsibilities to Christ in light of our faith. Therefore, this is a call for us to guard our own hearts. It is however, also a warning. Living the Christian life confident in our "do's and don'ts" is a spellbinding yet foolish trap. We drift into it unaware and often with good intentions. Activities like church attendance, tithing, and Bible-reading play a role in our walk with Christ, the question is why do we do them. Do you know?

Continue as you began for that's been God's way all along

Justification before God has always been by faith, but never faith collaborating with good works. All justifying relationships with God —not just yours—are based on faith in him. In verses 6–9, Paul takes us back before God's law to show us faith in him has always been the operating principle to satisfy him. Only those who believe like Abraham did, will receive the blessing Abraham received! The books of the law testify to this truth as well.[2] Living life trusting in our good works is the very opposite of living by faith. The consequences of good works are very different as well: curses as opposed to redemption! You cannot supplement faith in Jesus with a dose of "good living." These two approaches repel one another.

1. Luke 24:25–27
2. Galatians 3:10–14

Discoveries

Now we have completed our fifth excavation into the book of Galatians. It is again time to stop digging and carefully examine what we have learned and what difference it can make in our lives. Pick the questions that will be most helpful for you or your community.

Connecting with the community

Here are some discussion questions to help you better understand the text. Do not merely reflect on them as an individual but rather think of each question, when applicable, in terms of your family, your community, your nation, and your church.

1. The apostle Paul calls the Galatians *foolish* in verse 1. What reason or reasons does he offer in this section for such a strong rebuke?

2. What purpose does the story of Abraham serve in Paul's argument? How is that story related to the cross of Christ?

3. Consider the three proofs of justification by faith alone that Paul presents. Which of the three do you find most compelling? Why?

4. How was the way in which the Galatians received salvation an argument in favor of Paul's gospel proclamation? Do our own experiences apply in the same manner today?

5. What is the significance of the word *bewitched* used by Paul to describe the Galatian's mindset? Do you see any ways in which believers today appear to be bewitched by a different gospel? Do you know of any cultures that still use this concept of the evil eye?

6. What are the two opposing ways to approach God contrasted in this study? Do you see evidence of both in your community? If so, how?

7. How is Paul's reasoning an example of a diatribe? Is this approach useful today for persuading or convincing someone of the truth of the gospel? If so, how?

8. From Galatians 3:6–9 we deduce that the Judaizers were appealing to the Mosaic Law in order to defend their doctrine. What is the error in their understanding of the Old Testament and in particular, the purpose of the Mosaic Law?

9. Consider your normal church experience in the community where you worship. Make a list of the things Christians are expected to do in your community. Your list may include things such as: church attendance, attending yearly conferences, baptism, communion, etc. What is the relationship of these activities to the message of the gospel? Which of these actions are thought to be a necessary part of the gospel message? Should they be?

10. If every Christian begins by faith, how can he or she continue to live by faith? What does a life of faith look like? What is the function of good works in relation to faith?

11. Consider your Christian walk up to this point in your life. Have there been times when you have stopped living in accordance to your faith in the gospel? If so, how? What caused you to go down such a road? Did a pastor or Bible teacher lead you astray? Could you now say that your actions then where foolish as Paul categorized the Galatian's actions?

12. Consider the faith and practice of the Christian churches in your local area. Do they proclaim a different gospel? Are any of them proclaiming a works-based justification? If so, what works are being required? What is their source for these ideas?

Probing deeper

These exercises are to help you look deeper into some of the secondary issues of our passage and may require reading from the rest of Scripture. Consider each of these questions in terms of yourself, your family, your community, your nation, and your church.

1. Read and prayerfully meditate on the following passages from the letters of Paul: 1 Corinthians 1:17–18; Galatians 5:11, 6:12–14; Ephesians 2:16; Philippians 2:8, 3:18; Colossians 1:20, 2:14. Why do you think the crucifixion is so important to Paul and to his argument in Galatians 3:1–14?

Notes, Observations & Questions

2. Read Romans 4:1–25 and observe carefully Paul's description of the relationship between works and faith with respect to justification. In what ways is Paul's argument in Romans similar to his argument here? In what other ways does the argument in Romans contribute to the argument in this passage of Galatians?

3. Paul uses the experience of Abraham in Genesis 15 and the words of David in Psalm 32 to support his position. In both cases, these Old Testament heroes receive blessing because of their faith because of God's doing and apart from their works. Read these two chapters. In what ways does the Old Testament ratify the message Paul preaches? Can you add any other Old Testament stories or passages that also support Paul's argument?

4. Study the following passages of Scripture. They deal with the very important concept of redemption: Leviticus 25:23–34; Numbers 3:40–51; Colossians 1:9–14; Galatians 3:10–14. What is the meaning and significance of the word *redemption*?

Bringing the story to life

Paul reminds the Galatians to continue as they began; in other words, to remember what brought them salvation which was faith in Christ, and then to continue with it. Come up with an object to use as an illustration in sharing your own testimony. A testimony tells people how you came to faith in Christ and specifically, what you believe. It is an opportunity to share the good news or gospel and its effects on your own life. The object may reflect who you were before Christ, an event that brought you to Christ, or the transformation in your character with the Spirit working in your life. The point of the object is to capture people's attention and to be reminded of your testimony when they encounter that object again. Once you have prayed and prepared, share your testimony with someone as to how you came to faith in Christ, what you believe about Christ, and how you are continuing in faith.

Memorizing the key

Commit to memory the key phrase for Galatians 3:1–14, which is:

> Justification before God has always been by faith

Learning the Bible includes remembering what issues Scripture addresses and where to find things. Memorizing the key phrases will help you to better understand and apply the key points of each book.

Observation journaling

This section will prepare you for *Field Study 7* by reading through the next section of Galatians. We have included three types of exercises: some for before you read, some for while you are reading and some for after you have completed the reading.

Before you read

Fill in the chart below with what you already know about the relationship between law and grace. This exercise will help you learn and remember as you encounter new information. You will fill in the new information after you have read the text.

Reading knowledge chart

	What I already know	What I have learned
What is the purpose of the law?		
What is the relationship between law and grace?		

While you are reading

On the following page, we have laid out the biblical text with wide margins so you can mark the text with questions, key terms, notes, and structures. We have removed all of the verse markings so you can read it without distractions and have laid out the text with spacing to help you see how the lines are related. Review the guidelines on *The art of active learning* section, page xi at the beginning of your *Field Notes* for some suggestions on reading, learning, and marking the text effectively.

Galatians 3:15–22

Brothers, let me give an example from everyday life: even with a man-made covenant, when it has been ratified no-one can set it aside or add anything to it. Now the promises were spoken to Abraham and to his offspring. Scripture does not say "and to offsprings," referring to many, but "and to your offspring," referring to one, who is Christ. What I am saying is this: The law that came 430 years later, does not set aside a covenant previously ratified by God, so as to nullify the promise.

For if the inheritance is based on law, then it is no longer based on a promise; but God in his grace gave it to Abraham by means of a promise. Why then was the law given? It was added because of transgressions, until the arrival of the offspring to whom the promise had been made. It was put into effect through angels by an intermediary. Now an intermediary is not for one party only, but God is one. Is the law then opposed to the promises of God? Absolutely not! For if a law had been given that could impart life, then righteousness would certainly have been based on the law. But the Scripture imprisoned all things under sin, so that the promise by faith in Jesus Christ might be given to those who believe.

Notes, Observations & Questions

Summarize the text here

95

After you have read

1. Go back to your *reading knowledge chart* on page 94 and fill in anything that you have learned while reading through this section of Galatians. Compare it with what you already knew to see what the text has revealed so far.

2. Write out Galatians 3:15–22 from the previous page or your own Bible into a journal word for word. This practice will help you to remember and understand what you have just read. This week, journal your thoughts on how you came to faith. Specifically, what role did you play in being justified before God? How should your justification make you act? Do you act in this way? Why or why not?

3. Now read Galatians 3:15–22 in your own Bible. Continue to reread it each day until you get to *Field Study 7*. This will reinforce the learning of Scripture and help you in retention.

Pray

As we learn the Word of God, it is essential that we communicate with him through prayer. First, consider writing a prayer, psalm, or poem to God. What would God have you pray in light of his justification through Christ's death on the cross? Pray for your church, your nation, your community, your family and yourself. Try to pray with a friend or family member or even in a small group. Consider this sample prayer:

Dear Heavenly Father,

Studying your Word today reminded me of when I first believed. Thank you for stepping in to my life then. Help me to live today with the same attitude and passion I had then. It brings so much joy and assurance to my soul to know that my faith response to you is but another example of what you have desired all along. Thank you for reminding me of the experience of Abraham and the testimony of the Old Testament Scriptures. A righteous standing before you has always been only by faith in you. There has never been another way! Why is it I so easily live as if more is required? Forgive me for this. I pray that the Holy Spirit will help me this week to live confident in you and rejoicing in the hope that I have in Jesus Christ, Amen.

Excavate the Site

Galatians 3:15–22

Even the law points to justification by faith

Galatians 3:15–22

FIELD STUDY 7

How is the text arranged?

Our previous study examined three of the five pieces of evidence offered by Paul to demonstrate that justification before God is by faith in Jesus Christ. As significant as the evidence of the Galatian believers' experience, Abraham's experience, and the Scriptural record are, Paul has even more support to come. In this *Field Study*, we look at two more proofs. Paul continues to present the gospel as he defends it. Make sure you read the text several times. Use the guide provided. It helps break up the biblical text into its logical progression.

Galatians 3:15–22

Section	Bible Text
Proof Four: How covenants work in everyday legal practice	
Analogy from man-made covenants	¹⁵ Brothers, let me give an example from everyday life: even with a man-made covenant, when it has been ratified no-one can set it aside or add anything to it.
Connection to Abraham	¹⁶ Now the promises were spoken to Abraham and to his offspring. Scripture does not say "and to offsprings," referring to many, but "and to your offspring," referring to one, who is Christ.
Explanation	¹⁷ What I am saying is this: The law that came 430 years later, does not set aside a covenant previously ratified by God, so as to nullify the promise. ¹⁸ For if the inheritance is based on law, then it is no longer based on a promise; but God in his grace gave it to Abraham by means of a promise.

$Galatians\ 3:15-22$

Section	Bible Text
Proof Five: The real purpose of the Law	
Purpose 1	[19] Why then was the law given? It was added because of transgressions,
Purpose 2	until the arrival of the offspring to whom the promise had been made. It was put into effect through angels by an intermediary. [20] Now an intermediary is not for one party only, but God is one.
Objection Response	[21] Is the law then opposed to the promises of God? Absolutely not! For if a law had been given that could impart life, then righteousness would certainly have been based on the law.
Purpose 1 and 2 reiterated	[22] But the Scripture imprisoned all things under sin, so that the promise by faith in Jesus Christ might be given to those who believe.

The Promises to Abraham

Paul refers back to God's promises to Abraham, which concerns the issues of land, descendants, and blessing. They emerge in the story of Abraham recorded in Genesis 12–22. In Galatians, Paul is focusing primarily on the third issue, the promise to bless the nations through Abraham's descendant whom Christians believe to be Jesus Christ. This blessing of justification for the nations through Jesus is received as Abraham received it—by faith. Look at Genesis 12:1–3.

Let's look briefly at these two pieces of evidence.

How covenants work in everyday legal practice: Paul's fourth proof uses a contemporary analogy to demonstrate the permanence of God's covenant with Abraham. God keeps his promises! The law that came after the promise does not change it. Inheriting the blessing of justification by faith is according to the promise, which finds fulfillment in Abraham's ultimate *offspring*, Jesus Christ.

The real purpose of the law: The final proof Paul provides is launched from the law itself. Paul presents the purpose of the law to argue that it was never intended to be used as the Galatians desired. The law exposed man's need for a Savior but was never to be the savior. It was not *added* to the promises of God to Abraham but rather it came into history with its own purpose.

We will examine these in detail a little later. Before then, let's study some important issues crucial to understanding our passage.

2091 God calls Abraham?

1925 God calls Abraham?

Receiving the Law on Mount Sinai? 1446

Receiving the Law on Mount Sinai? 1260

What is this passage saying?
What are some key terms and phrases?

Take some time now to study and meditate on the following terms. They are crucial to the meaning and significance of this text.

Meaning of Key Terms

Key word or phrase	Meaning and significance
Covenant (3:15)	There were different types of *covenants* in the ancient world just like there are today. Since Paul introduces the term *inheritance* in verse 18, it appears he is specifically referring to a "will" or "testament" type of a covenant. These are *unilateral* type covenants. Applied to covenants, this term means that only one of the parties involved in the covenant is making the promises while the other is merely the recipient of its benefits. By using this meaning of the word *covenant*, Paul provides an analogy from everyday life. He refers to a man-made covenant that cannot be altered or annulled when signed to illustrate the permanence of God's covenant with Abraham.
Offspring or seed (3:16)	A key issue in Paul's argument here hinges on his use of the word *offspring* or *seed*. You see, the word *offspring* or *seed* is a collective singular. This means that it can refer to *one* or *many*—just like the English word *sheep,* which can be singular or plural. Here, Paul argues that God's promises were made to Abraham and his one *offspring*, Jesus Christ. God's promises for the nations are only in Jesus Christ, Abraham's ultimate *offspring*. In this way, those from the nations who believe by faith inherit the promise in Christ and are also referred to as *offspring*. Therefore, Paul refers to Jesus as Abraham's one *offspring* in verse 16 but later in verse 29, he refers to believers, those who belong to Christ by faith, as Abraham's multiple *offspring*.
Added (3:15, 19)	Paul argues through the analogy of a human covenant that things cannot be *added* to the promises of God since they were already ratified. He then goes on to say that the law was *added* "because of transgressions" in verse 19. Did you notice? The use of the same term seems to create a contradiction. Was Paul confused or contradictory? The apparent contradiction is only in English. Paul uses two different Greek verbs in verse 15 and 19 to avoid this very situation. The problem is that English only has one word to translate both! In Romans 5:20 Paul describes the entrance of the law with a third verb—*came in*. Paul is not confused nor is he contradicting himself. The law was added to history with a purpose but not so that it could supplement God's promise.

Alfred Nobel's Last Will and Testament
This is Alfred Nobel's last will and testament dated November 27th, 1895. In it he endows his fortune of almost $200 million US to create five yearly prizes for those who confer the *greatest benefit to mankind* which became the Nobel Prizes. This is a good example of a unilateral will or covenant.

Usages of Seed

Usage	Meaning
Natural Seed	Physical descendants of Abraham. Jews. (Genesis 12:1–3)
Natural-Spiritual Seed	Physical descendants of Abraham who have faith. Believing Jews. (Romans 9:6)
Spiritual Seed	Believers who are Gentiles. Not physical descendants of Abraham but share his faith. (Galatians 3:6–9)
Ultimate Seed	Jesus Christ. (Galatians 3:16)

Two Different Words

Verse 15   **epidiatassetai** / *επιδιατασσεται* = Added

Verse 19   **eprosetethe** / *επροσετεθη* = Added

1250	1100	950	800	650	500 B.C.

Saul becomes king 1050

David becomes king 1010

Solomon becomes king 971

930 The kingdom divides

722 Northern kingdom falls to Assyria

Southern kingdom falls to Babylon and the temple is destroyed 586

Meaning of Key Terms

Key word or phrase	Meaning and significance
Paul's discussion of the purpose of the law (3:19–22)	In Galatians 3:19, Paul begins to discuss the true biblical purpose of the law. This discussion will continue into chapter 4. It is important for you to understand that Paul is not presenting all the purposes of the law here. He just explains what is necessary to the point at hand. In other writings, like Romans, we see Paul describing other purposes for the law. For example, in our passage in verse 19, the purpose presented is "because of transgressions," that is, the law exposes sin. Yet, from Romans 4:15 we know that in exposing sin, the law's purpose is to bring wrath. Moreover, Romans 5:20 indicates that another purpose for the law was to increase sin! Paul's discussion here is not comprehensive regarding the purpose of the law.

The Law from Angels?

There are several ancient Jewish sources that include the idea that the law was given through angels. For example the Jewish historian Josephus writes:

"And for ourselves, we have learned from God the most excellent of our doctrines, and the most holy part of our law, by angels or ambassadors."
Josephus, Antiquities, 15.5.3

Other Angel Writings

The *Book of Jubilees* is another ancient Jewish document written in Hebrew in the second century B.C. It contains a fictional recounting of the material from Genesis 1 to Exodus 12. While not being factual, it does help us understand what some Jews believed. It reads:

*"And He said to the angel of the presence: **Write for Moses** from the beginning of creation till My sanctuary has been built among them for all eternity."*
(The Book of Jubilees, i.27)

What about the culture?

Did you know first century Jews believed that Moses did not receive the law directly from God? They believed there were intermediaries, other than Moses between God and Israel. Paul uses this Jewish idea of mediators in the giving of the law as a way to show the law's inferiority to the promise of Abraham. It was commonly accepted that Moses received the law from God through angels. Therefore, there were several stages of mediation at Mount Sinai. God gave the law to angels, they gave it to Moses, and finally Moses took it to Israel. The angels represent God and Moses represents Israel. Note the comments by the first century Jewish historian Josephus as well as the ancient Jewish work the *Book of Jubilees* on the side of the page. The New Testament moves in this direction as well. Galatians 3:19–20, Hebrews 2:2 and Stephen in Acts 7:53 affirm the Jewish belief that the law was mediated to Moses through angels. What is interesting is that the Exodus account is silent on this. Only Deuteronomy 33:2 allows for this understanding in the Old Testament.

Deuteronomy 33:2

The LORD came from Sinai and revealed himself to Israel from Seir; he shone forth from Mount Paran, and came forth with ten thousand holy ones. With his right hand he gave a fiery law to them.

B.C. 2000   1850   1700   1550   1400   1250

2091 God calls Abraham?

1925 God calls Abraham?

Receiving the Law on Mount Sinai? 1446

Receiving the Law on Mount Sinai? 1260

100

What is the explanation?

Let's examine how the two pieces of evidence Paul presents here further his point that the central message of the gospel is justification by faith through Jesus Christ apart from works of the law.

8) *Proof Four:* The Galatians, or the troublemakers among them, could argue that the law came after Abraham's faith encounter with God and therefore should replace or be added to the faith placed in the promise. In order to help the Galatian believers understand how invalid this objection would be, Paul invokes a human example from normal legal practice. They would agree that once a typical human covenant was approved and signed, one could not disregard or alter it. Its terms had to stand just as when it was officially sanctioned. So it is with God's promises to Abraham and his *offspring*. It's a covenant that stands as initially established, and among its original stipulations, was that justification is by faith in God. Now, Paul is aware that one could counter-argue this explanation by saying God's promises to Abraham and his *offspring* were already fulfilled before the law was given. This would imply that the covenant was fulfilled by his immediate *offspring* and therefore was completed. Thus, the Law of Moses would be the latest operating principle given by God, one that replaced the experience of Abraham.

Paul, however, does not let them off the hook. The *offspring* anticipated in God's covenant with Abraham is Jesus Christ. Therefore, the covenant was not complete before Moses received the law. The law was given and ratified by God, and came 430 years after his promises to Abraham, but does not cancel or invalidate those initial promises. Inheriting God's promised blessing of justification for the nations follows the principle Abraham demonstrated when his promise was given. The law does not change this. God's promise is received by grace through faith in Abraham's ultimate *offspring*, Jesus Christ. Just as every day covenants cannot be altered or disregarded, God's promise to Abraham to justify by faith alone is still operative.

Moses and the Law

Moses brought the law down from Mount Sinai as recorded in Exodus 19–24. Because of the involvement of Moses in receiving God's law on behalf of Israel, it became known as the *law of Moses*.

Gustave Doré, 1832–1883

1250   1100   950   800   650   500   B.C.

Saul becomes king 1050   930 The kingdom divides   722 Northern kingdom falls to Assyria
David becomes king 1010   Southern kingdom falls to Babylon and the temple is destroyed 586
Solomon becomes king 971

101

Moses and the Law

Israel's acceptance of God's offer to partner with him as his representative nation in the world meant a commitment to live according to this law. The story of Israel in the Old Testament is presented in light of Israel's obedience or disobedience to this law.

Rembrandt Harmenszoon van Rijn, 1659

If you are following Paul's reasoning so far, there is a question that should continually tease you. Answering it wrongly is why the Galatians' were embracing a works-based gospel! The question is this: What then is the purpose of the law, Paul?

Proof Five: According to Paul, the law does not grant the Spirit, it does not justify, and it does not replace faith. Rather, the law places one under a curse.[1] So what's the point of the law? Paul asks another potential objection in order to answer it. First, the law entered history to reveal transgressions. The law provided a concrete expression of God's standard and showed all deviations to be sin. While sin preceded the law's arrival, the law clearly exposed wrongdoing and in this sense, increased sin. Second, Paul explains that the law entered history to fulfill a temporary function. Therefore, its purpose ended with the coming of Abraham's *offspring*, Jesus Christ.[2] What Paul means by this *temporary* purpose is vague at this point but he returns to clarify this in verse 22 as well as in the analogies that will follow in 3:23–4:7.

The third thing Paul declares concerning the law does not concern its purpose but rather its importance. Because of the way in which the law was received, it is evident that it is inferior. The law was given through intermediaries and involved two parties with mutual responsibilities and obligations. The promise of justification on the other hand was given directly from God and rested only in his promise.[3] Now, verse 21 raises the next logical question: Does all this mean that there is conflict between God's law and God's promise? Definitely not! Both find their origin

James Wasserman, 2009

Mount Sinai

The traditional location of Mount Sinai is near Saint Catherine's Monastery in the Sinai Peninsula within the boundaries of modern day Egypt. It is also known in the Scriptures as Mount Horeb.

1. Deuteronomy 27:26, Romans 5:12–21
2. Galatians 3:19
3. Galatians 3:20

B.C.	1	A.D.	10	20	30	40	50

5? Birth of Jesus

4–6? Birth of Paul

John the Baptist begins his ministry 28–29?

Jesus begins his ministry 28–30?

Jesus is crucified and resurrected 30–33?

33–34? Paul encounters Christ on Damascus road

46–47? First Mis Journey

Paul writes Galatians 48?

in God. But the law was never intended to make a person righteous before God. There is only tension if one misuses the law.

Paul ends this section by returning to the reason for the law clarifying the two-pronged purpose already mentioned. The entrance of the written law into history for a period, reveals man's enslaved condition to sin and drives him to look to the coming *offspring* of Abraham, which is Jesus. By faith in Christ, believers receive the promise of justification before God.

What is God saying?

In the previous section of the letter, we discovered three evidences in favor of justification by faith in Christ. This new section adds two more proofs. Overall, God through Paul is loud and clear. Five times, he declares the gospel message is that justification is by faith alone in Jesus Christ:

300+ interpretations?

Did you know there are over 300 interpretations of Galatians 3:20? Contextually, the phrase "but God is one" is not a statement on God's *being* but a contrast with the preceding verse. The previous phrase indicates an intermediary is present only when two parties are coming together. The assumption is that there are respective commitments being made. This refers to the Law of Moses. Given the "but God is one" phrase stands in contrast to this, by implication it refers to the fact that the commitments of the promise to Abraham rest solely on one, God.

Where else does this happen in Scripture?

Paul's teaching on justification might appear contradictory to the teaching of James but is in fact in agreement with it. James 2:24 reads, "You see that a man is justified by works and not by faith alone." James and Paul agree that justification before God is by faith in Jesus Christ. This is also clear at the Jerusalem Council in Acts 15. One cannot strip this verse from its context and place it against Paul. James' point regarding the works of the law is the equivalent of Paul's formula in Galatians when he writes "faith expressing itself through love" (5:6). Both expressions recognize that those who are justified by God through faith must live outwardly for him.

Contextually, all James is saying is that genuine faith is manifested in works. It's not that one needs the law to be justified but that it makes evident who the justified are by the way they live their lives. Paul and James would cry out alongside the Reformers that faith alone justifies, but faith that justifies is never alone.

Romans 5:20

Now the law came in so that transgression would increase, but where sin increased, grace abounded all the more.

James the Brother of Jesus
The author of the epistle of James is understood to be the son of Mary and Joseph, the half-brother of Jesus. As a key leader in Jerusalem, James presided over the Jerusalem Council in Acts 15.

49? Jerusalem Council
60–62? Paul arrives in Rome under house arrest
70 Temple is destroyed
John writes Revelation 95–96?
50–52? Second Missionary Journey by Paul
64 Fire in Rome
79 Pompeii and Herculaneum are destroyed by Vesuvius eruption

Martin Luther

Lucas Cranach the Elder, 1472–1553

The famous Protestant reformer Martin Luther believed misunderstanding the law led to the corrupt situation that the Church found itself in.

1. *Your personal experience* in receiving the Spirit testifies that justification is by faith in what God does, not in what you do.

2. *The experience of father Abraham* testifies that justification is by faith in what God does, not in what you do.

3. *The Old Testament Scriptures* testify that justification is by faith in what God does, not in what you do.

4. *The way in which covenants work in everyday legal use* demonstrates that justification is by faith in what God does, not in what you do.

5. *The purpose of the law itself* testifies that justification is by faith in what God does, not in what you do.

Where else does this happen in history?

Martin Luther is a perfect example of this same problem of living imprisoned by religious laws because of a misunderstanding of the purpose of the law. He dedicated his life to satisfying God. He longed for salvation. He turned to the church of his day, the Roman Catholic Church, and became a monk. He fasted, prayed, tithed, went to mass, listed his sins in great detail for confession, and even went on a pilgrimage to Rome to climb the *Scala Sancta*, the *Sacred Stairway*. All this was to abide by a system of religious conduct taught by the Church and born out of wrongly understanding God's law. It was as Luther climbed the *Scala Sancta* on his knees to reach God that he feared his works would not work. It was then he believed Romans 1:17, "the righteous will live by faith." Luther, among others, reacted to a church that, among other things, was confused about God's purpose in the law.

Praetorium Stairs

James Tissot, 1886–1894

These are believed to be the stairs that Jesus ascended to appear before Pontius Pilate. Legend has it that Constantine's mother, St. Helena had them brought to Rome from Jerusalem as a Sacred Stairway.

Scala Sancta

Diana Bentzer, 2004

The *Scala Sancta* or Sacred Stairway was supposedly moved to Rome around A.D. 326. Now faithful followers of Jesus are to climb these on hands and knees to allegedly decrease punishment for already forgiven sins.

Paul's argument here so far is in keeping with what John sees and hears through words of praise in the heavenly scene disclosed to him in Revelation 5. Jesus alone as a sacrificed lamb purchases men for God with his blood. Man's merits are not taken into account alongside of Jesus' work in the throne room of heaven. Salvation is a work of God alone.

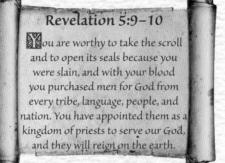

Revelation 5:9–10

You are worthy to take the scroll and to open its seals because you were slain, and with your blood you purchased men for God from every tribe, language, people, and nation. You have appointed them as a kingdom of priests to serve our God, and they will reign on the earth.

Lamb of God

The Lamb of God or *Agnus Dei* provides the visual reminder of the work of Christ, especially to a Jewish audience. Jesus alone paid for the redemption of sin.

God's promise to Abraham of blessing the nations with an upright standing before him by faith in his provision of Jesus Christ still stands. The subsequent arrival of the law is altogether separate from the gospel though it has a role to play. Clear distinctions must be maintained. Here is what the well-known reformer Martin Luther says:

> As I often insist, therefore, these two, the Law and the promise, must be very carefully distinguished; for they are as far apart in time, place, person, and all features as heaven and earth, the beginning of the world and its end... For unless the Gospel is clearly distinguished from the Law, Christian doctrine cannot be kept sound.

(Martin Luther, *Lectures on Galatians*, 1535, ed. Jaroslav Pelikan, Hilton C. Oswald and Helmut Lehmann, 1999)

What does God want?

Here are a few applications derived from our study that should be applied to our daily Christian walk. Remember that Paul continues to argue in favor of the same principle from several different angles. There is much overlap here with what God already declared previously in the epistle, but repetition signals importance. God makes the same point repeatedly and deliberately. Think about how these applications relate to you personally.

You can only lean on God's promise when you live by faith

God made a promise. He is reliable and will not annul, ignore, or replace his own word. He will do what he said he would do. He will justify those who come before him through faith in Jesus Christ.

That is precisely what he promised. There is comfort and security in the truth that a right standing before God depends on God alone. Therefore, it is a foolish thing to put your trust in that which is not a part of his promise. Only when you live by faith do you lean on God's commitment to you. Are you living by faith?

Legalism reverses the purpose of the law of God.

There is a lawful way and an unlawful way to use the law. The unlawful way to use the law is to run to good works to feel like you measure up before God. The "lawful" way to use the law is to run by faith to the grace of God in the Lord Jesus Christ for life. It is ironic that those desiring to uphold God's law, disrespected the intention he had for it. The law is like a medical MRI scanner. It reveals a condition within. Living by law is powerless to impress God, just as a medical scanner or X-ray machine cannot heal a sick body. The law exposes our helpless state before God and makes us yearn for delivery by faith in him. It brings us to our knees seeking God's grace. To live like God is satisfied by a mixture of faith and good works is to blend Scriptural teachings illegitimately. It is to misunderstand God. Do you misuse God's law?

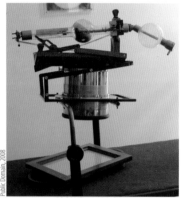

Old X-Ray Machine

The development of x-ray technology began in the late 1880's with an interest in seeing inside the body. Today, x-rays are used widely in the medical profession along with other uses such as security. Many airports use the technology to see what is inside unopened luggage.

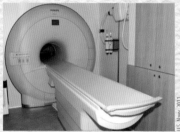

MRI Scanner

MRI stands for magnetic resonance imaging. It is a process used in medical imaging to view the internal structure of the body.

Discoveries

Now we have completed our sixth excavation into the book of Galatians. It is again time to stop digging and carefully examine what we have learned and what difference it can make in our lives. Pick the questions that will be most helpful for you or your community.

Connecting with the community

Here are some discussion questions to help you better understand the text. Do not merely reflect on them as an individual but rather think of each question, when applicable, in terms of your family, your community, your nation, and your church.

1. Analyze carefully the content of Galatians 3:15. What feature or characteristic of a man-made covenant does the apostle highlight? Why is it important?

2. In verse 16, Paul talks about the promises spoken to Abraham. Explain in your own words the relationship of this verse to the concept of the ratification of covenants mentioned in verse 15. In other words, what is the relationship that exists between the ratification of a covenant and promises?

3. According to Galatians 3:16, who is the offspring of Abraham to whom the promises were made? Discuss with your group how this is relevant to Paul's argument. Why is it important to understand the connection that exists between the promises made to Abraham and the blessings of the gospel of Christ?

4. If the Law of Moses was not part of the original promise to Abraham, what is/was its purpose? Is there any relationship between the law and the gospel?

5. Prayerfully meditate on verses 17–18. What is the covenant previously ratified by God of which Paul speaks in verse 17? In what way could the Law of Moses be thought as nullifying the promise previously made by God? Why is that not the case?

6. What relationship exists between the promises of Abraham and

the Law of Moses? Are they complementary? Are they contrary? Are they distinct? Defend your answer from the argument made by Paul in this section of the letter.

7. According to Galatians 3:19, what is the purpose of the law in God's plan of salvation? Why is the law so important to a Christian's everyday life? Discuss with your group any ways in which God used or is using the law in your life to lead you to the gospel.

8. What is the relationship that exists between living by faith and resting in the promises of God? Do you feel this describes the way you currently practice your Christian faith? Can you mention any examples of the way your faith is seen in your life and how this is evidence of your reliance on God's promises?

9. What is legalism? Can you think of any examples of its existence in your church community? Discuss in your group the significance of the affirmation of Paul regarding the inability of the law to impart life. How is this truth related to the problem of legalism in the church?

10. Do you have any tendencies to a particular form of legalism? What good things are you prone to misuse and therefore corrupt into legalistic practices?

11. Legalistic practices are usually linked to the cultural setting where they appear. Circumcision was a legalistic tendency in Jewish communities. Can you identify any cultural legalistic tendencies of your community?

Probing deeper

These exercises are to help you look deeper into some of the secondary issues of our passage and may require reading from the rest of Scripture.

1. Read Genesis 12:1–3 and Genesis 17:1–27. If the promises where made by covenant to Abraham and Christ, centuries before the Law of Moses was given, how is this an argument in favor of Paul's gospel? What is the relationship that exists between the promises to Abraham and the gospel message?

Notes, Observations & Questions

2. Study carefully the teaching of the Bible with respect to covenants in Galatians 3:15–16; Genesis 15:1–21; 2 Samuel 7:1–17; Hebrews 6:13–20. From what you learn in these texts, what is the relationship between covenants and promises? When you consider the covenants with Abraham and David, who makes the promises in these covenants? Discuss in your group why this is so important when we consider the hope God offers to us in the promises of the gospel.

3. Review Paul's arguments in Galatians 1 in favor of his gospel. Why is it significant that the law was mediated through angels rather than being directly revealed by God?

4. So far, we have mentioned five proofs presented by Paul in favor of the divine authority of his commission and message. Take some time now to review these proofs and discuss with others in your church or small group the ways in which these proofs help you value the gospel and seek to protect its purity.

Bringing the story to life

Part of understanding Galatians 3:15–22 requires an understanding of a covenant. Your assignment is to create a modern day unilateral covenant between you and God. You may work on this as a group. Make a one-page document that lays out the covenantal terms of your salvation. All of the requirements for your covenant must be placed on Christ. All of the benefit should be yours. Refer back to Galatians 3:15–22 as well as the verses about covenants mentioned in our *Probing Deeper* section.

The purpose is to document what Christ has done in saving you. By making it in the form of a legal covenant, it will help you to appreciate how unique Christ's work on the cross is. When your covenant is complete, take time to show it to someone and explain its significance.

Memorizing the key

Commit to memory the key phrase for this *Field Study*. The key phrase for Galatians 3:15–22 is:

> Even the law points to justification by faith

Learning the Bible includes remembering what issues Scripture addresses and where to find things. Memorizing the key phrases will help you to better understand and apply the key points of each book.

Observation journaling

This section will prepare you for *Field Study 8* by reading through the next section of Galatians. We have included three types of exercises: some for before you read, some for while you are reading and some for after you have completed the reading.

Before you read

Review the key terms from *Field Studies* 5 through 7 to insure you remember all of them. This will help you to follow the message that God is communicating through Paul's letter to the Galatian churches.

The key terms:

- From *Field Study 5* are on page 67–68.

- From *Field Study 6* are on page 83–84.

- From *Field Study 7* are on page 99–100.

Which key terms and definitions have been particularly helpful in understanding the message of Galatians? Why?

While you are reading

On the following page, we have laid out the biblical text with wide margins so you can mark the text with questions, key terms, notes, and structures. We have removed all of the verse markings so you can read it without distractions and have laid out the text with spacing to help you see how the lines are related. Review the guidelines on *The art of active learning* section, page xi at the beginning of your *Field Notes* for some suggestions on reading, learning, and marking the text effectively.

Galatians 3:23–4:7

Now before faith came, we were kept in custody under the law, being imprisoned until the coming faith would be revealed. So then, the law was our guardian until Christ came, so that we might be justified by faith. But now that faith has come, we are no longer under a guardian. For you are all sons of God through faith in Christ Jesus.

For all of you who were baptized into Christ have clothed yourselves with Christ. There is neither Jew nor Greek, there is neither slave nor free, there is neither male nor female, for you are all one in Christ Jesus. And if you belong to Christ, then you are Abraham's offspring, heirs according to the promise.

Chapter 4

Now I mean that the heir, as long as he is a child, is no different from a slave, though he is owner of everything. But he is under guardians and managers until the date set by his father. So also we, when we were children, were enslaved to the elementary principles of the world. But when the fullness of time had come, God sent his Son, born of a woman, born under the law, to redeem those who were under the law, so that we might receive adoption as sons. Because you are sons, God has sent the Spirit of his Son into our hearts, calling out, "Abba! Father!" So you are no longer a slave, but a son, and if a son then also an heir through God.

Notes, Observations & Questions

Summarize the text here

Notes, Observations & Questions

After you have read

1. Journaling is another way to help us learn. Write out Galatians 3:23–4:7 from the previous page or your own Bible into a journal word for word. This practice will help you to remember and understand what you have just read. This week, journal your thoughts as you consider the freedom that we have in Jesus Christ and how it affects you, your family, your community, your nation, and your church. Write down what God wants you to do with that freedom and then act accordingly.

2. Now read Galatians 3:23–4:7 in your own Bible. Continue to reread it each day until you get to *Field Study 8*. This will reinforce the learning of Scripture and help you in retention.

Pray

As we learn the Word of God, it is essential that we communicate with him through prayer. First, consider writing a prayer, psalm, or poem to God. What would God have you pray in light of the importance of living by faith? Pray for your church, your nation, your community, your family and yourself. Consider this sample prayer:

God Almighty,

Again you remind me of the wonderful truth that I stand before you declared holy because of the Lord Jesus Christ. You clearly want me to remember this and live in light of it. I can see that only when I live by faith do I live leaning on what you have promised. You will do what you promised to do only according to the terms of your promise. This makes sense and is fair. It also fills me with joy and hope for you can be trusted. I ask you, God, to help me and the people of my church understand your purpose in the Law. It is such a difficult concept for us to grasp and there is so much attention devoted to it in the Old Testament that it can be confusing. There are so many problems within our churches because of misunderstanding. Holy Spirit, please guide my mind. Help me to understand the purposes of the law as you, God, intended it not as I make it. I need your help in this, Lord, Amen.

Galatians 3:23–4:7

FIELD STUDY 8

How is the text arranged?

In the previous section of Galatians, Paul took us to the books of Moses in order to prove that justification is by faith in Jesus Christ and not by works of the law. He also examined the purpose of the law in history. This is a difficult topic and is at the heart of the Galatian problem. These churches did not understand the purpose of the law. For this reason, Paul slows down and clarifies the issue even further through several analogies that we will explore in this *Field Study*. Read the text several times. Use a pen to mark out divisions as you see them and then compare your divisions with ours below.

Galatians 3:23–4:7

Section	Bible Text
Fifth Proof Clarified: Analogies of the Purpose of the Law	

The law as our jailor	²³ Now before faith came,
	     we were kept in custody under the law, being
	     imprisoned until the coming faith would be revealed.

The law as our slave-attendant: From child-minded to sonship	²⁴ So then, the law was our guardian until Christ came,
	     so that we might be justified by faith.
	 ²⁵ But now that faith has come,
	     we are no longer under a guardian.
	 ²⁶ For you are all sons of God
	     through faith in Christ Jesus.

Galatians 3:23–4:7

Section	Bible Text
The law as our slave-attendant: From child-minded to sonship	[27] For all of you who were baptized into Christ have clothed yourselves with Christ. [28] There is neither Jew nor Greek, there is neither slave nor free, there is neither male nor female, for you are all one in Christ Jesus. [29] And if you belong to Christ, then you are Abraham's offspring, heirs according to the promise.
Guardians and trustees: From child to adopted son with inheritance rights	[1] Now I mean that the heir, as long as he is a child, is no different from a slave, though he is owner of everything. [2] But he is under guardians and managers until the date set by his father. [3] So also we, when we were children, were enslaved to the elementary principles of the world. [4] But when the fullness of time had come, God sent his Son, born of a woman, born under the law, [5] to redeem those who were under the law, so that we might receive adoption as sons. [6] Because you are sons, God has sent the Spirit of his Son into our hearts, calling out, "Abba! Father!" [7] So you are no longer a slave, but a son, and if a son then also an heir through God.

As our excavation unfolds, we will examine Paul's analogies carefully. At this point, note the general divisions that are evident from the outline and form the backbone of this study.

In verse 22, Paul refers to the law as imprisoning all under sin. He uses (23) this *jailor* imagery in verse 23 to transition the Galatians into his next main section. There he uses the image of a house slave, a well-known role in ancient society that serves to clarify the temporary nature of the law.

At the beginning of chapter 4, Paul uses yet another familiar analogy, (4:1) that of a guardian or trustee. Through this image, the temporary function of the law is stressed even further. Let's examine this portion of the letter in greater detail now.

Baptismal Pool

This traditional Jewish purification bath or *mikveh* was discovered in Jerusalem just south of the Temple Mount. Some have wondered if these ritual baths may have been used by early Jewish Christians for baptisms.

Todd Bolen, www.BiblePlaces.com

B.C. 2000	1850	1700	1550	1400	1250

2091 God calls Abraham?

Receiving the Law on Mount Sinai? 1446

1925 God calls Abraham?

Receiving the Law on Mount Sinai? 1260

What is this passage saying?
What are some key terms and phrases?

Take some time now to study and meditate on the following concepts. Alongside of the cultural issues that follow, these key terms are essential to grasping the meaning and significance of this text.

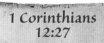

1 Corinthians 12:27

Now you are Christ's body, each of you is a member of it.

Meaning of Key Terms

Key word or phrase	Meaning and significance
Union with Christ (revisited– 3:27)	Paul has already discussed the topic of the believer's union with Christ in Galatians 2:20. Here we can learn another aspect of it. Paul often describes believers as being *in Christ*. This is because their standing before God is founded upon a faith-based union with Jesus Christ. They are united with him, participate in him, and are incorporated into him. Here, Paul refers to believers as those *baptized into Christ* and those who *put on Christ*. With this first image of baptism, Paul is not saying that the external act of water *baptism* is the doorway into a relationship with Jesus Christ. That interpretation would go against his entire argument so far with respect to circumcision. Rather, he is using this common rite, by which Christians publicly professed their faith in Jesus, as a metaphor that identifies them as believers. No one enters into a relationship with Jesus through baptism. Baptism is a testimony to an already existent relationship with Christ through faith. To *put on Christ* is yet another figurative way of speaking about being justified by faith. Two separate issues may have influenced this imagery. Given the immediate metaphor of baptism, it could stem from the fact that one took off their outer garments for baptism as an act that spoke of a person's new identification with Jesus. Paul's image of *putting on Christ* portrays Christ clothing or covering the believer. The broader context of sonship, however, may be in mind. When a child became an adult, it was a Roman custom for him to remove the childhood robe and put on the adult robe. This new robe symbolized his new status as a son with all of the inheritance rights. Whatever the background to *put on Christ* is, just like *baptized into Christ*, its basic purpose is to refer to believers in this passage.

The Body of Christ

A helpful way in which Paul talks about our union with Christ is through the metaphor of the body. Believers are the body of Christ, of which he is the head. Though the body has many parts, it is still one body.

Vitruvian Man

This famous drawing by Leonardo da Vinci reminds us of Paul's imagery for the church. Da Vinci thought that the anatomy of the human body was an analogy of how the universe worked. Paul reminds us that the human body is an analogy of the church with everyone attached to each other and led by Christ who is the head.

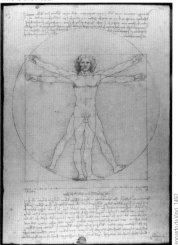

Leonardo da Vinci, 1492

| 1250 | 1100 | 950 | 800 | 650 | 500 B.C. |

Saul becomes king 1050
David becomes king 1010
Solomon becomes king 971

930 The kingdom divides

722 Northern kingdom falls to Assyria
Southern kingdom falls to Babylon and the temple is destroyed 586

115

The Historical Perspective

Christ arrived on the scene in a world very different than it had ever been before. The world was united by a network of Roman roads that facilitated the movement of the gospel. It was governed by an empire that brought peace or *pax romana* on a scale previously unknown, which was enforced by the Roman army. It was also a world in which inhabitants, despite their ethnic diversity, shared Greek as their common language.

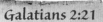

Galatians 2:21

I do not set aside the grace of God, for if righteousness comes through the law, Christ died for nothing!

Pedagogue

The term *pedagogue* literally means *to lead the child*. Pedagogues were like private tutors very loyal to their masters. For this reason, they were entrusted with the care of the master's sons. A famous pedagogue of antiquity was a man called Sicinnus. He was the slave-attendant to the sons of the Greek leader Themistocles who defeated the Persians at the battle of Salamis in 480 B.C. Sicinnus, a Persian himself, played the crucial role in the victory by deceiving the Persian king, Xerxes, at the request of his master.

Meaning of Key Terms

Key word or phrase	Meaning and significance
Elementary principles (4:3)	The way Paul uses the phrase *elementary principles* recalls the state of childhood in order to describe the experience of man under the law, before the coming of faith in Christ. The phrase simply means *the basics*. Within the childhood analogy Paul uses, *the basics* were things like the alphabet. The child needs to first learn the ABC's in order to build language and intelligent communication. Paul compares life under the law to a child's life under the ABC's in elementary school. There was a time in history when the law functioned like this. However, since the arrival of justification by faith in Christ, the Galatians were no longer in this stage.
Fullness of time (4:4)	This phrase speaks of the *completeness* of a particular time. It is placed in contrast to infancy's ABC's stage, which is over and completed. A new stage has begun. A transition occurs at the right time in history from one stage to another. In our passage, God's intervention in Christ inaugurates this transition. Yet, the Galatian believers were acting as though living under the law was still operative; as if God had not yet intervened climactically in Christ. This is another way of proclaiming the message of Galatians 2:21. God has intervened in history at precisely the right time, and in doing so, the temporary purpose of the law has been fulfilled. There are no grounds for trying to mix law and faith anymore.

What about the culture?

The analogies Paul employs in this text are somewhat alien to our culture. It is important we devote some time to understand them now so that we may discover what Paul means by what he says.

The second analogy Paul uses is that of a slave-attendant or *pedagogue*.[1] In the ancient Roman world, well-to-do families selected reliable slaves to be *pedagogues* and take responsibility for the infant boys in the household. The infants had no rights, responsibilities, nor privileges yet. Their slave-attendants woke, washed, dressed, and fed them. Although they taught them manners and took them to and from school safely, they were not formal educators as the term implies today. They were, however, in charge of helping the child grow to become a responsible citizen who bore the family name well. These pedagogues prepared boys for the privileges and responsibilities of

1.   Galatians 3:24

B.C.	1	A.D.	10	20	30	40	50

5? Birth of Jesus		John the Baptist begins his ministry 28–29?		33–34? Paul encounters Christ on Damascus road	46–47? First Mi Journey

4–6? Birth of Paul

Jesus begins his ministry 28–30?

Paul writes Galatians 48?

116

Jesus is crucified and resurrected 30–33?

Roman Roads

The Romans built a vast network of roads across their conquered realms to facilitate the movement of their troops and trade. It is estimated 50 thousand miles of paved roads spread out across their empire. Some of these form part of the foundations of roads used today. Roman roads provided the infrastructure for the movement of the gospel across the known world.

Roman Army

The Roman army were the police force of the world of the first century A.D. Their presence around their conquered lands assured relative peace on a level never seen before.

sonship in that family when the right time came. The closest parallel today is perhaps a live-in nanny.

Paul also uses the analogy of guardians and trustees in describing the purpose of the law.[2] This leads into a discussion of adoption and sonship. In the Roman world at that time, a boy born into a free and affluent family was also under the authority of other guardians in charge of his person and interests. During infancy, the child had no independence and was subject to slaves even though he theoretically had a birthright to inherit the entire estate.

Unlike the practice of many ancient and contemporary societies that fix the legal age of adulthood without exceptions, the Romans allowed the father of the boy to determine when he believed the time was just right. The fixed age was fourteen, but the father could adjust it. A distinction, therefore, was made between a child and a son. When the father appointed this time, a ceremony called the *liberalia* was prepared, in which the boys took off their childhood toga or *praetexta* and put on the adult toga or *virilis*. The taking off and putting on was indicative of putting away childhood and embracing adulthood. The act of doing so was deemed an adoption to sonship. Unlike many cultures today, a father adopted his own boy or anybody else, to sonship. Adoption signaled a change in status to a free individual with

Example of a Roman Toga

The Roman toga was a wool garment of cloth, 6 m/20 ft in length, which was wrapped around the body and worn over a linen tunic. By the second century B.C., it was only allowed to be worn by male Roman citizens.

2. Galatians 4:2

50   60   70   80   90   100 A.D.

49? Jerusalem Council

60–62? Paul arrives in Rome under house arrest

70 Temple is destroyed

John writes Revelation 95–96?

50–52? Second Missionary Journey by Paul

64 Fire in Rome

79 Pompeii and Herculaneum are destroyed by Vesuvius eruption

117

Jean-Léon Gérôme, 1867

The Death of Julius Caesar

Caesar Augustus lived from 63 B.C. to A.D. 14 and was the most influential Roman ruler that ever lived. His rule followed that of Julius Caesar who was assassinated on the March 15th in Rome. Augustus inherited his position upon adoption by Julius even though he was not his natural son. This pattern of adopting one's successor as a son became common.

A Jewish Prayer

The Babylonian Talmud is a written record of Jewish thought and oral law recorded around A.D. 200. It reads:

"A man is bound to say the following three blessings daily: *'Blessed art thou who hast not made me a heathen, who hast not made me a woman and who hast not made me a slave.'*"

(Babylonian Talmud, Tractate Menahoth 43b, Eli Cashdan, Concino Press, 1989)

While this prayer was written after the first century A.D., it may have been a well known attitude in Paul's day. In Galatians, Paul is reversing the Jewish mindset and prayer.

the full rights of inheritance of the father's estate. It is important to grasp the significance of this analogy since it permeates Paul's description of the movement from life under the law to faith in Christ.

The final background issue relevant to the meaning of this passage concerns certain social distinctions made in the first century. Jews, for example, looked down on Gentiles believing that God did as well. Even though Gentiles could, through circumcision, convert to Judaism to gain access to God, it was still believed that being a *born Jew* was better than being a *converted Jew*. The problem in Galatia clearly indicates this mindset in the church. Society in general distinguished between male and female as well as between being free and being a slave. Women and slaves had little value or status. Both the Jews and the Greeks had this mindset. The Greeks made the distinction between themselves and non-Greeks whom they called *barbarians*. Have a look at the Jewish prayer of thanksgiving on the side bar—an attitude no doubt Paul exhibited before faith in Christ. This is what makes verse 28 so shocking to Paul's readers. God unwinds man's illegitimate social hierarchies. Before God, all are equal regardless of race, gender, and socio-economic status.[1] This statement is not removing the roles, for example, between men and women. It is a statement that declares all people equal in status and value before God.

What is the explanation?

We are now ready to dig deeper into the meaning of our passage. Paul (22 briefly described the role of the law in verse 22 as a *jailor*. The law locked all up under the dominion of the sin it exposed. This imagery continues in verse 23. Before Christ's arrival with the gospel of justification by faith, both the Galatians who were Gentiles and Jews like Paul were imprisoned. They were under the law's custody.

1.   Galatians 3:28; Ephesians 2:11–22

Custodian language transitions Paul into another helpful analogy of the purpose of the law—a domestic comparison.

6) The law functioned like a child's nanny until the arrival of Christ; caring for the child until the coming of justification by faith in Jesus. Now that faith in Christ has come, the child no longer needs a nanny. The child has grown up. Jew and Gentile believers alike are no longer in a stage of infancy; rather, they are adult sons. That is to say, a faith union with Jesus Christ, God's Son, grants divine sonship to believers now. Paul explains that *sons of God* are believers who have been baptized into Christ and put on Christ. He highlights two things: the first is that *sons of God* are equal before God. Man's hierarchies of worth are irrelevant in Christ. There is neither superior nor inferior status, just equality before God. The second is that *sons of God* are heirs. If Jesus as Abraham's *offspring* is the recipient of God's promise for the nations, then those from the nations who participate by faith in him are his heirs. A son of Abraham is one who is united to Christ by faith—an heir of his will.

7) Paul's domestic analogy to explain the law's purpose—a child under a nanny—gives way to another. This time the analogy comes from the Roman custom of adoption into sonship. As a child, the boy is under the authority of slave guardians and trustees until his father declares otherwise even though by birthright he theoretically owns the complete family estate. These circumstances are comparable to man's situation under the law; he is like a child learning the basics of life awaiting declaration of sonship. Just like a Roman father set a precise date to adopt his boy to sonship, so God intervened at the right time in history. He sent his own Son, born of a woman at a point in history that placed him under the law. Paul is connecting God's intervention in history in the sending of his Son to the fulfillment of his commitment after the fall of humanity in Genesis 3:15. The curse upon the serpent who deceived Adam and Eve shows God's intention to intervene in history to defeat the curse of sin in his creation. Only God could do this, and he accomplished it by sending his own Son, Jesus Christ. God promised he would do this through the *seed* or *offspring* of the woman. Therefore, God's Son was born of a woman. God said he would reverse the curse of sin now revealed in the law. So God's Son was born under the law.

Gentiles and the Law

How can Paul declare that Gentiles were under the law before the coming of Christ? Was the law not given exclusively to Israel? Non-Jews were able to join the community of God's people in the era of the law. They could approach God but only by converting to the Hebrew faith. An essential act of conversion was being circumcised.

Genesis 3:15

And I will put enmity between you and the woman, and between your offspring and her offspring; he will bruise his head and you will strike his heel.

Paul concludes this section offering two purposes God accomplished by sending his Son. The first one was to buy back those under the curse of the law. In buying them, he also adopts them as sons. And in adopting them, Gentile and Jewish believers alike now receive the Spirit who alone assures them of their intimate Father-son relationship—one in which they can call out to God as their Father. The Galatian believers were to remember they are no longer subject to the law like the jailor, nanny, and guardian/trustee analogies illustrated. They are sons of God who are heirs of his promise.

What is God saying?

Using helpful illustrations, God shows us again his purposes for the law. Aside from incarcerating man to expose how rampant sin is in humanity, the law's function was clearly temporary. It functioned like an infant's caregiver until sonship by faith in Jesus Christ had been received. It also worked like a guardian or trustee, supervising man in his infancy until adoption as sons of God was granted. This can only be accomplished by faith in Christ. The law served the interests of

2 Corinthians 6:18

And I will be a father to you, and you will be my sons and daughters says the Lord Almighty.

Where else is this taught in Scripture?

The teaching that believers are adopted as sons with inheritance rights before God occurs elsewhere in Paul's writings. In Romans chapter 8, Paul deals with life in the Spirit. The certainty of one's future inheritance as a child of God is assured by the Spirit of God himself who resides within the Christian. In 2 Corinthians 6:18, Paul paraphrases the Old Testament to show that as adopted sons in God's family, we are to live responsibly before him (2 Samuel 7:14 and Isaiah 43:6). God had always planned to adopt believers into his family. Thus, Paul continually borrows the legal concept of adoption into sonship in the first century and uses it to describe the relationship between a believer and God the Father through faith in Jesus Christ.

For all who are led by the Spirit of God are sons of God. For you did not receive the spirit of slavery leading to fear again, but you received the Spirit of adoption as sons by whom we cry "Abba! Father!" The Spirit himself bears witness with our spirit that we are children of God. And if children, then heirs, heirs of God and fellow heirs with Christ, if indeed we suffer with him so that we may also be glorified with him. For I consider that our present sufferings are not worth comparing with the glory that will be revealed to us. For the creation waits in eager expectation for the revealing of the sons of God. For the creation was subjected to futility, not willingly but because God subjected it, in hope that the creation itself will also be set free from its bondage to decay into the glorious freedom of the children of God.

Where else does this happen in history?

In the 4th century A.D., the Roman Emperor Constantine converted to Christianity. This had positive and negative repercussions in the Christian church. On the positive side, widespread persecution of Christians stopped. Some of the most violent Christian persecutions had occurred under Constantine's predecessor, Diocletian. However, there were long-term detrimental consequences too. The church became so attached to the state that it was impossible to separate the two. The practical result of this union was that those born into the Roman Empire were deemed Christian by birth and infant baptism, regardless of faith; a sort of cultural Christianity emerged. Cultural Christianity is still a problem today. It is a mindset that defines Christianity without need for a faith response to Jesus Christ. With such a view, birth into a Christian nation or Christian home classifies one as a Christian. This ignores the truth that one is adopted into God's family only by God's grace through faith. Cultural Christians assume they are sons and daughters of God without the process of adoption. Sonship is not a status one is born into physically; nor is it inherited from parents, the society around you, or the nation you are from. It is a gift received by faith.

Emperor Constantine

Constantine was Roman Emperor from 306 to 337 and was said to have converted to Christianity in 312 at the Battle of Milvian Bridge where he had a vision of a cross.

the promise; it prepared mankind for the arrival of God's promise. Its function was temporary.

The very form in which the law was presented to Israel in Exodus 19–24 borrows an analogy from the ancient world. Its form matches up with conditional covenants between surrounding nations. By borrowing an analogy of conditional contracts existing at the time, the form spoke of the conditional nature of the covenant of the law anticipating its temporary function. Failure on the part of Israel nullified God's commitments within it, and Israel failed before she ever set out from Sinai.

The coming of faith in Jesus ends the era of the law's supervision. It also ends illegitimate, man-made categories of worth. In Christ, believers are now sons. Sons are no longer supervised; they are full heirs.

What does God want?

Here are a few applicational points to consider in light of our dig

through this passage of Scripture. Remember to be intentional about applying them to your life. What God teaches us is not for informational purposes. He wants us to be transformed.

Put childish things away!

Just as we don't expect a mature adult to play with dolls or little toy cars, believers are not to live as though they lived in a pre-Christian era under the supervision of a nanny. When you live the Christian life trying to earn God's approval through rules and practices—even good ones—you are acting like a spiritual baby. Legalism is the lifestyle of immature Christians. It is not an expression of maturity but infancy. It's as though you do not comprehend God's intervention in history and in your life through Jesus Christ. You know God wants you to live a godly life but now you live as if your good living earns you a right to God and his blessing. It doesn't. It's time to stop. It's time to grow up. You are a son of God—an heir of his promises—so it's time to put the little dolls and cars of legalism away. Live by faith in Christ, he lives in you!

Pisidian Antioch Cardo

A *cardo* was a Roman street running north-south. If geography allowed, it served as the main street and lined with various shops and outlets. Paul and Barnabas would have walked down this *cardo* when they visited this Galatian city in Acts 13–14.

Enjoy your adoption into God's family!

God intervened in history and offered redemption to mankind. If you have received his offer in Christ, he has stepped into your life and adopted you as his son or daughter. Do you understand the implications of being a child of God? Believers in Jesus Christ should be the most joyful people on the planet, and the most optimistic, and the most hopeful even in the midst of suffering. We should be the most understanding and gracious too. We have been adopted by God! We have a relationship—a personal relationship— with the living God and an inheritance through him. We have the right to call on him as our loving heavenly Father. Are you living in the joy of your relationship with God? You have a privileged, eternal future with him!

Todd Bolen, www.BiblePlaces.com

Discoveries

Notes, Observations & Questions

Now we have completed our seventh excavation into the book of Galatians. It is again time to stop digging and carefully examine what we have learned and what difference it can make in our lives. Pick the questions that will be most helpful for you or your community.

Connecting with the community

Here are some discussion questions to help you better understand the text. Do not merely reflect on them as an individual but rather think of each question, when applicable, in terms of your family, your community, your nation, and your church.

1. In verse 23, Paul describes the as law keeping mankind in custody and imprisoned. How did the law do this? Why did the law have to serve this function in the history of mankind to prepare for Christ?

2. Explain the phrase "so that we might be justified by faith" in verse 24b to what Paul said in verses 23 and 24a. How does the law take us to Christ? Share in your group any particular ways in which the law of God has accomplished this in your own life.

3. Meditate on the descriptions of Christ's work for us in verses 27–29. What is the importance of these descriptions? How real is the principle, "you are all one in Christ Jesus" in your community or church? In what ways is this issue a struggle for your group or community?

4. What does the phrase "you belong to Christ" in Galatians 3:29 mean? How is it significant in your life and the life of your church today?

5. Review the explanation of verse 9 in this study. What is the significance of the phrase "elementary principles?"

6. If the time of Christ's first coming was "the fullness of time," in what stage of salvation history do we now live? What stage of salvation history does the law belong to?

7. Review the section at the beginning of the *Field Study* called, What about the culture? Is there any way in which the function of the law still applies today?

8. Consider Paul's analogy in Galatians 3:23–29 regarding the law as a nanny to a child. Is this analogy useful in your cultural context? Could you think of any other illustration that would better illustrate the same principle in your community?

Probing deeper

These exercises are to help you look deeper into some of the secondary issues of our passage and may require reading from the rest of Scripture. This will help you connect some of the concepts that Paul addresses in Galatians with other passages in the Bible. Consider each of these questions in terms of yourself, your family, your community, your nation, and your church.

1. Read Romans 3:9–4:25 and Galatians 4:1–7. From what you learn from these two passages, discuss the following questions in your group or community: In what sense is the purpose of the law temporary? How has it fulfilled its purpose in God's plan? How can believers learn from it today if its purpose was limited and temporary?

2. Compare Hebrews 5:11–14 with Galatians 3:23–4:7. In what ways do Christians tend to be childish today? What are the marks of a mature Christian that no longer lives like a child?

3. Read Ephesians 1:1–3 and meditate on the concept of adoption. In what way does this concept help you understand God's love for you? How does the realization that you are an adopted child of God help you understand the blessedness of your relationship with God? How does it teach you about the glorious, gracious work of Christ on your behalf?

4. Read Romans 8:15–23; 9:1–5 and Ephesians 1:5–6. Can you think of any other benefits that you have received from the gospel that are better and more transcendent than being adopted into God's family? If the church is the family of adopted children of God by faith, how does such a reality guide and dictate the relationship between its members? How should they relate and treat each other considering the passages you just read?

Notes, Observations & Questions

Bringing the story to life

Galatians 3:23–4:7 calls us to put away our childish legalism. While the message is clear, sometimes its application can be hard. Many people within Christianity have misunderstood the gospel and have lived their entire lives under legalism.

Reflect on your own Christian life. Do you have legalistic tendencies in which you think that you are earning God's favor with certain actions or activities that you participate in? Make a list of things that you do to try to appease God. Your list may only be a few things or it might be very long. It is helpful to take the time to think through your behavior and the motivations behind your actions. There may be one area in your life where this is more dominant; for example, volunteering. You may constantly offer to help when volunteers are required but you do it completely for the wrong reason. You might be willing to help, but you think God expects you to do this and it helps keep your salvation.

Instead of a list, it may be that a certain object represents your tendencies towards legalism. Whether it's a list or a specific object representing your legalism, the goal is to destroy it. This could be especially effective if you are studying Galatians in a group or class. Gather everyone together and read Galatians 3:23–4:7. Allow your list or your object to represent your tendencies to train and earn salvation from God. Together as a group, renounce this sin and embrace the completed work of Christ for salvation. Then destroy the list or object. Maybe it's possible to have a bonfire. The purpose is to create a conscious memory of surrendering this faulty type of thinking. It is the exact same problem as those in Galatia had. Recognize that it is the work of Christ alone that saves you. Let the destruction of your list mark a change in your thinking.

Memorizing the key

Commit to memory the key phrase for this *Field Study*. The key phrase for Galatians 3:23–4:7 is:

> The law prepared us for the gospel of Jesus

Learning the Bible includes remembering what issues Scripture addresses and where to find things. Memorizing the key phrases will help you to better understand and apply the key points of each book.

Notes, Observations & Questions

Observation journaling

This section will prepare you for *Field Study 9* by reading through the next section of Galatians. We have included three types of exercises: some for before you read, some for while you are reading and some for after you have completed the reading.

Before you read

Paul makes several contrasts in Galatians 3:23–4:7. All of them have to do with before Christ and after Christ. On the timeline below, list each contrast Paul makes as either *before Christ* or *after Christ*.

Before Christ   *After Christ*

While you are reading

Below and on the following page, we have laid out the biblical text with wide margins so you can mark the text with questions, key terms, notes, and structures. We have removed all of the verse markings so you can read it without distractions and have laid out the text with spacing to help you see how the lines are related. Review the guidelines on *The art of active learning* section, page xi at the beginning of your *Field Notes* for some suggestions on reading, learning, and marking the text effectively.

Galatians 4:8–31

Formerly, when you did not know God, you were enslaved to those who by nature are not gods. But now that you have come to know God, or rather to be known by God, how is it that you turn back again to the weak and worthless elementary principles of the world? Do you want to be enslaved to them all over again? You are observing days and months and seasons and years! I fear for you that I may have labored over you in vain.

Brothers, I beg of you, become as I am, for I also have become as you are. You have done me no wrong. You know it was because of a bodily illness that I first preached the gospel to you, and even though my condition was

Notes, Observations & Questions

a trial to you, you did not despise or reject me, but received me as an angel of God, as Christ Jesus Himself. Where then is that sense of blessing you had? For I can testify that if it were possible, you would have gouged out your eyes and given them to me. So have I then become your enemy by telling you the truth? Those people are zealous for you, but for no good purpose. They want to shut you out so that you may be zealous for them. It is always good to be zealous for a good purpose, and not only when I am present with you. My children, for whom I am again undergoing birth pains until Christ is formed in you, I wish I could be present with you now and change my tone, because I am perplexed about you.

Tell me, you who want to be under the law, do you not listen to the law? For it is written that Abraham had two sons, one by the slave woman and the other by the free woman. But the son by the slave woman was born according to the flesh, while the son by the free woman was born through the promise. These things may be interpreted allegorically, for the women represent two covenants. One is from Mount Sinai bearing children who are to be slaves; she is Hagar. Now Hagar represents Mount Sinai in Arabia and corresponds to the present Jerusalem, for she is in slavery with her children. But the Jerusalem above is free, and she is our mother. For it is written, "Rejoice, O barren woman who does not bear; break forth and cry aloud, you who have no birth pains; because more are the children of the desolate woman than of her who has a husband." Now you, brothers, like Isaac, are children of promise. But just as at that time the one born according to the flesh persecuted the one who was born according to the Spirit, so it is the same now. But what does the Scripture say? "Cast out the slave woman and her son, for the son of the slave woman shall not share the inheritance with the son of the free woman." Therefore, brothers, we are not children of the slave woman but of the free woman.

After you have read

1. Take time to summarize Galatians 4:8–31. This process will help you to understand what you have just read and make sense of it.

2. By this point, you have seen some of the benefits of journaling. Write out Galatians 4:8–31 from the previous pages or your own Bible into a journal word for word. This practice will help you to remember and understand what you have just read. This week, journal your thoughts as you reflect on what role legalistic thinking has had in your life. Is it something you have struggled with? Journal your thoughts about embracing the clear teaching of Paul when it comes to trusting completely in the work of Christ alone.

3. Now read Galatians 4:8–31 in your own Bible. Continue to reread it each day until you get to *Field Study 9*. This will reinforce the learning of Scripture and help you in retention.

Pray

As we continue to learn the Word of God, we must continue to communicate with him through prayer. Write a prayer, psalm, or poem to God. Pray about the purpose of the law in your life and the life of your church, your nation, your community, and your family. Pray with at least one other person if possible. Consider this sample prayer:

Lord Almighty,

I was struggling to understand the purpose of the law in my life and you helped me today. Thank you. The illustrations of a prison guard, a child-minder, and a guardian and trustee helped me understand the temporary function of the Old Testament law until the arrival of the Lord Jesus Christ in history. I can see that the law prepared for his arrival. I rejoice, however, in the truth that adoption into your family with full inheritance rights of life with you is by faith in the Lord Jesus Christ. Praise be to you! Help me, please, by the power of the Spirit, to live like an adult son. Help me to grow up. I know my do's and don'ts cannot earn me an inheritance with you. Help me to enjoy the wonderful truth that my inheritance is because of you. I am a member of your family. I desire to enjoy that status and help others do so too. I love you Lord, Amen.

Field Study 9

Galatians 3–4:
   The Gospel of Justification by Faith
    3:1–14 Proof 1, 2, 3
    3:15–22 Proof 4, 5
    3:23–4:7 Proof 5 clarified
    4:8–31 So what? Concluding Appeals

Galatians 4:8–31

FIELD STUDY 9

How is the text arranged?

In the previous sections of his letter to the Galatians, we have seen Paul present a barrage of evidence to demonstrate that justification before God is by faith in Jesus Christ apart from works of the law. The remaining verses of chapter 4 conclude this central section of the letter with a series of appeals. Paul's affection for the Galatians and passion for the truth of the gospel are unmistakable. These appeals are full of emotion and are important both for them and for us. Read these verses slowly.

Galatians 4:8–31

Section	Bible Text

Appeal 1: Don't go back to slavery	⁸ Formerly, when you did not know God,
	    you were enslaved to those who by nature are not gods.
	⁹ But now that you have come to know God,
	   or rather to be known by God,
	how is it that you turn back again to the weak
	   and worthless elementary principles of the world?
	Do you want to be enslaved to them all over again?
	¹⁰ You are observing days and months and seasons and years!
	¹¹ I fear for you that I may have labored over you in vain.

Appeal 2: Live as believers not under a system of law.	¹² Brothers, I beg of you, become as I am,
	   for I also have become as you are.
	   You have done me no wrong.
	¹³ You know it was because of a bodily illness
	   that I first preached the gospel to you,
	    ¹⁴ and even though my condition was a trial to you,
	   you did not despise or reject me, but received me
	   as an angel of God, as Christ Jesus Himself.

Commands to Action

In verse 12, Paul uses the first command or *imperative* in the letter when he tells the Galatians, *"become as I am."* From this point on, Paul begins to use the imperative more often as he calls the Galatians to specific actions. Commands will become very prominent by chapter six.

Body Ailment

There have been several suggestions as to what ailment Paul suffered. Some scholars suggest that the apostle had contracted malaria and arrived to the region of Galatia wanting to recover. Others have suggested that Paul may have been struggling with an eye problem.

Galatians 4:8–31

Section	Bible Text
Appeal 2: Live as believers not under a system of law. (continued)	¹⁵ Where then is that sense of blessing you had? For I can testify that if it were possible, you would have gouged out your eyes and given them to me. ¹⁶ So have I then become your enemy by telling you the truth? ¹⁷ Those people are zealous for you, but for no good purpose. They want to shut you out so that you may be zealous for them. ¹⁸ It is always good to be zealous for a good purpose, and not only when I am present with you. ¹⁹ My children, for whom I am again undergoing birth pains until Christ is formed in you, ²⁰ I wish I could be present with you now and change my tone, because I am perplexed about you.
Appeal 3: Get rid of legalism and its advocates	²¹ Tell me, you who want to be under the law, do you not listen to the law? ²² For it is written that Abraham had two sons, one by the slave woman and the other by the free woman. ²³ But the son by the slave woman was born according to the flesh, while the son by the free woman was born through the promise. ²⁴ These things may be interpreted allegorically, for the women represent two covenants. One is from Mount Sinai bearing children who are to be slaves; she is Hagar. ²⁵ Now Hagar represents Mount Sinai in Arabia and corresponds to the present Jerusalem, for she is in slavery with her children. ²⁶ But the Jerusalem above is free, and she is our mother. ²⁷ For it is written, "Rejoice, O barren woman who does not bear; break forth and cry aloud, you who have no birth pains; because more are the children of the desolate woman than of her who has a husband." ²⁸ Now you, brothers, like Isaac, are children of promise. ²⁹ But just as at that time the one born according to the flesh persecuted the one who was born according to the Spirit, so it is the same now. ³⁰ But what does the Scripture say? "Cast out the slave woman and her son, for the son of the slave woman shall not share the inheritance with the son of the free woman." ³¹ Therefore, brothers, we are not children of the slave woman but of the free woman.

Sarah Sends Hagar Away

The story of Sarah giving her maidservant Hagar to Abraham in an attempt to fulfill God's promise of a son, serves at least two purposes. First, it recounts the event to help understand the origin of Ishmael, and secondly, it serves as an illustration of two covenants.

James Joseph Jacques Tissot, 1896–1902

B.C. 2000	1850	1700	1550	1400	1250

2091 God calls Abraham?

1925 God calls Abraham?

Receiving the Law on Mount Sinai? 1446

Receiving the Law on Mount Sinai? 1260

As you can see from the outline, Paul closes out the central section of the letter to Galatians with three appeals. In the first appeal, the apostle exhorts the Galatians not to subject themselves to slavery again since God has already delivered them by their faith. The second appeal rises out of their personal history and mutual affection. Paul desired that the Galatians live by faith rather than a system of laws that required them to renounce their Gentile birth and become Jews. Finally, the third appeal takes the Galatians back to the story of Abraham's family. The two women who bore him sons model two types of approaches to God for justification.

What is this passage saying?

What are some key terms and phrases?

Take some time now and explore these key words and phrases, which will build up your understanding of what God is saying.

Meaning of Key Terms

Key word or phrase	Meaning and significance
Observing "days and months and seasons and years" (4:10)	The Galatians are described as observing "days and months and seasons and years." Embracing life under the Jewish law did not just mean obeying rules but also observing the practices and festivities of Israel. In the Old Testament, God was included on Israel's weekly, monthly, seasonal, and annual calendar. This emphasis was divinely established to remind God's people of his work among them. God was separating his people for his service; they were to collaborate with him in his purposes in and for the world. The Jews kept special days like the Sabbath on a weekly basis. They observed New Moons with monthly sacrifices. They had festivals like Passover or Tabernacles in different seasons, and observed a Sabbatical year every seven years, and a Jubilee year every 50th year. Even as a believer, Paul observed some of these events by choice, as part of his Jewish heritage, celebrating God's work among his people (Acts 20:16). For the Galatians though, *their participation was wrongly motivated*. Given what we know from the letter of Galatians, their practice was fuelled by a belief that faith in Christ was insufficient. You can see how this could easily happen with young Christians under false teachers who taught the Scriptures but misunderstood their relationship to Jesus Christ.

Meaning of Key Terms

Key word or phrase	Meaning and significance
What was Paul's illness? (4:13)	Paul was ill when the Galatians first met him. His illness was so disturbing that Paul thought it natural that they should despise him, or literally *spit out* in disgust. We are not sure what Paul's illness was, but there are some interesting options. Paul may have had malaria since it was common in the region of Perga where he docked when he first arrived from Cyprus (Acts 13:13). Malarial fever causes awful headaches. Paul may have struggled with epileptic seizures since people were known to *spit out* against epileptics out of fear of demonic contamination. It may have been some type of eye illness such as *ophthalmia*. We do know Paul had eye problems later in life (Acts 23:3–5), and Paul does say that the Galatians loved him so much, they were willing to give him their own eyes if it were possible. There is also no way of knowing whether this experience was the same thing Paul alludes to in 2 Corinthians as the *thorn in the flesh* which he pleaded with God to remove from him (12:7–10). Paul suffered illness, perhaps long-term illness. Believers are not immune from it.
Two Jerusalems? (4:25, 26)	Paul contrasts the *present Jerusalem* with a *heavenly Jerusalem*. *Present Jerusalem* represented bondage, not only due to its Roman military occupation but because its inhabitants live under religious bondage. Judaism enforced a rule of bondage to the law. The *heavenly Jerusalem* on the other hand represents freedom. It is the dwelling place of God and of all those whom he liberates from slavery by faith in Christ. Paul is not the only New Testament author who talks of a heavenly Jerusalem. Consider Hebrews 11:10, 16; 12:22; Revelation 3:12; 21:2.

Hebrews 12:22–23

But you have come to Mount Zion, the city of the living God, the heavenly Jerusalem, and to myriads of angels, to the assembly and congregation of the firstborn, who are enrolled in heaven, and to God, the judge of all, and to the spirits of the righteous made perfect

Kimon Berlin, 2006

The New Jerusalem
This 14th century tapestry depicts the apostle John watching as the New Jerusalem descends from God.

Revelation 21:2

And I saw the holy city, the new Jerusalem, coming down out of heaven from God, prepared as a bride adorned for her husband.

What about the culture?

Paul interprets the story of Abraham allegorically.[1] What Paul means by the term *allegorically* is important to understand. The biblical world of the first century was a Graeco-Roman society, a Greek saturated culture ruled by Romans. There existed a Greek formal method of interpreting texts called the *allegorical method*. This approach looked for hidden spiritual meanings behind the text often ignoring the literal meaning intended all along. It was the Greek's way of dealing with tensions in their historical and religious literary heritage, and was often arbitrary and imaginative. It also sprung from their tendency to view the immediate physical realm as inherently evil and from their desire

1. Galatians 4:24

B.C.	1	A.D.	10	20	30	40	50
5? Birth of Jesus				John the Baptist begins his ministry 28–29?		33–34? Paul encounters Christ on Damascus road	46–47? First Mi
		4–6? Birth of Paul		Jesus begins his ministry 28–30?			Journey
				Jesus is crucified and resurrected 30–33?		Paul writes Galatians 48?	

to strive for the spiritual and pure non-material realm.

Philo was a key Jewish writer in the first century who interpreted the Jewish Scriptures for his people using the allegorical method. Unfortunately, Christian writers throughout the ages have done this illegitimately as well. *The formal allegorical method of interpretation is dangerous, and Paul is not endorsing it here.* Paul's *allegorical* practice in this text is more precisely known as *typology.* It is a way of reading a text where legitimate patterns are seen in the relationship between prior events or characters, which prefigure ones that follow. Paul accepts the story of Abraham as historical, but in its broader sense—and yet still within God's original intended meaning—Hagar and Sarah can be said to represent two ways of pursuing justification. This was not an added or spiritualized meaning. God intended this all along!

Philo of Alexandria

Philo was a Jew born in Alexandria and lived from 20 B.C. to A.D. 50 as a Hellenistic biblical philosopher. He used the allegorical method to attempt to harmonize Greek philosophy with the Hebrew Scriptures.

Origen Adamantius

Origen was born in Alexandria and lived from A.D. 185–232. He was a Christian scholar and theologian who used both a literal and an illegitimate allegorical method for interpreting Scriptures.

What is the explanation?

Let's go a little deeper into understanding our passage in this *Field Study.* Remember that these appeals conclude Paul's sustained argument so far.

1) *Paul's first appeal:* Paul reminds the Galatian believers of their condition before faith in Christ.[2] They were slaves in bondage to demonic spirits.[3] Sadly, although seeking a deity, they did not know the real God. That was not their condition anymore. Now they knew God. What is more important, God knew them. It is no wonder that Paul is startled that they would return to live as if they were under a weak and inferior system. Why would an adopted son and heir of God live according to a way of life that did not have the power to satisfy God or grant an inheritance? It seems these Galatian believers were already living motivated to please God through Jewish religious observances. Paul rightly feared his work among them would be practically useless if they chose to live legalistically. The force of his

2.   Galatians 4:8
3.   1 Corinthians 10:20

| 50 | 60 | 70 | 80 | 90 | 100 A.D. |

49?   Jerusalem Council

50–52?   Second Missionary Journey by Paul

60–62?   Paul arrives in Rome under house arrest

64   Fire in Rome

70   Temple is destroyed

79   Pompeii and Herculaneum are destroyed by Vesuvius eruption

John writes Revelation 95–96?

133

Non-gods

Paul's comment about being enslaved to those who are not gods in Galatians 4:8 may refer back to Acts 14:11–13. Paul and Barnabas were in the Galatian city of Lystra and healed a man who was lame from birth. The Galatians there assumed Paul and Barnabas were the Greek gods Zeus and Hermes because of their miraculous power.

Paul's Adjustment

Did you notice Paul's adjustment in verse 9, "now that you have come to know God, or rather to be known by God?" Paul is not correcting himself as he writes, since the Galatians do know God. He does clarify, however, that they only know God because God took the initiative in knowing them first. This is another way of declaring that God initiates the work of the gospel, just as we see in Romans 8:29.

Abraham's Age

Abraham was about 100 years old and Sarah about 90 when Isaac was born! Moreover, Sarah's old womb had never carried a child before. The miraculous nature of Isaac's birth is evident in that her childbearing years were long over. Hagar was presumably a much younger woman when Ishmael was born. It seems Abraham was around 86 when this happened.

Marie-Lan Nguyen, 2011

Hermes
In Greek mythology, Hermes was the son of Zeus. He was a herald or messenger of the gods to the humans.

Gardens of Versailles; seized during the French Revolution, 1793

An Image of Zeus
In ancient Greek mythology, Zeus was considered the "father of gods and men." He was the god of the sky and thunder, which is what he is holding in his right hand. He ruled the Olympians from Mount Olympus in Greece.

(1.

framed in verse 9: don't turn back to an enslaved condition by adding works of the law to faith in Christ to try to satisfy God!

Paul's second appeal: Paul and the Galatians have a relationship of deep affection. Paul appeals to this affection to beg these Gentile believers to live like he, a Jewish believer, now lived—not under an ethnically tied system of laws. Therefore, he reminds them of their first encounter. Paul first visited them while undergoing an illness. He believed the severity of his symptoms was enough for them to reject him in disgust. Yet, they received him as if he was Jesus Christ. They received him with joy and such affection that they would have given their own eyes for Paul! Now, they were treating him as if he was an enemy just because he spoke the truth to them.

Though there is nothing wrong with pursuing people with good intentions as Paul did, those courting the Galatians away from Paul and truth, were doing so for selfish purposes. Paul was distressed by this. He desired to

Romans 8:29

For those God foreknew he also predestined to be conformed to the image of his Son, so that his Son might be the firstborn among many brothers

2091 God calls Abraham?

Receiving the Law on Mount Sinai? 1446

1925 God calls Abraham?

Receiving the Law on Mount Sinai? 1260

selfish purposes. Paul was distressed by this. He desired to be present with them so that he could be firm and gentle in person—something a letter could not capture. He loved them as if he had given birth to them. Therefore, their attitude made him feel like he was in the pains of childbirth all over again. He was not hurt because his followers now rejected *him*. He was hurt because these beloved believers were rejecting the gospel by the way they wanted to live their Christian life.

3) *Paul's third appeal:* Lastly, in his third appeal, the apostle provides a picture from Scripture to recast the same message against legalism and make an appeal from it. He takes the Galatians back to the story of Abraham recorded in the books of the law, and asks that they understand what it declares. Abraham had two sons by two women. Hagar was a slave while Sarah was free. The slave woman bore a son named Ishmael, naturally; he was not born miraculously or fulfilling God's promise but out of Abraham's will. The son of the free woman, Isaac, was born supernaturally. That is, God opened Sarah's old womb to fulfill his promise in accordance with his will.

7) Paul interprets these two women *typologically* to represent two different covenants that produce two types of offspring. He focuses on the first directly and the Galatians can connect the dots on the second by implication. Hagar, the slave woman, represents the Mosaic Covenant, which was given on Mount Sinai, outside the Promised Land. Those under this law are slaves just like Hagar. Moreover, she represents the first century city of Jerusalem; a city whose offspring are enslaved not just to Rome but also to the rules of Judaism. The unstated implication of this verse is that Sarah, the free woman, represents the covenant or promise to Abraham. Those under it are free just like Sarah. She represents the heavenly Jerusalem whose offspring are free.

Use of the word "Law"

It is always important to note how the word *law* is used in a statement. At times, it refers to the actual covenant between God and Israel established through Moses at Mount Sinai. On other occasions, it refers to the actual Scriptural laws within that covenant. There are times when it refers to the first five books of the Bible—Genesis to Deuteronomy—also known as the Torah or the Pentateuch. In 4:21 Paul uses the term twice in two different ways. In the first, it refers to living under a system of law: the Mosaic Covenant. The second time is used to refer to a book in the Pentateuch—Genesis.

Mount Sinai

The traditional site of Mount Sinai is believed to be Jebel Musa in the Sinai Peninsula. This is attested as early as the 4th century A.D. in the writings of Egeria, a lady on pilgrimage in the lands of the Bible.

Berthold Werner, 2010

1250	1100	950	800	650	500 B.C.

Saul becomes king 1050 930 The kingdom divides 722 Northern kingdom falls to Assyria
David becomes king 1010 Southern kingdom falls to Babylon and the temple is destroyed 586
Solomon becomes king 971

135

Excavate the Site   Galatians 4:8–31
FIELD STUDY 9
Believers are to live in freedom not bondage

Paul's intention with this illustration is to show that the Galatian believers are just like Isaac. They are sons born according to God's faithful promise. Those troubling them with a false gospel of works are like Ishmael. They are living like the enslaved son born of Abraham's will trying to fulfill God's promise by self-effort. The Galatians were being persecuted by these troublemakers just as Isaac was by Ishmael. They should respond as God's Word declares in the Isaac-Ishmael encounter. They are to rid themselves of such a lifestyle. After all, believers are heirs because they are sons of the free woman; they are liberated by faith in Jesus in fulfillment of God's promise! Therefore, this picture from Scripture serves as an analogy of two opposite approaches to justification—one by law, the other by faith. Believers as children of the promise are to live by faith.

What is God saying?

God declares repeatedly in Galatians 3–4 that justification before him is by faith in Jesus Christ. This is in agreement with his promises to Abraham. Faith and works are not partners in justification. Jesus does not ask for help from the Law. In the verses we examined together in this study, God clearly expresses that he wants us to respond actively

Paul's Quotation of Isaiah

Why does Paul quote Isaiah 54:1? In this verse Isaiah anticipated Israel's prosperity after being liberated from her captivity in Babylon. Paul applies this experience to Sarah, who being initially barren, lived as though in exile. She will rejoice in the multitude of her liberated offspring.

Isaiah 54:1

"Shout for joy, O barren one, who has not given birth! Burst into song and cry aloud you who have not been in labor! For the children of the desolate woman will be more than the children of the married woman," says the LORD.

Where else is this taught in Scripture?

Romans 9:4–5

To them belong the adoption as sons, the glory, the covenants, the giving of the law, the Temple worship, and the promises. To them belong the patriarchs, and from them the human ancestry of Christ, who is God over all, blessed forever. Amen.

Even though God privileged Israel in their role and calling, their history shows that they often did not understand this (Romans 9:4–5). They often acted as though they deserved a relationship with God based on their own merit. This is the danger the Galatians were facing too. They were fortunate to be in a relationship with God by his grace, but were beginning to act as if maintaining it depended upon them.

The love Paul displays for the Galatians in these verses is characteristic of him toward other believers too. In 1 Corinthians 4:14–15 we see he cared deeply for the Corinthian believers. Paul loved those he labored to bring to faith in Christ. His interest in the well-being of those he led to Jesus Christ, be it the Corinthians or the Galatians, was pure.

1 Corinthians 4:14–15

I do not write these things to shame you but to correct you as my dear children. For though you have ten thousand guardians in Christ, you do not have many fathers, for in Christ Jesus I became your father through the gospel.

Romans 8:17

Now if we are children, then we are heirs, heirs of God and co-heirs with Christ, if indeed we share in his sufferings so that we may also share in his glory

to what he declares. Believers are not to live in slavery to any system other than that of faith. Moreover, God's system is not ethnically defined. One does not need to become a Jew to become a Christian. Therefore, believers like the Galatians are to remove any resemblance of legalism from their lives and fellowship. The importance of doing so cannot be minimized. False teaching, like sin, is contagious and spreads quickly.

In the Old Testament God made it very clear that he desired his people actively to rid themselves of evil influences that will corrupt them. If not, they will be unable to represent him accurately before the nations. For example, look at the story of Achan in Joshua 7, or at the reforms of Nehemiah.[1] Jesus also emphasizes to his followers, the dangers of being influenced by falsehood.[2] It hardens your heart to understanding God. Paul's call for the active removal of legalism cannot be taken lightly. This passage tells us that those free from bondage—be it the law or false gods—are to

Arab-Israeli Relationship

The ongoing tension between the Arabs and Israelis can be traced in part, all the way back to Abraham. While the Jews are descendants of Isaac, Arabs claim to be descendants from Ishmael.

Genesis 21:8–10

The child grew and was weaned. Abraham made a great feast on the day Isaac was weaned. But Sarah saw the son of Hagar the Egyptian, the son whom Hagar had borne to Abraham, mocking. So she said to Abraham, "Get rid of this slave woman with her son, for the son of this slave woman will not be an heir with my son Isaac!"

Where else does this happen in history?

The sacrificial love that Paul is expressing as coming from the Galatians can also be seen in other ancient works. Lucian of Samosata was a witty Greek writer of discourse and satire. In a work called *Toxaris* or *Friendship*, this ancient writer tells the story of a friendship between two men, Dandamis and Amizoces. During the course of a war, Amizoces is taken captive by the enemy. His dear friend Dandamis went to the enemy's chief to negotiate a ransom. However, Dandamis had nothing but himself to offer. The enemy's chief accepted Dandamis' eyes in exchange for Amizoces. Without hesitation, Dandamis allows the enemy to pluck out his eyes in order to rescue his friend. Amizoces could not bear the sight of his blinded friend, so he plucked his own eyes out as well.

Paul states in verse 15 that the Galatians would have gouged out their eyes and given them to him if possible. Lucian's story illustrates Paul's sentiments perfectly.

William Faithorne, 1600's

Lucian of Samosata
Lucian (A.D. 125–A.D. 180) was an Assyrian rhetorician and satirist who wrote in Greek.

1. Nehemiah 13:23–31
2. Mark 8:14–21

grow to enjoy their freedom in Christ. Children of promise are to live in freedom and never to desire to live in bondage.

What does God want?

There are two areas to consider as you think through what God wants you to do with what he says in this text. Remember that these are general principles. Make sure you make them specific to your life. The *Discoveries* section will help you with this as well. The second issue is particularly important. Be honest with yourself. We've framed the second as a question for you to answer.

Faith in Jesus is God's only acceptable means for life with him.

God's way is the way of faith in Christ. It is an act of grace. Life by faith in Jesus is his only gracious system for life with him; therefore, God exhorts us through Paul in several areas. First, think twice about living as a slave if he's made you a free son or daughter. Second, remember that being a Christian has nothing to do with nationality. Jewish believers, American believers, Spanish believers are all simply believers before God. If he makes no nationalistic or ethnic distinctions when it comes to value, we must be sure that we don't either. Lastly, remove legalism from your life and its promoters from your fellowship. Legalism is wrong and contagious. We are to be proactive in dealing with it.

Who are you most like? Ishmael? Isaac? Isaac living as Ishmael?

Paul indirectly applies these categories to the Galatians in our passage. There was a time when the Galatians did not know God and so were like Ishmael—sons of slavery or unbelievers. They then received the Spirit by faith and so became like Isaac—sons of promise or believers. Their problem was that now they were beginning to live like Ishmael when they were really like Isaac. This was inconsistent. Sons of promise should not live like sons of slavery. Therefore, we want you to consider which of these three categories best fits you. Take time to answer the following questions. Have you ever called out to God for salvation, by faith in Christ? If not, you're like Ishmael. You are still enslaved and separated from God. He offers you justification but only on his terms. If you have received God's gift of justification by faith, are you now living by faith? Or rather, are you now blending both faith and works? Are you like Isaac in your standing by faith before God but like Ishmael in your day-to-day living with God? These are important questions to answer. Take time to do so. God deems it important. You can be a citizen of the heavenly Jerusalem, an heir of God's promise, a son, or daughter of God by faith. If you are, then make sure you live by faith and not by works!

Discoveries

Now we have completed our eighth excavation into the book of Galatians. It is again time to stop digging and carefully examine what we have learned and the difference it can make in our lives. Pick the questions that will be most helpful for you or your community.

Connecting with the community

Here are some discussion questions to help you better understand the text. Do not merely reflect on them as an individual but rather think of each question, when applicable, in terms of your family, your community, your nation, and your church.

1. According to Galatians 4:8–9, the Galatians were turning back from the gospel and enslaving themselves to rituals again. Paul was astonished by their attitude. Why do you think they were doing this? Was it ignorance? If not, what reasons did they have to act in such a way? What can you learn from their decisions and behavior?

2. What does Paul mean by the phrase, "become as I am?" Why does he beg the Galatians to do this? How was that helpful to them?

3. Describe the Galatians' attitude toward Paul when they first met him. Why did they change? Have you ever changed your attitude or demeanor toward a pastor or Bible teacher? If so, why? Are these kinds of changes justifiable? Share experiences with those in your group where you have experienced situations such as these. What can you learn from Paul's teaching in this passage?

4. In Galatians 4:16, Paul infers that the reason the Galatians now rejected him was that he had confronted them truthfully. Why is it so hard to accept truthful correction? Are you teachable? When someone gives you an exhortation, do you treat such a person as an enemy even if he or she is right?

5. Explain Paul's argument in Galatians 4:21–28. Why is his illustration important? What can your church or community learn from it?

Notes, Observations & Questions

6. In Galatians 4:28, what does it mean to be children of the promise? If we, as the Galatians, are children of the promise, what benefits and responsibilities are bestowed upon us?

7. What was wrong with observing days and months and seasons and years? Why did this behavior discourage Paul so much? What were the Galatians doing when observing days and months and seasons and years? Can you think of any practices that churches today enforce as required and imply Christ's work is not sufficient?

8. Explain the way Paul uses the story of Abraham as an allegory? In what sense can it be said that this type of allegory was legitimate? Discuss the dangers of allegory?

9. Describe the way in which Sarah and Hagar represent the relationship between the two covenants (promise and law). Are these covenants related or complementary? Can they coexist?

Probing deeper

These exercises are to help you look deeper into some of the secondary issues of our passage and may require reading from the rest of Scripture.

1. Compare Paul's presentation of the gospel in 1 Corinthians 15:1–28 in comparison to Galatians 4:8–31. Are you currently enslaved by any doctrines alien to the gospel? If so, how did you get there? Are you under any teacher that is leading you away from the freedom of the true gospel? Can you identify the source of your wrong thinking? Are you willing to be freed by the gospel? What steps must you take to escape from such enslaving doctrines?

2. Review the narrative of the birth of Ishmael and Isaac in Genesis 16:1–18:15. What are the characteristics of a Christian who acts like an "Ishmael?" Do you believe you show any of these? If so, were you aware of it before this study? What steps must you take to change?

3. Are you living your Christian life like an "Isaac?" How do you know? If so, what can you do to encourage those around you to live in the freedom of the promises of the gospel?

4. Read the following passages: Galatians 4:24–26; Hebrews 11:11, 16; 12:22; Revelation 3:12; 21:2. Now review the notes in this *Field Study* regarding the two Jerusalems in the Key Terms. What is the relationship that exists between freedom and the new heavenly Jerusalem? Why is this significant for our Christian walk in the present according to Paul? If you follow Paul's argument, would you say that you are living in slavery of the present Jerusalem, or are you living in the freedom of the heavenly Jerusalem?

Bringing the story to life

Paul's example of living like Isaac or Ishmael is a powerful one. Survey at least five people who are not studying Galatians with you. They can be from your family, church, or anyone else. They do not have to be believers. The question that you are going to ask them is:

Who are you living most like: Ishmael? Isaac? or Isaac living like Ishmael?

Obviously, this will take some explanation for your survey to work. Read Galatians 4:8–31 to your survey participant and then take the time to explain carefully what Paul is saying. If necessary, go back and read Genesis 16:1–18:15 so that he or she knows the background story. Once your participant understands the question, record their thoughts on how they live. Keep them on task, answering the one question and how the characteristics of living like Ishmael or Isaac play out in their lives. Once you have surveyed at least five people, compare your findings with others in your group who are doing the same exercise. Share how you would answer the question and what you have learned from the exercise.

Memorizing the key

Commit to memory the key phrase for this *Field Study*. The key phrase for Galatians 4:8–31 is:

Believers are to live in freedom not bondage

Learning the Bible includes remembering what issues Scripture addresses and where to find things. Memorizing the key phrases will help you to better understand and apply the key points of each book.

Observation journaling

This section will prepare you for *Field Study 10* by reading through the next section of Galatians. We have included three types of exercises: some for before you read, some for while you are reading and some for after you have completed the reading.

Before you read

Review Galatians 4:8–31 and summarize the text with three statements according to the verses below. Make sure your statements are succinct and clear.

Statement 1:
(verses 8–11)

Statement 2:
(verses 12–20)

Statement 3:
(verses 21–31)

While you are reading

On the following page, we have laid out the biblical text with wide margins so you can mark the text with questions, key terms, notes, and structures. We have removed all of the verse markings so you can read it without distractions and have laid out the text with spacing to help you see how the lines are related. Review the guidelines on *The art of active learning* section, page xi at the beginning of your *Field Notes* for some suggestions on reading, learning, and marking the text effectively.

Galatians 5:1–15

For freedom Christ has set us free. Stand firm, then, and do not submit again to a yoke of slavery. Look! I, Paul, tell you that if you let yourselves be circumcised, Christ will be of no benefit to you. Again I testify to every man who lets himself be circumcised that he is obligated to keep the whole law. You who are trying to be justified by law have been alienated from Christ; you have fallen away from grace. For, through the Spirit, by faith, we eagerly await for the hope of righteousness. For in Christ Jesus neither circumcision nor uncircumcision counts for anything, but the only thing that matters is faith working through love.

You were running well. Who cut in on you and hindered you from obeying the truth? This kind of persuasion is not from the one who calls you. "A little yeast leavens the whole lump of dough." I am confident in the Lord that you will accept no other view than mine, and the one who is troubling you will bear his judgment, whoever he is. Now, brothers, if I am still preaching circumcision, why am I still being persecuted? In that case the offense of the cross has been removed. I wish the ones upsetting you would even emasculate themselves!

You, my brothers, were called to freedom. But do not use your freedom as an opportunity for the flesh; rather, through love serve one another. For the whole law can be fulfilled in a single command: "You shall love your neighbor as yourself." But if you keep on biting and devouring each other, watch out that you are not consumed by one other.

Notes, Observations & Questions

Summarize the text here

Notes, Observations & Questions

After you have read

1. Journaling is another way to help us learn. Write out Galatians 5:1–15 from the previous page or from your own Bible into a journal word for word. This practice will help you to remember and understand what you have just read. This week, journal your thoughts as you consider the difference between a life of freedom and bondage. Don't only think in terms of yourself, but also how Christian freedom and bondage affects your family, your community, your nation, and your church. Write down what God wants you to do with that freedom and then act accordingly.

2. Now read Galatians 5:1–15 in your own Bible. Continue to reread it each day until you get to *Field Study 10*. This will reinforce the learning of Scripture and help you in retention.

Pray

As we continue to learn the Word of God, it is essential that we communicate with him through prayer. Consider writing a prayer, psalm, or poem to God. What would God have you pray in light of the importance of not being in bondage to the law? Pray for your church, your nation, your community, your family and yourself. Consider this sample:

Dear God,

Now that I've studied your Word in Galatians for a little while, I also find it ridiculous to think that I would ever live my life as though 'faith in Jesus' needed a little dose of 'works of my own' to receive life with you. Forgive me for thinking this way in the past. I now know that as an heir of what you have promised I am to live in freedom not bondage. I find it hard, though, to live in freedom. I need your direction. Help me to yield to your Spirit every day so that I live a life of freedom your way. It is so easy to run to a system of rules and regulations because they are so concrete and measurable. I realize leaning on the Spirit, though, is the path of faith. All I ask is for your help in living this way. I also need your wisdom and help in removing traces of legalism in my family and church fellowship. I know it is there and dangerous. Do a work in the hearts of believers around me. Help me help them live in Christ's freedom. It is a difficult task that lies ahead. Help us, please, in the name of Christ, Amen.

Field Study 10

Galatians 5–6:
The Gospel of Sanctification by Faith
5:1–15 Freedom from legalism and sin
5:16–26 Freedom from flesh to Spirit
6:1–18 Freedom to serve

Galatians 5:1–15

FIELD STUDY 10

How is the text arranged?

We now begin our exploration of the last major section of the letter of Galatians. In chapters 1–2, Paul defended his own God-granted authority to convince the Galatians that his gospel was God's gospel. In chapters 3–4, Paul proved from several angles that the gospel is about justification by faith alone in Jesus Christ. In this final section, Paul turns to the implications of the gospel for daily Christian living. What we believe is evident in how we live! How then should a believer live the Christian life, in light of the teaching of Galatians? Read the passage several times. Think about its meaning and the implications of its message for your life. Look at the outline provided as it divides the passage up into its major movements.

Galatians 5:1–15

Section	Bible Text
A call to Christian freedom	¹ For freedom Christ has set us free. Stand firm, then, and do not submit again to a yoke of slavery.
Clarification 1: Freedom from legalism	
Consequences of living by law	² Look! I, Paul, tell you that if you let yourselves be circumcised, Christ will be of no benefit to you. ³ Again I testify to every man who lets himself be circumcised that he is obligated to keep the whole law. ⁴ You who are trying to be justified by law have been alienated from Christ; you have fallen away from grace.

Galatians 5:1–15

Section	Bible Text
Consequences of living by law (continued)	⁵ For, through the Spirit, by faith, we eagerly await for the hope of righteousness. ⁶ For in Christ Jesus neither circumcision nor uncircumcision counts for anything, but the only thing that matters is faith working through love. ⁷ You were running well. Who cut in on you and hindered you from obeying the truth? ⁸ This kind of persuasion is not from the one who calls you. ⁹ "A little yeast leavens the whole lump of dough." ¹⁰ I am confident in the Lord that you will accept no other view than mine, and the one who is troubling you will bear his judgment, whoever he is. ¹¹ Now, brothers, if I am still preaching circumcision, why am I still being persecuted? In that case the offense of the cross has been removed. ¹² I wish the ones upsetting you would even emasculate themselves!

Clarification 2

Freedom from a life of sin	¹³ You, my brothers, were called to freedom. But do not use your freedom as an opportunity for the flesh; rather, through love, serve one another. ¹⁴ For the whole law can be fulfilled in a single command: "You shall love your neighbor as yourself." ¹⁵ But if you keep on biting and devouring each other, watch out that you are not consumed by one other.

The Christian life of freedom: Paul transitions to a discussion about (1) Christian living with a general exhortation. *The Christian life is a life of freedom.* Believers, therefore, are to resist living as though they are under the law. This, after all, was not God's purpose in liberating them. This is the main point of the remainder of the letter. All else is clarification of what Christian freedom is and is not.

Clarification 1: The Christian life of freedom is not a lifestyle under (2– a system of laws. In this section, the apostle Paul outlines the consequences of living as believers according to legalism. Ultimately, trying to earn God's favor by attempting to keep a system of laws does not please God in any way.

Legalism

Legalism is living the Christian life with the mindset that one's personal conduct earns God's favor. It is often expressed in excessive concern for the smallest details of traditional laws yet with complete disregard for their underlying purposes.

B.C. 2000	1850	1700	1550	1400	1250

2091 God calls Abraham?

1925 God calls Abraham?

Receiving the Law on Mount Sinai? 1446

Receiving the Law on Mount Sinai? 1260

146

5) *Clarification 2:* The Christian life of freedom apart from the law does not mean believers can live indulging in sin. This is not the only other alternative. Rejecting living under law does not mean embracing a life of sin and licentiousness. A believer is able to satisfy the will of God expressed in the law, but only through a faith that works through love.

What is this passage saying?
What are some key terms and phrases?

It is important to consider some key terms, concepts, or phrases in our passage. Take time to study them. They are crucial to the meaning and significance of this text.

> ### Licentiousness
> Licentiousness is living the Christian life indulging in sin with the attitude that this is permissible because God will forgive you anyway.

Meaning of Key Terms

Key word or phrase	Meaning and significance
Stand firm (5:1)	The Galatian believers were exhorted to stand firm against the pressure of living the Christian life enslaved to the law. This was not a passive response despite the inactivity evoked in the imagery of a person standing. Paul often exhorts believers to take a stand—in the Lord (Philippians 4:1), in the faith (1 Corinthians 16:13), in solid teachings (2 Thessalonians 2:15), and against the schemes of the devil (Ephesians 6:11). After all, believers then and now live in this present evil age (Galatians 1:4). The picture of a soldier taking a stand against an attack, as in Ephesians 6, is helpful for it captures the importance of standing firm. To stand firm against life under the law allows believers to live in freedom.
Christ will be of no advantage… You are severed from Christ… You have fallen from grace (5:2, 4)	Paul's argument in Galatians so far does not allow these phrases to be interpreted as if it was possible for a believer to lose his or her salvation before God. The apostle is not talking about a change in state before God from saved to unsaved. He strongly argues salvation is something that God graciously grants as a gift to those who turn to Jesus Christ by faith. Here, Paul is talking about two systems of approaching or walking with God. Coming to God for justification according to law is not living according to grace. It is possible for a believer to live life as though he was not a believer. Paul is not talking about one's state before God but about two systems in which believers potentially live.

Petr Kratochvil, 2011

Standing Firm
Standing firm is not a passive and effortless activity. It requires discipline, attention, and commitment.

> ### John 10:28–29
> I give them eternal life, and they will never perish. No one will snatch them from my hand. My Father, who has given them to me, is greater than all, and no one is able to snatch them out of my Father's hand

1250   1100   950   800   650   500   B.C.

Saul becomes king 1050
David becomes king 1010
Solomon becomes king 971

930 The kingdom divides
722 Northern kingdom falls to Assyria
Southern kingdom falls to Babylon and the temple is destroyed 586

147

Faith and Works

This is Paul's way of expressing that faith is not opposed to works. He also mentions this truth in Ephesians 2:10. James also deals with this issue in James 2:14–18.

Ephesians 2:10

For we are his workmanship, created in Christ Jesus to do good works, which God prepared beforehand so we may do them.

Meaning of Key Terms

Key word or phrase	Meaning and significance
A faith that works (5:6, 13)	A believer is one who is justified by receiving salvation from God by faith. This person then lives out that salvation by faith. This is called *sanctification*. In Galatians 5:1–15, Paul presents three potential lifestyles available to a believer. Only one lifestyle is in accordance with God's will and properly represents the Christian life of freedom by faith. Believers are not to live under legalism. Neither are they to live as though licensed to sin even though these two are very real possibilities. Rather, believers are to live by a faith *working through love* (verse 6) or *through love, serve one another* (verse 13). The Christian life is one of responsibility to God and one another. Although as believers we are no longer enslaved to the law or to our sinful passions, we are still enslaved. We are enslaved to live for God, imitating Christ. Saving faith is not opposed to works in the Christian life. It is opposed to the false idea of *saving* works!
Fulfilling the whole law (5:14)	What does Paul mean by fulfilling the whole law through loving one another? Is he not opposed to the law in the life of a believer? How is it he desires we fulfill it through love? The word law is used in the Bible in different ways: to refer to the Mosaic covenant, to the actual Scriptural laws, to certain books in the Bible, to an era in history, and as an illegitimate means of justification. Paul is opposed to the illegitimate use of the law, not to the law itself. God gave the law. It was never intended to justify. The covenant was fulfilled in Christ, which ended that era. However, Paul argues from the books of the law that the Scriptural laws themselves were an expression of God's character and guidance on how to walk before him by faith (see also James 2:14–18). Jesus opposed its illegitimate use too in the Sermon on the Mount, and yet affirmed that loving God and loving people fulfilled the entire law. Paul focuses here on how believers can fulfill the Scriptural law that expresses God's character.

The Sermon on the Mount

The Sermon on the Mount in Matthew 5–7 presents the teachings of Jesus on the law.

Carl Heinrich Bloch, 1834–1890

What about the culture? Two background issues help us in our understanding of the passage. In the society of the New Testament, the accepted practice was that Gentiles were always circumcised as

Mark 12:29–31

Jesus answered, "The most important is: 'Hear, Israel, the Lord our God, the Lord is one. Love the Lord your God with all your heart, with all your soul, with all your mind, and with all your strength.' The second is this: 'Love your neighbor as yourself.' There is no other commandment greater than these."

B.C.	1	A.D.		10		20		30		40		50

5? Birth of Jesus

4–6? Birth of Paul

John the Baptist begins his ministry 28–29?

Jesus begins his ministry 28–30?

Jesus is crucified and resurrected 30–33?

33–34? Paul encounters Christ on Damascus road

Paul writes Galatians 48?

46–47? First Mis Journey

a prerequisite to embracing life with the God of the Jews. In fact, if a person was not circumcised, Jews deemed even complete obedience to the law worthless. This may be a reason why Paul talks about rendering Christ's work *worthless* if a believer lived according to the law. In doing so, he turns the argument on its head regarding *what* deemed *what* worthless! Look at the following quotes from the first century Jewish historian Josephus. He provides a window into the culture, which helps us understand this issue in early Christianity.

> "Hyrcanus [A Jewish military leader in the second century B.C.] took Dora and Marissa, cities of Idumea, and subdued all the Idumeans and permitted them to stay in that country if they would circumcise their genitals and make use of the laws of the Jews."

> "…for as he [a Jew called Eleazar] entered into his [A Gentile king Izates in first century A.D.] palace to greet him, and found him reading the law of Moses, he said to him "You do not consider, O king, that you unjustly break the principal of those laws, and are injurious to God himself [by omitting to be circumcised]; for you ought not only to read them, but chiefly to practice what they ask of you. How long will you continue uncircumcised? But if you have not yet read the law about circumcision, and do not know how great the impiety you are guilty of by neglecting it, read it now." When the king had heard what he said, he delayed the thing no longer, but retired to another room, and sent for a surgeon…"

(Josephus Antiquities 13.257 & 20.44–48 adapted from William Whiston's translation)

The Ten Commandments

The Ten Commandments, also known as the Decalogue, were given to Moses on Mount Sinai as recorded in Exodus 20.

Decalogue

It was believed that the Ten Commandments represented the 613 laws contained in the Jewish law. These ten laws are divided into two kinds. The first four deal with love for God. The next six deal with love for your neighbor. Thus, the summary of the law which Jesus provides as loving God and loving your neighbor in Mark 12:28–31 represents the entirety of the law.

The book of Acts makes it clear that, in the first century, Christians were persecuted by the Jews. For the Jew it was scandalous to believe their anticipated Messiah would die on a cross since such a death was a sign of God's curse.[1] It was for this reason that Jews persecuted those who preached that a person could be accepted by God by believing in a crucified Messiah. The fact that Paul was persecuted by Jews was therefore proof that he preached the correct gospel. It also showed that he no longer preached circumcision as he did before conversion. The cross caused an *offense*, a term that literally means *scandal*. On the other hand, it amused Greek Gentiles too as they thought it foolish to accept as God and Savior, a Jew who was not clever or powerful enough to evade death—what sort of God was he?[2] The society of the

1. Galatians 3:13; Deuteronomy 21:23
2. 1 Corinthians 1:18–30

49? Jerusalem Council   60–62? Paul arrives in Rome under house arrest   70 Temple is destroyed   John writes Revelation 95–96?

50–52? Second Missionary Journey by Paul   64 Fire in Rome   79 Pompeii and Herculaneum are destroyed by Vesuvius eruption

The Theology of the Cross

Martin Luther's *Theology of the Cross* is his most important original contribution to Christian theology. Luther declares that a true Christian theologian is only one who sees the work of God in history in the light of suffering and the cross. Luther declared, *crux sola est nostra theologia* or "only the cross is our theology." At the cross we learn that God hides himself in suffering and that his hand *is* actually manifested in events that superficially are evil. A theology of glory on the contrary, rejects the suffering of Christ and seeks to please God through the glory of human works. For Luther, these self-glorying works are the "enemies of the cross of Christ." It is exhibited in those who ultimately are rejecting the gift of God in Christ by seeking salvation in their own terms and strength. This was the false idea embraced by the Galatians.

first century, therefore, took offense at the message of the cross. Yet, the cross is the foundation upon which the gospel stands.

What is the explanation?

The Christian life of freedom: The first verse of chapter 5 is like a door hinge that swings the topic from *becoming* a believer to *living as* a believer in Jesus Christ. Jesus Christ came on a rescue mission; he came to liberate man from evil.[1] He set believers free from bondage to the law, sin, and sin's curse—the curse of death—so that they may live in freedom as heirs of God. In this verse, Paul presents his summary point for the remainder of the letter: *Christ freed believers so that they may live in freedom.* In light of this, believers are to resist returning to the burdensome life of slavery under a system of law.

Galatians 1:3–4

Grace and peace to you from God our Father and the Lord Jesus Christ, who gave himself for our sins to rescue us from this present evil age, according to the will of our God and Father.

Clarification 1: Freedom from legalism. There are consequences to living the Christian life under a system of law. In these verses, Paul has presented five examples of the dangers of legalism in the life of a Christian. He based his appeal now on his friendship with the churches of Galatia.

First, in Galatians 2:21 Paul declares that God's grace is rendered pointless if the works of the law are added to Christ's death. He now applies this truth to the specific situation in Galatia. *To embrace circumcision is to live as if Christ's death is unnecessary.* Second, to embrace just one aspect of the law, such as circumcision, out of religious duty logically forces one to accept all aspects of life under the law. It renders a believer a slave to the law. Third, to live legalistically is to live as if alienated from Christ. Only by living life by the Spirit through faith, can believers' experience daily assurance of their right standing before God. Therefore, physical circumcision is irrelevant when it comes to the issue of salvation. What counts is faith; a faith so genuine it pours out

Galatians 2:21

I do not set aside the grace of God, for if righteousness comes through the law, Christ died for nothing!

Galatians 1:6

I am astonished that you are so quickly deserting the one who called you by the grace of Christ, for a different gospel-

1. Galatians 1:3–4

The Phrygian goddess Cybele

In the nearby region of Phrygia, pagan worshippers of Cybele emasculated themselves as an act of worship to their false god.

with acts of love.[2] Fourth, living the Christian life under a system of law stifles the growth and maturity of the believer. It is a way of life, which cannot please God. Paul was confident the Galatians would be persuaded by his letter and heed his warning, while God would deal with the troublemakers.[3] Finally, living the Christian life under a system of law numbs the power of the cross of Christ. It is to live as if one is under Judaism. This was certainly not what Paul preached. For this reason, he sarcastically declares that if the Galatians believed cutting off a little bit of skin made them acceptable to God, then they should go ahead, cut the whole thing off, and please him even more! Christ died so that believers may live in freedom, and living under legalism is not Christian freedom.

5) *Clarification 2: Freedom from a life of sin.* A life of Christian freedom cannot be a life of legalism, or a life of irresponsible, immoral behavior. Paul already argued against these errors in Galatians 2:17. Here he does so again to be emphatic. The alternative to living without law is not living with a license to sin. Believers are called by God to freedom but they are not to use this freedom as an excuse for living as though they are still under the control of sin. They are to use their freedom to be devoted to the loving service of other people. Given the Galatians were adamant about being enslaved, Paul calls them to a righteous slavery. Loving service would also stop them from acting like wild animals toward one another.

2.   Galatians 5:4–6
3.   Galatians 5:7–10

Salvation

There are three aspects to the biblical concept of salvation. Justification is the *point* in time when an individual believes and is declared righteous before God. Sanctification is the *process* by which a believer is progressively made righteous by God. Glorification is that state of actually being righteous that will occur when a believer comes before God in heaven. In Galatians 3–4 Paul dealt with justification. In chapters 5–6 he addresses sanctification.

Paul's Analogies

Paul uses two analogies in this section of the letter. The first analogy is an athletic metaphor. The word *hinder* literally means *to cut in.* Paul is playing with the imagery of *cutting* in the act of circumcision to speak of *cutting in* and so tripping someone up in a race! The second analogy is a proverbial saying. Exodus 12:14–20 prohibited the use of yeast in bread at the Passover. It was a way of speaking of the removal of the spreading of evil influences among the people. Here Paul uses it to depict legalism as an evil influence that has no place in the Christian life.

Fighting Like Wild Animals

In Galatians 5:15, Paul uses the language of wild animals biting and fighting one another to call the Galatian believers to stop fighting among themselves. It is not appropriate for Christians to act like wild beasts constantly clashing against one another. It seems the spirit of legalism brought other tendencies with it: fighting and bickering.

151

What is God saying?

Galatians 5:1–15 serves as a transition from the topic of justification—how one becomes a believer in Jesus Christ, to the topic of sanctification—how one lives the Christian life. Through Paul, God reminded the Galatian believers of a key purpose for their liberation. God freed those who turned to him by faith in Jesus so that they may live in freedom. The Christian life of liberty is not living with the mindset that good works of the law complete or maintain one's standing before God. Nor is the Christian life of liberty living as

Where else is this taught in Scripture?

1 Corinthians 5:11

But now I am writing to you not to associate with anyone who calls himself a Christian who is sexually immoral or greedy, an idolater or a slanderer, a drunkard or a swindler. Do not even eat with such a person.

The book of Galatians deals primarily with the problem of legalism among the Galatian churches. Even the space Paul devotes to it in this passage relative to the issue of licentiousness illustrates this emphasis. In our passage, Paul devotes what we've classified as eleven verses to legalism and only three verses to licentiousness.

There is no indication the Galatians were exploiting their Christian freedom by indulging in things like drunkenness and sexual immorality and therefore Paul does not dwell on these problems. The book of 1 Corinthians, however, indicates a different problem among the Christians in Corinth. Their problem was licentiousness. It appears they were openly indulging in sin. The sins embraced by the Corinthian society became the practices of the church. Internal turmoil was ravaging the congregation. There were factions and divisions forming in the church. Members were indulging in different kinds of illegitimate sexual practices; Corinthian believers were even abusing the spiritual gifts they had received from God. Paul wrote to them with a similar purpose to the letter to Galatians. He wanted believers to grow in their Christ-likeness. Both books deal with the progressive sanctification of Christians despite the tendency to remain stagnant through turning to legalism or licentiousness. The licentiousness of the Corinthians and the legalism of the Galatians were at their core, the same problem. It could be said that the two extremes Christians gravitate toward as presented in Galatians 5:1–15 are but a representation of the letter of Galatians on the one hand and 1 Corinthians on the other.

1 Corinthians 6:9

Do you not know that the unrighteous will not inherit the kingdom of God? Do not be deceived! The sexually immoral, idolaters, adulterers, passive homosexual partners, practicing homosexuals, thieves, the greedy, drunkards, the slanderers, and swindlers will not inherit the kingdom of God.

1 Corinthians 5:1–2

It is actually reported that sexual immorality exists among you, and of a kind that is not even tolerated among pagans, for a man has his father's wife. And you are proud! Shouldn't you rather have been filled with sorrow and removed from your fellowship the man who did this?

Where else does this happen in history?

The early twentieth century provides a remarkable illustration of the illegitimate ways in which some Christians sought to live. Grigori Rasputin was a monk in the Russian Orthodox Church. Like other mainline Christian traditions, the Russian Orthodox Church became steeped in a multitude of religious practices and ceremonies. Avid adherence to these became for many but certainly not for all, the means through which an individual could satisfy God. That is, they became legalistic. Rasputin was born and raised in this type of environment. He chose to embrace the Orthodox Church following a period of penance in a monastery for criminal activity. In time, he became disillusioned with the established church and its clergy and became a wandering, spiritual mystic. His reputation as a holy man with healing powers grew across Russia. Rasputin gathered quite a large following and became highly influential in the political realm at the time of the First World War. Though he emerged out of a system steeped in legalistic tendencies he reacted strongly by turning to the other extreme. He was not guided by the Scriptures but by his own inner promptings. Rasputin became known for sexual promiscuity, drunkenness, and abuse of power through bribery. It was his belief that

Grigori Rasputin

Rasputin was a colorful figure who was known to some as a "mad monk" and to others as a mystic, prophet, and faith healer. He lived from 1869–1916.

if one yielded to sin and temptation one could then really fully experience repentance and salvation. Therefore, he lived licentiously without apology. He believed Russia itself would experience more of God's abounding grace if Russians sinned more. He justified his indulgence in sin by seeing it as granting God the opportunity to do what he believed God desires to do most: to graciously forgive.

though licensed by God to sin as one pleases. Rather, the Christian life of liberty must be a life of faith. It is a life of faith enslaved to Christ. Paul deals with the same issues at the end of Romans 5 and all the way through Romans 6.

The Galatian believers were to walk in fellowship with God in the manner they had entered their relationship with him, namely by faith in Jesus. Sanctification operates under the same terms as justification. Living by faith will result in a beautiful expression of the Christian life of liberty: sacrificial love.

What does God want?

We are now ready to consider some important implications of our study for daily Christian living. Remember that the issue is how a believer should live the Christian life. Here are some key applicational points:

Stand strong against the tendency toward legalism or licentiousness

God set you free so that you may live a life of love to him and to others. If you are a believer, you are an heir of God. Live like one. This does not just happen. The tendency is to drift and the result is living the Christian life incorrectly. Do you stand firm? Do you know what legalism is and how it manifests itself in your life? What about licentiousness? The society you live in might advocate it. Certainly, an important aspect in standing strong is recognizing what the gospel actually declares. Misunderstanding God's gospel inevitably leads to an ungodly life. Do you abuse the gospel?

Express your faith in Jesus through works of love

Saving faith is not opposed to works. God desires to produce works in your life. You do not avoid living the Christian life of freedom incorrectly by simply dodging legalism or licentiousness. Passivity is not God's will for your life either. As a believer, you have a responsibility to live for God and become like Christ. Do you? Is your service to God recognized as such by him? It is the motivation of your heart that renders a work either a faith-work or a legalistic act. God grants us the opportunity to express our faith in him by loving the people he has placed around us. Do you look for opportunities to show your love for God by serving and loving people?

Pisidian Antioch Nymphaeum

This is all that is left of the *nymphaeum* or monument to the nymphs. Greek mythology thought nymphs to be lessor female deities often associated with a landform such as mountains. Before Paul brought the gospel to this Galatian city, this is the type of worship that the people participated in.

Todd Bolen, www.BiblePlaces.com

Discoveries

Now we have completed our ninth excavation into the book of Galatians. It is again time to stop digging and carefully examine what we have learned and what difference it can make in our lives. Pick the questions that will be most helpful for you or your community.

Connecting with the community

Here are some discussion questions to help you better understand the text. Do not merely reflect on them as an individual but rather think of each question, when applicable, in terms of your family, your community, your nation, and your church.

1.   In Galatians 5:1, Paul exhorts the Galatians to stand firm in the freedom Christ bought for them. How could they accomplish that? How can you? What clues do you find in the text of Galatians? Share with your group to gather several ideas that you can apply as a community.

2.   According to verse 6, what is the only thing that matters with respect to righteousness in Christ? Consider in your group different ways in which your faith can show that it is working through love. Do you have a loving faith? How can you improve in this area of your Christian walk?

3.   What is the essence of the law? If the Galatians were so preoccupied with the law, why then where they not fulfilling its precepts in their relationships?

4.   If Christ has called the believers to freedom, how is that freedom lived out on a daily basis? Discuss in your group what a life of freedom looks like in comparison to a life of slavery to law and human precepts.

5.   Why is the law so contradictory to a life of freedom in the gospel?

6.   When the Galatians choose to embrace circumcision as part of their gospel, what does this addition imply about Christ's death and its benefits?

Notes, Observations & Questions

7. How can we avoid sinful behavior and at the same time stand firm in the freedom granted to us by our Lord Jesus Christ? What is the principle offered by Paul in Galatians 5:13? Share with your group specific ways in which you can live firm in the freedom Christ bought for you.

8. The Christian life must be lived avoiding two deviant behaviors: legalism and licentiousness. How can you avoid these two extremes?

9. If faith is manifested through loving actions, what steps can you take to live out your faith in love at your home, workplace, and church? Can you identify any areas or relationships in your life where your faith is weak? How can you strengthen your faith in such cases?

10. Make a list of the most important relationships in your life. How can you motivate each of your loved ones with the lessons you have learned in this *Field Study*?

Probing deeper

These exercises are to help you look deeper into some of the secondary issues of our passage and may require reading from the rest of Scripture. This will help you connect some of the concepts that Paul addresses in Galatians with other passages in the Bible. Consider each of these questions in terms of yourself, your family, your community, your nation, and your church.

1. Why did Paul infer from the Galatians attitude towards circumcision that they must also keep all of the law? Read Romans 2:25; Galatians 3:10–11, 21; Deuteronomy 27:26. If you were to choose only one thing to keep from the law, would you choose circumcision? If not, what would you choose? Would this be of any benefit to you with respect to salvation and justification?

2. Why was Paul still being persecuted? What part of his message made him unpopular and dangerous to others according to verse 11? Read 1 Corinthians 1:17–25. In view of Paul's teaching, why is the cross so paramount to the purity of the true gospel? How does it testify to the principle of justification by faith alone in Christ alone apart from works?

3. Read again Galatians 5:6, 13, and then read and meditate on Ephesians 2:8–10. What is the true biblical relationship between faith and works according to these texts? Consider your Christian walk at the present. Do you believe you are standing firm in the freedom Christ has granted you? Why or why not?

4. In our explanation of the text we mentioned that it is clear from the book of Acts that the Jews, Paul included, persecuted the Christians. Read Acts 4:1–31. What was the cause of this persecution? What does this fact teach you regarding the dangers of the gospel?

5. Read Galatians 5:1–15 carefully. Explain the relationship that exists between these concepts: freedom, faith, love, righteousness, and service. Work as a group. You could create a diagram showing the connection between the terms and their meaning.

Bringing the story to life

The command in Galatians 5:1–15 makes it very clear that we are to love and serve one another. Serving someone in love could include giving grace, forgiving, encouraging, visiting, helping, cleaning and an infinite number of other ideas.

Some people are easier to serve than others. Find someone, some family, or group who may not be particularly easy to serve and serve them. Maybe it is someone with special needs or someone who has a difficult personality; maybe it's someone who is homeless or needy. Use the gifts God has given you to serve. Maybe it is cooking a meal or fixing up a house. Maybe your service is just taking the time to listen and encourage someone. You can even do this project as a group. The important thing is to obey the command of Scripture to serve in love. Find a way to bring encouragement and in the process, remind them of the joy of being an adopted son or daughter of the God of all creation.

Memorizing the key

Commit to memory the key phrase for this *Field Study*. The key phrase for Galatians 5:1–15 is:

Christians are free from law and sin to live for God

Learning the Bible includes remembering what issues Scripture addresses and where to find things. Memorizing the key phrases will help you to better understand and apply the key points of each book.

Observation journaling

This section will prepare you for *Field Study 11* by reading through the next section of Galatians. We have included three types of exercises: some for before you read, some for while you are reading and some for after you have completed the reading.

Before you read

Fill in the chart below with what you already know about living by the flesh and living by the Spirit. This exercise will help you learn and remember as you encounter new information. You will fill in the new information after you have read the text.

Reading knowledge chart

	What I already know	What I have learned
Living according to the flesh		
Living according to the Spirit		

While you are reading

On the following page, we have laid out the biblical text with wide margins so you can mark the text with questions, key terms, notes, and structures. We have removed all of the verse markings so you can read it without distractions and have laid out the text with spacing to help you see how the lines are related. Review the guidelines on *The art of active learning* section, page xi at the beginning of your *Field Notes* for some suggestions on reading, learning, and marking the text effectively.

Galatians 5:16–26

But I say, walk by the Spirit, and you will not carry out the desires of the flesh. For the desires of the flesh are opposed to the Spirit, and the desires of the Spirit are against the flesh, for these are in opposition to each another, so that you do not do what you want. But if you are led by the Spirit, you are not under the law. Now the works of the flesh are obvious: sexual immorality, impurity and sensuality, idolatry, sorcery, enmity, strife, jealousy, fits of anger, rivalries, dissensions, divisions, envy, drunkenness, orgies, and things like these. I warn you, as I warned you before, that those who practice such things will not inherit the kingdom of God. But the fruit of the Spirit is love, joy, peace, patience, kindness, goodness, faithfulness, gentleness, and self-control. Against such things there is no law.

Now those who belong to Christ Jesus have crucified the flesh with its passions and desires. If we live by the Spirit, let us also keep in step with the Spirit. Let us not become conceited, provoking and envying one another.

Notes, Observations & Questions

Summarize the text here

After you have read

1. Go back to your *reading knowledge chart* on page 158 and fill in anything that you have learned while reading through this section of Galatians. Compare it with what you already knew to see what the text has revealed so far.

2. Write out Galatians 5:16–26 from the previous page or your own Bible into a journal word for word. This practice will help you to remember and understand what you have just read. This week, journal your thoughts on what it means to walk by the Spirit or live by the Spirit or keep in step with the Spirit.

3. Now read Galatians 5:16–26 in your own Bible. Continue to reread it each day until you get to *Field Study 11*. This will reinforce the learning of Scripture and help you in retention.

Pray

As we continue to learn the Word of God, it is essential that we communicate with him through prayer. Write a prayer, psalm, or poem to God expressing your desire to serve others in love. Pray for impact that your church can have in your community in serving through love. Pray for your church, your nation, your community, your family, and yourself. Try to pray with someone else throughout the week and consider this sample prayer:

Dear Heavenly Father,

What you are teaching me in Galatians is so relevant to my life. It is as though you wrote it directly to me! I desire to live in freedom but certainly struggle to do so without running to the extremes of either legalism or sin. In fact, sometimes I think that living by a set of rules will stop me sinning. I know rules have no power to do so, though, for only the Spirit does. So help me live out in the freedom you desire. Help me, help my family, help my church fellowship walk in fellowship with you by faith in Jesus for it is by this faith that we entered a relationship with you. I know that only then will we all be able to represent you before our nation and the watching world in an honoring manner. Help us express our life of freedom by faith constantly looking for opportunities to love others practically. Open my eyes to the opportunities all around me to show your love in Jesus Christ. Amen.

Excavate the Site
Galatians 5:16–26

Christians are free to live in step with the Spirit

Galatians 5:16–26

FIELD STUDY 11

How is the text arranged?

In the previous section of Galatians, we explored a few key issues of the Christian life. Paul reminded us that it is a life of freedom. God desires that we walk with him by faith. Such a life is not lived self-righteously, nor immorally, but rather as a life of faith expressed through love. A question that should rise in our minds at this point is, why are believers attracted to a lifestyle that goes against what God desires? Why is it so hard to live the Christian life in the freedom that God grants? Paul addresses this issue in this next section of the letter. He clarifies even further, what Christian freedom is and is not. In doing so, he as a masterful teacher, frames the Christian life as a *walk*—a life controlled by one of two opposing forces. This is very relevant since it is God himself who is showing us how to walk as believers! Let's study this issue together. Take a moment to read the passage with the guide provided.

Galatians 5:16–26

Section	Bible Text
Clarification 3: A life walking by the Spirit not the flesh	
The Christian life of freedom: general exhortation	¹⁶ But I say, walk by the Spirit, and you will not carry out the desires of the flesh.
Living by the Spirit contradicts living by the flesh	¹⁷ For the desires of the flesh are opposed to the Spirit, and the desires of the Spirit are against the flesh, for these are in opposition to each another, so that you do not do what you want. ¹⁸ But if you are led by the Spirit, you are not under the law.

Galatians 5:16–26

Section	Bible Text

The result of living by the flesh	¹⁹ Now the works of the flesh are obvious:
	     sexual immorality, impurity and sensuality,
	  ²⁰ idolatry, sorcery, enmity, strife, jealousy, fits of anger,
	     rivalries, dissensions, divisions,
	  ²¹ envy, drunkenness, orgies, and things like these.
	 I warn you, as I warned you before,
	     that those who practice such things
	         will not inherit the kingdom of God.

The result of living by the Spirit	²² But the fruit of the Spirit is
	     love, joy, peace,
	     patience, kindness, goodness,
	     faithfulness, ²³ gentleness, and self-control.
	         Against such things there is no law.

Concluding exhortation	²⁴ Now those who belong to Christ Jesus
	     have crucified the flesh with its passions and desires.
	  ²⁵ If we live by the Spirit,
	     let us also keep in step with the Spirit.
	  ²⁶ Let us not become conceited,
	         provoking and envying one another.

Our outline of the passage presents four sections. Paul begins this third clarification of the Christian life of freedom by exhorting the Galatian believers to live under the control and direction of the Spirit. The second section shows how walking in the flesh leads to slavery rather than freedom. The third section then demonstrates that the freedom of the Spirit produces the godly character and behavior that God desires in believers. Finally, Paul concludes the chapter with a renewed exhortation to the Galatians to walk by the Spirit.

What is this passage saying?
What are some key terms and phrases?
Take some time now to study and meditate on the following terms and concepts. Remember that understanding the meaning of the text begins with understanding these expressions. Paul has carefully chosen his words; therefore, we must understand them in their context in order to grasp the meaning of this passage.

B.C. 2000	1850	1700	1550	1400	1250

2091 God calls Abraham?

1925 God calls Abraham?

Receiving the Law on Mount Sinai? 1446

Receiving the Law on Mount Sinai? 1260

162

Meaning of Key Terms

Key word or phrase	Meaning and significance
Walk (5:16)	The word walk is used here as an idiom for *how a person lives* or *behaves in life*. The apostle uses three more verbs in this section that describe this same idea—*led* in verse 18, *live* in verse 25, and *keep in step* or *march* in verse 25. It is crucial to keep in mind that our passage is dealing with Christian living, or with the way a Christian should behave. This was the problem at the very core of the Galatians' error, and it is still a problem for Christians today.
Walking by the Spirit as opposed to the flesh (16–18, 26)	The believer can potentially choose two different walks for his or her life. Only one of them is according to God's will. Each walk results from the underlying influence controlling the believer. If the Holy Spirit is influencing and directing the Christian, the result is a walk pleasing to God. If, on the other hand, the flesh influences and directs the believer, then he or she will live in a manner not in keeping with God's desires. This struggle for control exists only in those in whom the Holy Spirit is present. Unbelievers are entirely under the control of the flesh. The flesh is that capacity in every person—corrupted by sin—to live life independent of God. Until believers receive a resurrected body, that sinful capacity remains in their lives. It was defeated but not destroyed at the moment of salvation. The flesh has no right to exercise control over the life of a Christian. Believers choose to submit themselves to it. The flesh is not something external to the believer—like a demon. It is the believer's own capacity to live life in disobedience to God. It is important to realize that living self-righteously under the law, or living licentiously and immorally are both expressions of walking according to the flesh. Legalists live the same *carnal* lives as those living licentiously.
Will not inherit the kingdom of God (5:21)	Paul ends the list of works of the flesh with words of caution. He declares that "those who do these things will not inherit the kingdom of God." This is a concept often used in reference to eternal life with God. However, this statement does not mean that a believer who sins by living according to the flesh will lose his or her salvation. Paul himself argues in Galatians that behavior does not determine justification, only faith does. Rather, Paul's intention is to contrast two lifestyles. The first one is not fitting of a Christian since it resembles the life of an unbeliever who has no fellowship or inheritance with God. It is the vices of pagans. The second lifestyle is God's desire for the believer. Since unbelievers will not inherit the kingdom of God, it is not right that those *who will do so*, should choose such an ungodly lifestyle.

Acts 24:24

But this I admit to you, that I worship the God of our ancestors as a follower of the Way (which they call a sect), believing everything that is according to the Law and that is written in the Prophets.

A Believer's Walk

The command to *walk* is used in several places in the New Testament including the following passages:
- Ephesians 4:1, 17
- Ephesians 5:8, 15
- 1 John 1:6, 7
- 1 John 2:6, 11

Each of these verses speak of a believer's *walk*. It is a common way of referring to one's lifestyle.

The Christian Life

The act of walking is an idiom for the Christian life. In the early church, Christianity was described as the *way* or the *path* upon which the walking occurs. Look at Acts 9:2 and 19:9. You walk the Christian life on the Christian path or way.

Paul Friel, 2004

Biblical Lists

The lists of vices and virtues are not the only lists Paul writes. We find similar lists in other Pauline letters:
- Romans 1:18–32; 13:13
- I Corinthians 5:9–11; 6:9, 10
- 2 Corinthians 12:20, 21
- Ephesians 4:19; 5:3–5
- Colossians 3:5–9
- I Thessalonians 2:3; 4:3–7
- I Timothy 1:9, 10; 6:4, 5
- 2 Timothy 3:2–5
- Titus 3:3, 9, 10

These lists are primarily tied to issues of character and were commonly used during the time of the New Testament.

What about the culture?

Lists of vices and virtues were common in the ancient world. Paul's lists of vices included in the New Testament were particularly appealing to his listeners since they were familiar with this type of writing from popular moral handbooks. Listing vices and virtues was a standard literary convention. For this reason, Paul declares in verse 19 that the works of the flesh are *well known* or *obvious*.

Philo of Alexandria
Philo (20 B.C. to A.D. 50) lived as a Hellenistic Jew focusing on Biblical philosophy.

An example of this type of writing is Philo, the first century Jewish writer, who provides a similar list in his work, *Sacrifices of Abel and Cain*. Only a short sample is provided here since, in his list, he cites 146 vices to avoid!

> Know, then, my good friend, that if you become a votary of pleasure you will be all these things: a bold, cunning, audacious, unsociable, uncourteous, inhuman, lawless, savage, ill-tempered, unrestrainable, worthless man; deaf to advice, foolish, full of evil acts...

(Philo, The Sacrifices of Abel and Cain, 32, translated by C.D. Yonge.)

What is the explanation?

Now that we have explored some key concepts relevant to this section of the letter, we are ready to dig deeper into the text. Remember that the main point made in Galatians 5–6 is that Christ has liberated believers so that they may live in freedom. We are dealing with what the Christian life of freedom involves. Our passage provides the third of four clarifications.

Paul exhorts the Galatian believers to allow the Spirit to influence and direct conduct. This is the key to living the Christian life of freedom, as God desires it. Only then does the believer live by a faith expressing itself through love. Only a lifestyle dependent upon, and empowered by the Spirit of God can please God. Walking by the Spirit is the antidote to life in the flesh, in either self-righteous or immoral living.

The Didache
The Didache is a late first or early second century work lost for centuries but rediscovered in the 19th century. It is a text composed by the second generation of Christians! It is also known as the *Teaching of the Twelve Apostles* and deals with issues such as Christian living, rituals, and church organization, providing a window into the early church. The section on the *Two Ways*, 1:1–6:3 illustrates another set of lists of vices and virtues.

B.C.	1	A.D.	10	20	30	40	50

5? Birth of Jesus

John the Baptist begins his ministry 28–29?

33–34? Paul encounters Christ on Damascus road

46–47? First Mi Journey

4–6? Birth of Paul

Jesus begins his ministry 28–30?

Paul writes Galatians 48?

Jesus is crucified and resurrected 30–33?

RULE OF THE COMMUNITY
QUMRAN 4.9-12 CAVE 1

⁹HOWEVER, TO THE SPIRIT OF DECEIT BELONG GREED, SLUGGISHNESS IN THE SERVICE OF JUSTICE, WICKEDNESS, FALSEHOOD, PRIDE, HAUGHTINESS OF HEART, DISHONESTY, TRICKERY, CRUELTY, ¹⁰MUCH INSINCERITY, IMPATIENCE, MUCH FOOLISHNESS, IMPUDENT ENTHUSIASM FOR APPALLING ACTS PERFORMED IN A LUSTFUL PASSION, FILTHY PATHS IN THE SERVICE OF IMPURITY, ¹¹BLASPHEMOUS TONGUE, BLINDNESS OF EYES, HARDNESS OF HEARING, STIFFNESS OF NECK, HARDNESS OF HEART IN ORDER TO WALK IN ALL THE PATHS OF DARKNESS AND EVIL CUNNING. AND THE VISITATION ¹²OF ALL THOSE WHO WALK IN IT WILL BE FOR AN ABUNDANCE OF AFFLICTIONS AT THE HANDS OF ALL THE ANGELS OF DESTRUCTION, FOR ETERNAL DAMNATION BY THE SCORCHING WRATH OF THE GOD OF REVENGES, FOR PERMANENT TERROR AND SHAME.

Rule of the Community

In the 1940's a series of caves by the Dead Sea were found to contain hundreds of jars with ancient scrolls in them. Many of these are portions of the Old Testament. A community of religious people lived here even before New Testament times! They had rule books to govern their lifestyle. *The Rule of the Community* contains a vice list too.

Life in the Flesh

Paul refers to *the effects of life in the flesh* as the "unfruitful works of darkness" in Ephesians 5:11.

Ministry of the Holy Spirit

In Galatians 3:1–14, Paul shows that the Holy Spirit has many ministries. Though he is present in the life of believers as a seal, guaranteeing the coming inheritance with God, this does not mean believers live on a day to day basis under his influence and direction. That is to say, the sealing of the Spirit is not the same as the filling of the Spirit or walking by the Spirit mentioned in Ephesians 1:13–14 and 5:18.

21) *The effects of life in the flesh:* The need to live in obedience to the Spirit is first illustrated by Paul in the negative. He provides the Galatians with a list of vices, which are examples of the kind of attitude and conduct of an individual not governed by the Spirit but by the desires of the flesh. The list is not exhaustive. Paul is not implying that a person living according to the flesh exhibits all of these characteristics at the same time. Rather, they serve as examples of the kind of works the flesh can produce. It certainly describes the kind of life prone to be practiced by those who have not trusted Christ by faith. Paul wants the Galatians to be aware of the fact that living according to the flesh is self-evident. As we examine the vices he lists, remember that the definitions represent the ancient understanding of the terms, and not necessarily how we use these words today.

49? Jerusalem Council

50–52? Second Missionary Journey by Paul

60–62? Paul arrives in Rome under house arrest

64 Fire in Rome

70 Temple is destroyed

79 Pompeii and Herculaneum are destroyed by Vesuvius eruption

John writes Revelation 95–96?

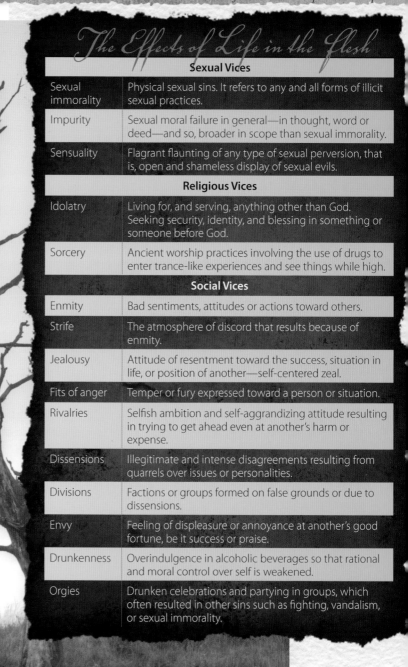

The Effects of Life in the Flesh

Sexual Vices	
Sexual immorality	Physical sexual sins. It refers to any and all forms of illicit sexual practices.
Impurity	Sexual moral failure in general—in thought, word or deed—and so, broader in scope than sexual immorality.
Sensuality	Flagrant flaunting of any type of sexual perversion, that is, open and shameless display of sexual evils.
Religious Vices	
Idolatry	Living for, and serving, anything other than God. Seeking security, identity, and blessing in something or someone before God.
Sorcery	Ancient worship practices involving the use of drugs to enter trance-like experiences and see things while high.
Social Vices	
Enmity	Bad sentiments, attitudes or actions toward others.
Strife	The atmosphere of discord that results because of enmity.
Jealousy	Attitude of resentment toward the success, situation in life, or position of another—self-centered zeal.
Fits of anger	Temper or fury expressed toward a person or situation.
Rivalries	Selfish ambition and self-aggrandizing attitude resulting in trying to get ahead even at another's harm or expense.
Dissensions	Illegitimate and intense disagreements resulting from quarrels over issues or personalities.
Divisions	Factions or groups formed on false grounds or due to dissensions.
Envy	Feeling of displeasure or annoyance at another's good fortune, be it success or praise.
Drunkenness	Overindulgence in alcoholic beverages so that rational and moral control over self is weakened.
Orgies	Drunken celebrations and partying in groups, which often resulted in other sins such as fighting, vandalism, or sexual immorality.

Life in the Flesh

3) *The fruit of life in the Spirit:* In sharp contrast to the works of the flesh, Paul presents a description of the type of life the Spirit produces in the believer who walks under his influence and control. The list is a portrait of the Christian life of freedom God desires for his children. It is a life of faith that expresses itself through love. It is important we note that this fruit is produced by the Spirit in those believers that submit their lives to him. The law served many purposes but one aspect that is often overlooked is that it reveals the will and heart of God. If the Galatian believers walked continually by the Spirit there would be no need for them to seek life under the legislations of law anyway. God himself would produce a lifestyle in conformity with his desires in those leaning on him by faith. Here is the list the Holy Spirit inspired Paul to write.

The Fruit of Love

Grammatically it is valid to render the fruit of the Spirit simply as *love.* If love is the fruit of the Spirit, the other eight virtues are expressions of this love. This fits Paul's previous description of the Christian life as a life of faith expressing itself through love. It is also consistent with Paul's emphasis on a life of love as a fulfilment of God's law (5:14) as well as with the pre-eminence of love in 1 Corinthians 13.

The fruit of Life in the Spirit

Love	Unconditional and costly affection toward God and people despite merit in that person or current circumstances.
Joy	Deep-seated gladness or attitude of delight irrespective of circumstances.
Peace	Tranquillity of mind and heart despite the surrounding situation.
Patience	Long-suffering or forbearing, usually with people.
Kindness	Graciousness, benevolence, and compassion toward others irrespective of their merit.
Goodness	Inner and outer moral excellence.
Faithfulness	The trait of being loyal, dependable, reliable, and trustworthy.
Gentleness	Considerate of, and toward, others.
Self-control	The ability to exercise mastery or discipline over self in all areas of life.

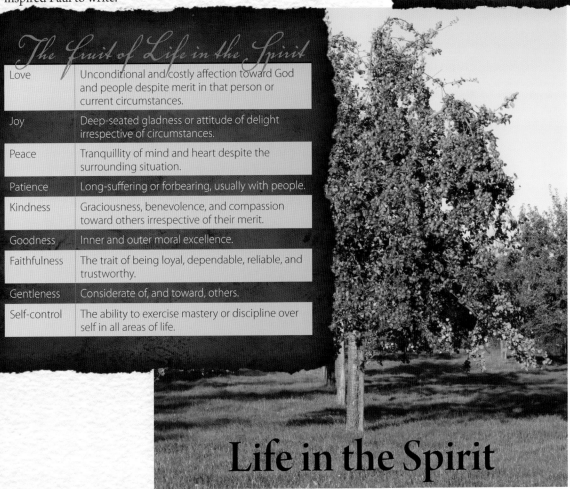

Life in the Spirit

Concluding exhortation: Paul concludes this, his third clarification of what the Christian life of freedom is, with the same exhortation he used to begin it. He exhorts the Christians in Galatia to live by the Spirit. They were to "keep in step with the Spirit" on a daily basis. Only under the Spirit's influence and direction would their wrongful treatment of others—and of Paul—cease. After all, the flesh lost its right to control them when they believed by faith in Jesus Christ. Their sinful nature was crucified by their union with Jesus. Though the flesh remains in the present age as a reality in the life of every believer, it has no right to master him or her. Only by walking by the Spirit is the allurement of the flesh crucified.

Where else is this taught in Scripture?

God repeatedly expresses his desire for us to walk in a manner that pleases him. Even though Paul argued that Abraham received justification before God by faith, (Genesis 15:6), it is clear that God also desired that he live an upright and godly life (Genesis 17).

> ### Genesis 17:1–2
> God tells Abraham, "I am God Almighty. Walk before me and be blameless."

One of the first books Jews study from a young age is the book of Leviticus. Although its ceremonies and practices are confusing to us today and thus we tend to ignore it, Leviticus is a clear command from God to an already redeemed people to live life in a manner that pleases him. This means to live in a way that reflects his character. God calls those he rescues by grace to live godly lives. A brief outline of Leviticus shows this point. Everything within the book has to do with manifestations of holy living in his people in that era of life under the law.

> ### Leviticus 11:45
> You are to be holy, for I am holy.

Abraham
God called Abraham to a life of holiness and purity, not to gain salvation, but in response to being saved.

Worship before God in holiness (Chapters 1–16)
Walk before God in holiness (Chapters 17–27)

> Therefore, prepare your minds for action by being self-controlled, and set your hope fully on the grace that will be brought to you when Jesus Christ is revealed. As obedient children, do not be conformed to the evil urges you had when you lived in ignorance, but like the Holy One who called you, you also be holy in all your conduct, for it is written, "You shall be holy, for I am holy."

Where else does this happen in history?

In the 6th century A.D., Pope Gregory I revised an existing list of sins, and classified all manner of sin under the so-called *Seven Deadly Sins*. His list was intended to be a way of teaching people of the seriousness of wrongdoing. It was but another way of listing sin so that men and women would be prepared to fight it. It was never intended to be exhaustive but meant to rank the degree to which the sin offended love. From most serious to least, Gregory's list was pride, envy, anger, sadness, avarice (greed), gluttony, and lust. The intentions of Gregory the Great in promulgating the list were sincere.

Proverbs 6:16–19

There are six things that the LORD hates, seven that are detestable to him: haughty eyes, a lying tongue, and hands that shed innocent blood, a heart that devises wicked plans, feet that are quick to run to evil, a false witness who utters lies, and a person who spreads discord among brothers.

Solomon's writing in Proverbs 6 may be where Gregory got the idea of seven deadly sins. Listing virtues and vices is a helpful way of analyzing conduct as long as we are motivated by the life of the Spirit.

Francisco de Zurbarán, 1626–1627

Gregory the Great
Pope Gregory (A.D. 540–604) was a man committed to holy and righteous living, worship, missions, and meeting the needs of the poor.

What is God saying?

God wants his people to live in freedom. He defines the Christian life of liberty as a life of faith expressing itself through love. Yet, believers drift toward illegitimate lifestyles, be it legalism or licentiousness. The reason for such drifting is the conflict that rages inside the believer. It is the conflict between the Holy Spirit and the flesh. Through Paul's words to the Galatians here, God accomplishes two things. First, he informs us of the reason why the Christian life of freedom is a difficult walk. Second, he clarifies further what he means by the Christian life. It is a life led by the Spirit and therefore producing his fruit. It is not a life influenced by, and producing the works of, the flesh. On the contrary, it is a life that is becoming more and more like Jesus Christ.

The Life of Christ

The fruit of the Spirit is a portrait of the life of Christ. He displays:
- Love, Ephesians 5:1–2
- Joy, Hebrews 12:2
- Peace, Luke 1:68–79
- Patience, 1 Timothy 1:16
- Kindness, Ephesians 4:32
- Goodness, Colossians 1:27
- Faithfulness, Matthew 26:39
- Gentleness, 2 Corinthians 10:1
- Self-control, Matthew 4; 27:40

The fruit of the Spirit is perfectly modeled in the life of Jesus.

What does God want?

We continue to explore the Christian life of liberty as it relates to us. How does God want believers to live life? Applying several key issues from this text into your life will help you engage with what God desires of you.

Be aware of the conflict that rages within the life of a believer

Conflict rages within you. You cannot wake every morning assuming all is calm because the sun is shining and the birds are chirping. Danger lurks within you if you are a Christian. You possess the capacity, even as a believer, to live today in rebellion to God. It is inconsistent with your standing in Christ but a reality nonetheless. Today you may be tempted to lose your temper, sacrifice your integrity, hurt others with your words, feast your eyes on what is illegitimate, perhaps even envy someone else's life or be jealous of their success. All of this is possible even though you may have spent a few minutes in the Scriptures. If you are a believer, are you aware of the battle that rages in your soul? Are you at war with the God you say you love? You are a child of God living in a world of sin. Sin still appeals to your flesh. Be careful today of what you feed your heart. Don't live ignorant of the danger.

God's solution to your daily conflict is himself. Lean on him.

The Holy Spirit resides in the life of the believer. He desires to influence and direct your lifestyle so that Christ-likeness is evident in you. Your outer lifestyle, after all, is but an expression of who controls your inner life. Every morning God awaits your commitment to rely on him. He's already there. Let him guide your decision-making, plans, activities, family life, dreams, ambitions, and day to day walk. Only when he controls your will and affections will his godly fruit be produced in you. When his fruit is produced in you, Jesus Christ is reproduced through you. And only then is your life in keeping with his desires. Live in dependence upon him. He is always available.

Discoveries

Now we have completed our tenth excavation into the book of Galatians. It is again time to stop digging and carefully examine what we have learned and the difference it can make in our lives. Pick the questions that will be most helpful for you or your community.

Connecting with the community

Here are some discussion questions to help you better understand the text. Do not merely reflect on them as an individual but rather think of each question, when applicable, in terms of your family, your community, your nation, and your church.

1. What is the two-part essential exhortation of Paul in this section of the letter according to verse 16? Explain what you need to do to fulfill this exhortation. Discuss with your group and make a list if necessary.

2. What kind of relationship exists between the flesh and the Spirit in the life of the believer according to verses 17–18? Can you fulfill the desires of the flesh and those of the Spirit at the same time? How does this relationship manifest in the daily life of believers?

3. Read the list of sins mentioned in verses 19–21. Try to make an ordered list that names each of these sins according to the way you perceive their gravity. Begin with the worst sins and end with the sins that are not as bad. Do you think God agrees with you? Discuss this topic with your group. Does everyone agree? Why or why not?

4. Explain the significance of the statement in verse 21, "those who do these things will not inherit the kingdom of God." What is the purpose of this warning?

5. What is the evident result of a life that walks by the Spirit according to verses 22–23? Discuss with your group which of these manifestations of the fruit of the Spirit are evident in your church. How about your nation?

6. Meditate on the list of sins described as the "works of the flesh." Discuss which sins tend to entangle you. As a group, prayerfully confess to the Lord any sinful tendencies you identify in your lives from this list. Embrace the grace of the gospel and its power to clean you and give you victory over any sin.

7. In previous chapters, the apostle Paul emphasized the gift of freedom we have received from Christ. How does a life full of the Spirit of God manifest such freedom? Be specific. It might help you to think of the works of the flesh and meditate on how they enslave, and then you can explain how the fruit of the Spirit expresses freedom.

8. Are you aware of the battle between your flesh and the Spirit of God in your daily life? Do you feel this tension to fight for holiness? How are you currently living, pleasing the flesh or submitting to the Spirit? What reasons do you have for your answer?

9. Think of ways you can pursue love in your relationships. How can you manifest the fruit of the Spirit in the events of common daily life? What does it mean to lean on the Spirit? How can your group demonstrate this reliance on God in the coming days?

Probing deeper

These exercises are to help you look deeper into some of the secondary issues of our passage and may require reading from the rest of Scripture. This will help you connect some of the concepts that Paul addresses in Galatians with other passages in the Bible. Consider each of these questions in terms of yourself, your family, your community, your nation, and your church.

1. Read the story of Sodom and Gomorrah in Genesis 19:1–29 and then meditate on the affirmations of Ezekiel 16:49. What can you learn from these texts about the nature of sin? Can you find any correlation between the different sins mentioned in Galatians 5:19–21 and the rest of these passages?

2. Read James 1:13–15. Is there a progression in sin? In other words, can you start sinning in a certain way and then progress into others? How so?

3. Read the fruit of *life in the Spirit* described in verses 22–23. Now look at the life of Jesus as portrayed in the Gospel of Mark. Come up with at least five illustrations from Mark of Jesus demonstrating the fruit of the Spirit. First list the specific fruit, and then list how Jesus displayed that particular fruit.

4. Read 1 Corinthians 13:1–13 and compare it with the fruit of the Spirit listed in Galatians 5:22–23. Can you see how love is a demonstration of the other eight characteristics of the Spirit? Is this kind of love demonstrated in the various ministries of your church? How about in your own life? Would others say that this is the type of love that marks your life?

Bringing the story to life

In Galatians 5:16–26, Paul provides lists of what the life of the flesh and the life of the Spirit look like. As believers, we are clearly in an ongoing battle against our flesh. Create an action plan to help you combat your flesh. Begin by being honest with yourself about what your sinful tendencies are using Paul's list in verses 19–21. Once you have determined which deeds of the flesh you are most prone to, come up with a way to combat those tendencies *in the strength of the Spirit*. Your action plan may include some of the following:

- Fleeing the tempting situation
- Going on a prayer walk to combat the fleshly desires
- Singing hymns of praise and adoration to God
- Removing or limiting opportunities in your life to be exposed to what tempts you
- Creating an accountability person or group whom you can pray with and call on when tempted

Write out your action plan and put it somewhere where you can read it when being tempted. Write out in full Galatians 5:19–23 on your action plan to remind you of the difference between the deeds of the flesh and the deeds of the Spirit. Put your action plan into action!

Memorizing the key

Commit to memory the key phrase for this *Field Study*. The key phrase for Galatians 5:16–26 is:

> Christians are free to live in step with the Spirit

Learning the Bible includes remembering what issues Scripture addresses and where to find things. Memorizing the key phrases will help you to better understand and apply the key points of each book.

Notes, Observations & Questions

Observation journaling

This section will prepare you for *Field Study 12* by reading through the next section of Galatians. We have included three types of exercises: some for before you read, some for while you are reading and some for after you have completed the reading.

Before you read

Review the key terms from *Field Studies 8* through 11 to insure you remember all of them. This will help you to follow the message that God is communicating through Paul's letter to the Galatian churches.

The key terms:

- From *Field Study 8* are on page 116–117.

- From *Field Study 9* are on page 132–133.

- From *Field Study 10* are on page 148–149.

- From *Field Study 11* are on page 164.

Which key terms and definitions have been particularly helpful in understanding the message of Galatians? Why?

While you are reading

On the following page, we have laid out the biblical text with wide margins so you can mark the text with questions, key terms, notes, and structures. We have removed all of the verse markings so you can read it without distractions and have laid out the text with spacing to help you see how the lines are related. Review the guidelines on *The art of active learning* section, page xi at the beginning of your *Field Notes* for some suggestions on reading, learning, and marking the text effectively.

Galatians 6:1–18

Brothers, if anyone is caught in a sin, you who are spiritual should restore him gently. But watch yourself, lest you also be tempted. Carry one another's burdens, and in this way you will fulfill the law of Christ. For if anyone thinks he is something when he is nothing, he deceives himself. But each one should test his own work, and then he can take pride in himself and not compare himself to somebody else. For each one will have to carry his own load.

Anyone who is taught the word must share all good things with the one who teaches it. Do not be deceived. God is not mocked. A man reaps what he sows. For the one who sows to please his flesh, from the flesh will reap destruction, but the one who sows to the Spirit, will reap eternal life from the Spirit. Let us not grow weary in doing good, for in due time we will reap if we do not give up. So then, as we have opportunity, let us do good to all people, especially to those who are of the household of faith.

See with what large letters I am writing to you with my own hand! Those who want to make a good impression in the flesh are trying to compel you to be circumcised. They do so only to avoid being persecuted for the cross of Christ. For those who are circumcised do not even keep the law themselves, but they want you to be circumcised that they may boast about your flesh. But may I never boast except in the cross of our Lord Jesus Christ, through which the world has been crucified to me, and I to the world. For neither circumcision nor uncircumcision counts for anything; what counts is a new creation. And all who walk by this rule, peace and mercy be upon them, and upon the Israel of God. From now on let no one cause me trouble, for I bear on my body the brand-marks of Jesus. The grace of our Lord Jesus Christ be with your spirit, brothers. Amen.

Notes, Observations & Questions

Notes, Observations & Questions

After you have read

1. Take time to summarize Galatians 6:1–18. This process will help you to understand what you have just read and make sense of it.

2. By this point, you have seen some of the benefits of journaling. Write Galatians 6:1–18 from the previous pages or your own Bible into a journal word for word. This practice will help you to remember and understand what you have just read. This week, journal your thoughts as you reflect on the battle that you go through with the deeds of the flesh versus the deeds of the Spirit. Journal about how you see the Holy Spirit working in your life and what fruit of the Spirit needs to be developed in your character.

3. Now read Galatians 6:1–18 in your own Bible. Continue to reread it each day until you get to *Field Study 12*. This will reinforce the learning of Scripture and help you in retention.

Pray

As we learn the Word of God, it is essential that we communicate with him through prayer. Consider writing a prayer, psalm, or poem to God. What would God have you pray in light of the Christian freedom in which he desires you to live? Pray for the Holy Spirit to manifest his fruit in the life of your church, your nation, your community, your family and yourself. Pray together with a group if you can. Consider this prayer as a sample:

Lord,

Thank you for providing concrete guidance on how to live the Christian life of freedom. I desire to live this way. This passage in Galatians certainly helped me understand the struggle within my own heart. Thank you. I can see that the drift toward a lifestyle that does not honor you results from my yielding away from your Spirit to my sinful nature. Forgive me for doing that so often. Help me wake every morning with a desire to submit to the Holy Spirit. I know that then, and only then, will my life, the life of my family and friends, and even the life within my church fellowship be one that bears the fruit you desire and deserve. Help us to lean on you while in this conflict for only in you is there victory. I long to represent you well. Help me for in the name of Jesus Christ I pray, Amen.

Galatians 6:1–18

FIELD STUDY 12

How is the text arranged?

We arrive at our last *Field Study* exploring the text of the letter of Galatians. In his last words to these believers, Paul continues to examine the Christian life of freedom and presents further clarification on what such freedom looks like in concrete terms. It's as though he is answering the question, how should the Spirit-led life, defined in Galatians 5, affect my interactions with others? Enjoy reading our final passage in Galatians. Try to use several Bible versions as you consider the guide provided.

Galatians 6:1–18

Section	Bible Text
Clarification 4: Freedom to serve others by...	

Restoring the fallen	¹ Brothers, if anyone is caught in a sin,
	        you who are spiritual should restore him gently.
	        But watch yourself, lest you also be tempted.

Bearing other's burdens	² Carry one another's burdens, and in this way you will fulfill the law of Christ.
Watching your attitude	³ For if anyone thinks he is something when he is nothing, he deceives himself.

Living as accountable to God alone	⁴ But each one should test his own work,
	        and then he can take pride in himself
	        and not compare himself to somebody else.
	⁵ For each one will have to carry his own load.

Looking after Bible teachers	⁶ Anyone who is taught the word must share all good things with the one who teaches it.

Galatians 6:1–18

Section	Bible Text
Living for eternal reward rather than temporary satisfaction	[7] Do not be deceived. God is not mocked. A man reaps what he sows. [8] For the one who sows to please his flesh, from the flesh will reap destruction, but the one who sows to the Spirit, will reap eternal life from the Spirit.
Doing good continually	[9] Let us not grow weary in doing good, for in due time we will reap if we do not give up.
Doing good to Christians	[10] So then, as we have opportunity, let us do good to all people, especially to those who are of the household of faith.
Closing Words	
Contrasting motivation behind advocates of the false gospel and Paul	[11] See with what large letters I am writing to you with my own hand! [12] Those who want to make a good impression in the flesh are trying to compel you to be circumcised. They do so only to avoid being persecuted for the cross of Christ. [13] For those who are circumcised do not even keep the law themselves, but they want you to be circumcised that they may boast about your flesh. [14] But may I never boast except in the cross of our Lord Jesus Christ, through which the world has been crucified to me, and I to the world. [15] For neither circumcision nor uncircumcision counts for anything; what counts is a new creation. [16] And all who walk by this rule, peace and mercy be upon them, and upon the Israel of God. [17] From now on let no one cause me trouble, for I bear on my body the brand-marks of Jesus.
Closing blessing	[18] The grace of our Lord Jesus Christ be with your spirit, brothers. Amen.

The initial verses of Galatians 6 contain the fourth clarification regarding the Christian life of freedom and declare, through several examples, that it is a life of service to others. Such a lifestyle is the evidence and result of living by the Spirit. Paul then proceeds to expose the wrongful motivations that these Judaizers had in the advancement of their law-based gospel. Finally, he closes his message with a warning and a blessing.

B.C. 2000   1850   1700   1550   1400   1250

2091 God calls Abraham?

1925 God calls Abraham?

Receiving the Law on Mount Sinai? 1446

Receiving the Law on Mount Sinai? 1260

What is this passage saying?

What are some key terms and phrases?

Let's study the following issues together. They will help you understand the passage more clearly, when we look at the explanation of the text.

Meaning of Key Terms

Key word or phrase	Meaning and significance
Fulfill the law of Christ (6:2)	Freedom from life under the law should not lead to lawlessness. God is not opposed to the law, only to its illegitimate use. Here, Paul indicates that bearing each others burdens fulfills the law of Christ. What does this mean? In the context of Galatians, this is another way of restating the truth found in Galatians 5:14: *Believers should live to love others.* Living according to the standards and expectations of Jesus Christ is to live to love God and people. This is the fulfillment of the law that God desires. A life that fulfills the law of Christ is a life of faith expressed through love.
Reaping corruption from the flesh and eternal life from the Spirit (6:8)	In the New Testament, the concept of eternal life is used in the following ways: First, it is used of the life with God that he shares as a gift with those who believe and that is fully realized in the future (John 10:28). Second, eternal life is the *quality* of life a believer experiences in the present. In this case, the concept hinges on whether he walks in fellowship with God by the Spirit (Galatians 6:8). All believers will receive the gift of eternal life. However, only those who walk in fellowship with God experience aspects of it even now. The double meaning of this concept affects the understanding of what Paul means by reaping corruption. In the first use, Paul is not saying a believer who lives in the flesh does not receive eternal life in the future with God. He is saying, however, that a believer forfeits current experiences of that life when he or she lives in a way ultimately destructive to Christian growth.
Boasting in the cross of Christ not the flesh (6:13–14)	First century society took offense at the message of the cross. We saw this in Galatians 5. Jews were offended by the idea of a Jewish Messiah hung on a cross since this spoke of God's curse upon him. Gentiles likewise, were amused at the claim that God would die in such shame and powerlessness. For this reason, the false teachers advocated a gospel that minimized the cross in order to fit in with society. In doing so, their gospel was more appealing to the world. Rather than boasting in what God did through Christ on the cross, they boasted in their own good works. This is the work of the flesh. However, society was in some sense right.

(continued on next page)

Sowing and Reaping

These two words together present a law of agriculture as it is applied to human behavior. The Galatians thought that their current beliefs and actions would not have negative consequences. But Paul wants them to acknowledge that this is not the case. Whoever thinks their actions can't have negative effects is deceived. Sowing behaviors like legalism will always reap negative consequences.

Todd Bolen, www.BiblePlaces.com

Harvest

In the days when the Bible was written, people lived off the land. Sowing and reaping were a matter of survival for most people. This made Paul's illustration very powerful.

The Cross

The Roman cross was the instrument used to kill Jesus. While it was meant to be a humiliating and excruciating death, Paul teaches that the event is worthy of boasting because of what God accomplished through it.

Meaning of Key Terms

Key word or phrase	Meaning and significance
Boasting in the cross of Christ not the flesh *(continued)*	At the cross, the curse of sin fell on the Jewish Messiah, Jesus Christ, *so that* such a curse would not fall on those who turn to him by faith. At the cross, God also took on shame and frailty *in order to* undo the shame and powerlessness of man's condition under sin.
The Israel of God (6:16)	The phrase *peace and mercy be upon them, and upon the Israel of God* must be clarified. Two groups are identified in this verse. Both groups are part of one overall body even though the distinction made here is important. Note how the repetition of *upon… and upon* highlights the distinction. The second group is not a further qualification or a repetition of the first. We know this because the word *Israel* is used 65 times in the New Testament always in reference to physical Jews. Therefore, the phrase is a reference either to the nation, or to that believing remnant of Jews within it. This means that the phrase, *Israel of God* cannot be an idiom that describes the church as a whole since the church in general is never referred to as Israel. Paul is referring to believing Jews, that is, Christian Jews. It is therefore understandable that he singles them out for a special mention. Especially since he could be accused of sounding anti-Semitic in Galatians! Jewish and Gentile Christians who live according to what Paul taught experience God's peace and mercy. They are equal before God.

Romans 9:6

But it is not as though the word of God had failed. For not all who are descended from Israel are Israel.

Acts 14:19

But Jews came from Antioch and Iconium, and after persuading the crowds, they stoned Paul and dragged him out of the city, supposing that he was dead.

What about the culture?

One interesting cultural aspect of this text is found in Galatians 6:17. In this verse, Paul affirms that he bears on his body "the brand-marks of Jesus." These marks, unlike circumcision, meant something. They did not grant God's salvation to Paul, but they did prove his passionate service to God as his Master. It is possible that some of these marks were acquired while ministering among the Galatians themselves. Slavery in the ancient world was widespread and slaves were branded by their masters. These scars labeled the slave as the property of another. Paul refers to his scars as a statement of his relationship with God. Paul was a slave, branded for God.

Other ancient authors also used this imagery. Look at this interesting parallel from the first century Jewish historian Josephus. In it, Antipater displays his loyalty to Caesar through marks on his body:

B.C.	1	A.D.	10	20	30	40	50

5? Birth of Jesus

4–6? Birth of Paul

John the Baptist begins his ministry 28–29?

Jesus begins his ministry 28–30?

Jesus is crucified and resurrected 30–33?

33–34? Paul encounters Christ on Damascus road

Paul writes Galatians 48?

46–47? First Mis Journey

Roman Mosaic of Slaves

This is a second century Roman mosaic from Dougga, Tunisia. It shows two slaves carrying wine jars wearing typical slave clothing along with others carrying towels and flowers. Slaves were very much a part of Roman life.

But Antipater threw away his garments, and showed the multitude of the wounds he had, and said, that as to his goodwill to Caesar, he had no occasion to say a word, because his body cried aloud, though he said nothing himself.

(Josephus, Jewish War, 1.197

translated by William Whiston)

The Roman Slave Market

Roman slave markets were places where people were bought and sold. Slaves served in a variety of roles from manual labor to domestic services such as accounting.

What is the explanation?

Let's take some time again to dig even deeper into the meaning of this passage.

Clarification 4: Freedom to serve others. In this portion of the text, the apostle Paul presents several direct and practical ways in which the believer can live out his or her Christian freedom as an expression of his or her walk in the Spirit.

(1) The apostle begins this fourth clarification encouraging "those who are spiritual," that is, those that walk by the Spirit, to deal with those that have been caught in some sin. He does not want the Galatians to condemn such persons but to *restore* them with gentleness —a characteristic of the fruit of the Spirit. The term *restore* is used of the mending of nets in Matthew 4:21. This is helpful for it provides a visual example, which highlights the remedial, not harmful, nature of the treatment. The attitude of those who are doing the restoration must be one that acknowledges that they too, though they are spiritual, may fall into sin. After all, a spiritual person is continually aware of the subtle dangers of sin.

(3) Paul also encourages the Galatian believers to ease one another's burdens. In doing so, they would serve others as Christ would. Burden bearing is a Christ-like quality that expresses the love expected of

Sin

The term used for sin in Galatians 6:1 indicates an inadvertent or isolated sin. It is not habitual sinning. Moreover, it is not a sin that brings the church into public shame since in such a case Paul advises differently. See 1 Corinthians 5:5; Romans 16:17.

50 — 60 — 70 — 80 — 90 — 100 A.D.

| 49? Jerusalem Council | 60–62? Paul arrives in Rome under house arrest | 70 Temple is destroyed | John writes Revelation 95–96? |
| 50–52? Second Missionary Journey by Paul | 64 Fire in Rome | 79 | Pompeii and Herculaneum are destroyed by Vesuvius eruption |

181

those who desire to fulfill Christ's will in their lives. The danger of burden bearing in sinful matters is that the flesh can exploit this initial expression of love by developing an attitude of conceit rather than compassion. Moreover, conceit removes any desire to serve others. Therefore, Paul also encourages the Galatian believers to examine themselves continually to make sure a spirit of arrogance and elitism does not develop in their hearts.

Believers are to live in light of their personal responsibility before God for it is to him that they will render an account of their behavior without any consideration or comparison to anyone else. As members of the body of Christ, there is an obligation for each part of the body to do its share of work. Therefore, bearing one another's burdens is accomplished when everyone bears his or her own load.[1]

(4-

Next, Paul writes emphatically about how a believer who is led by the Spirit, is free to serve others. Serving one another includes an obligation to support those who are teachers of the Word with good things. It may be that the Galatians were neglecting those who taught God's Word because of the influence of the Judaizers. Just as Jesus taught, burden bearing includes looking after the teachers of the Word.[2]

(6)

While a believer may be able to deceive other believers, God cannot be conned or ridiculed. Ananias and his wife Sapphira demonstrated this when God struck them dead. This was a lesson to the early church regarding God's discipline upon those who thought they could mislead him and his people. God knows the intentions of the heart.

(7-

Ananias and Sapphira

Ananias and his wife Sapphira were struck down by God as a lesson to the early church of God's discipline upon those who thought they could con him and his people. Read about it in Acts 5:1–11.

Raphael, 1515

Serving others means you do not deceive others with ulterior motives. It also means you do not compare yourself to others since a believer will render account for his or her life of service to God on personal merit, without consideration or comparison to others. Christians have the freedom to decide for themselves how to be of service by looking *tirelessly* for opportunities to do good, particularly toward other believers, and leaving the rewards up to God.

1. Galatians 6:2
2. Matthew 10:10

The apostle closes the letter with a series of exhortations that show the way in which the freedom of walking by the Spirit is made evident in the life of the believer. *The common denominator is service.* God grants believers the freedom to serve one another.

Closing words: Paul closes out the letter in these verses, but even here he does not relent against the corruptors of the gospel. In order to emphasize the importance of his message in this letter, Paul directs attention to the size of the words he writes by his own hand.

Papyrus 46

Papyrus 46 is one of the oldest New Testament manuscripts. It contains most of Paul's epistles, including all of Galatians. It was copied in Greek on papyrus around A.D. 200.

Public Domain

1 Corinthians 16:21

I, Paul, send this greeting with my own hand.

3) One last time Paul wants the Galatians to consider that those preaching a law-based gospel and emphasizing circumcision simply wanted to put on an outward show to please men. Their goal was to escape persecution. Judaism, after all, was identified by the rite of circumcision and was a legal religion under Rome. It was illegal to persecute a Jew, and Romans assumed those circumcised were Jews. Militant Jews were also less likely to persecute someone who was circumcised because they would assume that person was adhering to the Jewish law. These Judaizers also had a second motive behind their "gospel;" they wanted to boast about the Galatians' enslavement. Again, Paul connects their zeal to cut man's bodily flesh to a selfish motivation of their sinful flesh. They were putting on a show to impress man and God and receive personal praise. The perception of godliness was all that mattered to them.

6) Paul on the other hand, believed that the *only legitimate source of boasting for a believer is the cross of the Lord Jesus Christ*. When believers are united with Christ by faith, they die to the world and the world dies to them. Therefore, their only noble object of boasting must be God's work in Christ on the cross, even though the cross offended Jews and amused Gentiles. Ultimately, circumcision for religious purposes was irrelevant for those in Christ. What mattered was that

Dictation

Paul often dictated his letters to a scribe or *amanuensis*, picking up the pen himself just for the final greeting (see 1 Corinthians 16:21). This was a common practice in the ancient world. We do not know whether Paul dictates Galatians up to this point and then finishes it himself, or if he wrote the entire letter without the use of a scribe.

A Show in the Flesh

Note Paul's play on words. The term *flesh* is used here simply to refer to the physical body. Circumcision is an act on the physical body. But Paul uses the term with an eye on the other sense of *flesh*—that corrupt capacity to live life apart from God. He connects their desire to cut man's bodily flesh to living according to the *flesh*—their sinful disposition.

Jewish Law

If you need to be reminded about tensions surrounding the law, look back to the section entitled, *What about the culture?* in *Field Study 5*.

those who were united to Christ by faith, and therefore dead to the world, were now new creations. All believers who live according to what Paul teaches here will live in the experience of God's peace and mercy.

Finally, Paul ends the letter to the Galatians with a request and a blessing. He calls for the end of personal attacks on him. He bore legitimate physical marks for his commitment to Jesus.[1] Unlike circumcision in the eyes of his opponents, Paul did not deem these badges of godliness as a reason for boasting and self-exaltation but rather as proof of his devotion to Jesus. His final words reiterated again his understanding of the gospel. The gospel is all about the grace of God flowing through Jesus to man—the man of faith.

Where else is this taught in Scripture?

Paul's letters are always practical. The deep theological truths he passed on are always seasoned with application. God wants us to do something with what he declares. The way Paul structures his letters generally indicates a double emphasis that begins with Christian doctrine and leads to Christian duty. Look at the following outlines for the Letter of Romans and Ephesians.

Romans
Introductory Greeting and Preview (1:1–17)
Doctrine: Teaching on Salvation (1:18–11:36)
Duty: Christian Living (12:1–15:13)
Words of farewell (15:14–16:27)

Ephesians
Introductory Greeting (1:1–2)
Doctrine: Teaching on the Church (1:3–3:21)
Duty: Christian Living (4:1–6:20)
Words of farewell (6:21)

Romans 12:1

Therefore, I urge you brothers, by the mercies of God, to present your bodies as living sacrifices, holy and pleasing to God, which is your spiritual service.

Ephesians 4:1

I, therefore, a prisoner for the Lord, urge you to walk in a manner worthy of the calling with which you have been called...

Notice the verses in each letter that transition from doctrine to duty. Paul shows how one lives their Christian life is an extension of what they believe.

1. 2 Corinthians 6:3–10; 11:16–33

Where else does this happen in history?

A classic example of a life so radically transformed by the grace of God that it was lived out in grateful service of others is that of John Newton. He was born in London, England, in 1725 and spent the early years of his life in radical rebellion toward God. The only Christian influence on his life was from his mother, but she died when he was a young boy. His father showed little interest in him or God. Therefore, John sailed the seas with merchant ships and the Royal Navy, living without moral constraint and losing all sensitivity and compassion toward man as he worked aboard, and then captained, slave ships. At sea while transporting slaves for sale, John found himself in the clutch of death. It was then that he turned to God for salvation. Love and gratitude toward God motivated his life from that point on. He committed himself to living for God and entered full-time Christian service. He became a minister in the Church of England, a slave abolitionist, a writer, and hymnist. It is his hymn writing what makes him well known today. John was so amazed at God's grace in Christ upon his life that he never got over it. His most famous hymn *Amazing Grace* recorded this attitude for posterity. It has also verbalized the sentiments of many Christians since. John Newton lived out his love for God through service to others.

John Henry Newton
Newton was a British sailor and an Anglican clergyman who lived from 1725–1807.

What is God saying?

God liberates those who turn to him by faith in Jesus so that they may live in the freedom of the Spirit. The Christian life is not a life of legalism or licentiousness. Both of these are the result of living under the influence of the flesh. Freedom is found in living by faith expressing itself through love, and this is only possible in dependence upon the Holy Spirit. Life in the Spirit is also a life of service to others. This is one of the ways in which we walk by the Spirit! In this fourth and final clarification, God reminds us a true Christian life has multiple ways in which to express freedom in service to others, especially other believers.

Serving others was the essence of Christ's life. He declared that he did not come to be served but to serve and give his life as a ransom for many.[2] He also modeled service toward others from the humility of washing feet,[3] to ultimately dying on a cross.[4] In doing so, he fulfilled the Old Testament prophecies, which spoke of the Servant of the

2. Mark 10:45
3. John 13:1–17
4. Matthew 27:50

AMAZING GRACE
(ORIGINAL LYRICS)

Amazing grace, how sweet the sound
That sav'd a wretch like me!
I once was lost, but now am found,
Was blind, but now I see.

'Twas grace that taught my heart to fear,
And grace my fears reliev'd;
How precious did that grace appear,
The hour I first believ'd!

Thro' many dangers, toils and snares,
I have already come;
'Tis grace has brought me safe thus far,
And grace will lead me home.

The Lord has promis'd good to me,
His word my hope secures;
He will my shield and portion be,
As long as life endures.

Yes, when this flesh and heart shall fail,
And mortal life shall cease;
I shall possess, within the veil,
A life of joy and peace.

The earth shall soon dissolve like snow,
The sun forbear to shine;
But God, who call'd me here below,
Will be forever mine.

John Newton, Olney Hymns (London: W. Oliver, 1779)

Lord.[1] Those who walk by the Spirit in the way Christ did, live a life of service. In light of this, a proper understanding of the cross of Christ focuses the believer on serving others which gives glory to God for what he has done. Christians are not to boast about one's personal service or self-exaltation but exclusively on the praise of Christ. God has freed you to serve.

What does God want?

This final *Field Study* on the text of Galatians also makes demands upon our lives. God wants us to respond actively to his instruction. Once again, we must focus on the issue of how a believer should live a Spirit-led life of freedom. Take time to consider these questions and the way they relate to your life.

Express your freedom in Christ through service to others

The Christian life of freedom is a life of service. God wants Christians to be active. Open your eyes. Look around you. Where there are people, there are also many opportunities to serve. It is your responsibility to use your freedom to do so. Who can you help restore? Who is burdened with loneliness, ill health, or financial strain? How can you alleviate someone's difficulty? Have you encouraged someone you know who is in ministry? Do you financially support those in Christian work? All of these examples need the practical help of fellow believers. How do you make sure your actions lived before others does not make a mockery of God? Can you think of simple ways of blessing someone else's day? There are endless opportunities to live by faith through love today. But, it doesn't just happen. Be proactive in your pursuit of holiness while walking under the leadership of the Spirit of God.

Scarred for the cross of Christ?

In a world rampant with sin, life is hard. It was for Jesus and for Paul. This is still the case today for those who live for Christ. In a sense, it is as though the world is out to get you. Guess what? It is! Living against the desires of society will result in cuts, bruises, and perhaps more. We live in hostile territory. Don't assume the antagonism and difficulty you face in life is an indicator of God's distance. It may be a testimony of your devotion to God in the midst of a godless society. Paul models the right attitude for us. Rather than pleasing society or wallowing in self-pity, he rejoiced in the cross despite the painful side effects. The cross of Christ is worth living for. The scars it brings are simply badges of love. Paul lived sacrificially for Christ's glory. He bore scars for his master. Do you?

1.   Isaiah 42:1–4; 49:1–6; 50:4–9; 52:13–53:12; 61:1–3

Discoveries

Now you have completed your eleventh and final excavation into the book of Galatians. It is again time to stop digging and carefully examine what we have learned and what difference it can make in our lives. Pick the questions that will be most helpful for you or your community.

Connecting with the community

Here are some discussion questions to help you better understand the text. Do not merely reflect on them as an individual but rather think of each question, when applicable, in terms of your family, your community, your nation, and your church.

1. According to Galatians 6:1, what is the appropriate response of a Christian when a fellow believer is caught in a sin? Do you believe this is the normal response in the evangelical churches in your community? Do you think that this principle must be only applied to certain sins but not others?

2. In verse 2, the Galatians are encouraged to carry one another's burdens. What does this command entail? How is it done by an individual? How is it done by a church?

3. Read Galatians 6:3–5. What is the relationship between carrying one another's burdens in verse 2 and carrying your own load in verse 5?

4. Verse 9 contains yet another exhortation. Paul wants the Galatians to persevere in doing good tirelessly. Why do you think the apostle mentions this towards the end of his letter to the Galatians? Why is this important?

5. Paul uses the familiar agricultural law of sowing and reaping. What is the only way for the Galatians (and us) to be rescued from the consequences of what we have sown? In other words, if we always reap what we sow, and our tendencies are always for our own flesh, what is the only way to break the pattern of having to reap the destruction of our sin?

Notes, Observations & Questions

6. How often and how easily do you grow weary in doing good? When this happens, what causes such discouragement? Do you believe Paul has offered any solutions to weariness in this letter?

7. Can you describe the way in which verse 14 summarizes the message of the entire letter? What is it that makes Paul feel and think this way about the cross? Do you feel the same? Could you make this expression truly your own?

8. Review the explanation of the phrase "the law of Christ." Why is this significant? How is it related to the concept of freedom that was so predominant in chapter 5 of the letter? How can law and freedom coexist?

9. How does this last chapter portray a Christian walk that avoids both legalism and licentiousness? How can you model this life within your church? How should your church model this?

10. Are you currently serving other believers in your local church? If so, what have you learned from Galatians 6:10 that can make you, by God's grace, a better servant of Christ? If you are not serving, why? How can you start living a life of service to God and others? What must change?

11. How is the cross of Christ relevant in your life and/or ministry? Do you think you live a cross-centered life?

Probing deeper

These exercises are to help you look deeper into some of the secondary issues of our passage and may require reading from the rest of Scripture. This will help you connect some of the concepts that Paul addresses in Galatians with other passages in the Bible. Consider each of these questions in terms of yourself, your family, your community, your nation, and your church.

1. The declaration in Galatians 6:7, "a man reaps what he sows" has been called the law of reaping and sowing. Study the life of Samson in Judges 14–16. How is his life an example of this principle? Now, do you think this is a principle that is universally true? How does this principle affect your own life and actions?

Notes, Observations & Questions

2. Read these passages from the prophet Isaiah: 42:1–4; 49:1–6;
    50:4–9; 52:13–53:12; 61:1–3. What picture is being portrayed
    by Isaiah? Consider the narrative of Jesus washing his disciples'
    feet in John 13:1–17. How can we model service like Christ in our
    own lives or within our churches?

3. In Galatians 6:17 Paul speaks of bearing on himself the marks of
    the Lord Jesus Christ. Read Acts 14:1–20; 2 Corinthians 6:1–10;
    11:16–33. Imagine for a moment being in some of the situations
    described in these passages. Do you believe you would be willing
    to bear such marks for the sake of the Lord Jesus? How much are
    you willing to risk for the sake of the gospel? What implications
    does this have for how you live?

Bringing the story to life

In Galatians 6:17, Paul speaks about bearing the marks of Christ
on his body. We know from several passages in the New Testament
that Paul was persecuted on many occasions because of the gospel
of Christ. Today, there are Christians all around the world who are
persecuted for their faith. Do some research to learn about somewhere
in the world where Christians are being persecuted for their faith.
Use any resource available to you. Your pastor may be helpful for this.
Prepare to report to your Bible study group about what you have
learned. In your report, be sure to share these four things:

1. Who is being persecuted? It may be a church, certain pastors,
    or simply believers in a specific area.
2. Where is this persecution occurring? It may be a country,
    area, or region. Be as specific as you can.
3. What form is the persecuting taking? Is it imprisonment,
    burning of churches, injustices, or other means of
    persecution?
4. How can we pray for these believers who are bearing the
    marks of Christ today?

Share your report with other believers and commit to praying for our
persecuted brothers and sisters around the world.

Memorizing the key

Commit to memory the key phrase for this *Field Study*. The key phrase
for Galatians 6:1–18 is:

Christians are free to serve one another

Observation journaling

This section will help you review and remember the key verses in the book of Galatians. We have included three types of exercises: some for before you read, some for while you are reading and some for after you have completed the reading.

Before you read

Review the entire book of Galatians in your own Bible. Write a single sentence to summarize each of the six chapters.

Summary sentence for chapter 1:

Summary sentence for chapter 2:

Summary sentence for chapter 3:

Summary sentence for chapter 4:

Summary sentence for chapter 5:

Summary sentence for chapter 6:

While you are reading

On the following page, we have laid out key verses from the book of Galatians with wide margins so you can mark the text with questions, key terms, notes, and structures. Review the guidelines on *The art of active learning* section, page xi at the beginning of your *Field Notes* for some suggestions on reading, learning, and marking the text effectively.

Key Galatian Passages

Galatians 2:20–21

I have been crucified with Christ and it is no longer I who live, but Christ who lives in me. The life I live in the body, I live by faith in the Son of God, who loved me and gave himself for me. I do not set aside the grace of God, for if righteousness comes through the law, Christ died for nothing!

Galatians 3:3

Are you so foolish? After beginning with the Spirit, are you now being perfected by the flesh?

Galatians 4:19

My children, for whom I am again undergoing birth pains until Christ is formed in you,

Galatians 5:1

For freedom Christ has set us free. Stand firm, then, and do not submit again to a yoke of slavery.

Galatians 5:6b

But the only thing that matters is faith working through love.

Galatians 5:13

You, my brothers, were called to freedom. But do not use your freedom as an opportunity for the flesh; rather, through love serve one another.

Galatians 6:2

Carry one another's burdens, and in this way you will fulfill the law of Christ.

Notes, Observations & Questions

Summarize the text here

Notes, Observations & Questions

After you have read

1. Journaling is another way that we encourage you to learn. By this point, you have written down the entire book of Galatians. What have you learned so far from this ancient letter? This week, journal your thoughts as you consider God's message to the people of Galatia and what that has to do with us today. Write down how God would want you to respond to this letter and then take action accordingly.

2. Now read all of Galatians in your own Bible. Be sure you have reread the book completely before you begin the final *Field Study*. This will reinforce the learning of Scripture and help you retain it.

Pray

As we have learned the Word of God, it is essential that we communicate with him through prayer. Consider writing a prayer, psalm, or poem to God in response to the messages of Galatians. This week, pray that God would work in your heart as you respond to his call to serve others because of your freedom in Christ. Pray that you, your family, and your church would exemplify service to your community, and your nation. Make an effort to pray with at least one other person this week. Consider this sample prayer as you pray:

Father,

I often think that just because I am a Christian that life should be easy for me. I realize that this is not a promise of yours within this fallen state of the world. I am challenged by Paul's self-sacrificial living and amazing attitude in the face of ongoing struggle. Help me remember on a daily basis that I too live in a world that is hostile to you. I too need to respond with the right attitude. Help me also look for opportunities to serve you through serving others so that I too can stand scarred for your Name's sake. You have given us multiple ways of serving one another. Please bring needy people and needy causes my way today. Help me to see them and discern how I can help even if it costs me. Create in me a growing longing to boast in the Lord Jesus Christ before all those you bring my way. Thank you, Father, for the Lord Jesus Christ. Amen.

Field Study 13

Reviewing Galatians
  1–2 Defending the true Gospel
  3–4 The Gospel: Justification by faith
  5–6 The Gospel: Sanctification by faith

The Message
FIELD STUDY 13

We arrive at our last *Field Study* in Galatians. Having finished our excavation of the book, we are ready to analyze all of our findings. Together we've explored the significance and uniqueness of the gospel of Jesus Christ in this letter. We have dug into its teaching and have been challenged about its implications for daily life. Let's now bring all of our excavated gems together by answering some key questions.

What is the contribution to Scripture?
From Genesis to Revelation: The story of history

The human heart longs for salvation *because it is lost*. We know life is not as it should be. But this was not always the case. God's wish for humanity in creation was not to be lost, suffer, and die. His desire was that man and woman could enjoy life under God's authority serving as his representative rulers over a wonderful creation. Mankind was created to enjoy life, not to fear death. God created us to walk with him, not to be isolated from him.

Adam and Eve's willful rebellion against God's desires plunged mankind, and therefore creation, into this lost condition. When mankind chose life without God that is exactly what we received. God allowed his own created beings, made in his image, to rebel. However, God graciously declared his intention, for the sake of his name, to undo the intrusion of evil into his creation through a descendant of Eve. Man's embracing of evil and rebellion against God deserved separation from him. However, God would not

Genesis 3:15

And I will put enmity between you and the woman, and between your offspring and her offspring; he will bruise your head and you will strike his heel.

The Garden of Eden
God placed his most prized creation, Adam and Eve, in a garden of perfect order and tranquility.

Jacob Savery, 1601

James Joseph Jacques Tissot, 1886–1894

Mount Moriah

Mount Moriah is the place where the Lord led Abraham for the binding of Isaac for sacrifice in Genesis 22, and where God intervened with his own provision. This mountain is traditionally believed to be the location where the Temple Mount is situated in Jerusalem today. God provided his own Son for sacrifice many years later on Mount Moriah, which Abraham had named "The LORD will provide."

Genesis 22:14

And Abraham called the name of that place, "the LORD will provide." As it is said to this day, "On the mountain of the LORD it will be provided

allow Satan and sin to have the last say. A descendent of Eve would come, crush Satan, and destroy the curse of sin over man.

The divine intention to undo the intrusion of evil in his creation was also expressed as a promise to Abraham, the promise to bless the nations through him.

Now the LORD said to Abram, "Go out from your country, from your relatives, and from you father's household to the land I will show you. Then I will make you into a great nation, and I will bless you, and I will make your name great, so that you will be a blessing. I will bless those who bless you but the one who dishonors you I will curse, and in you all the families of the earth will be blessed."

Genesis 12:1–3

One who was a descendant of Abraham and before that, a descendant of Eve, would be the channel of blessing to the nations. God would provide a son to Abraham through whom he would restore mankind to life under God. Abraham believed God *himself* would fulfill the terms of his promise. This was illustrated to Abraham when he was called to take Isaac to Mount Moriah and sacrifice his son. God faithfully intervened providing an alternate sacrifice. Abraham's faith in God was evident through obedience. As such, Abraham's faith modeled for mankind what God wants from people so that they can experience the blessings of his promise.

Genesis 15:6

Abram believed the LORD, the LORD credited his response of faith as righteousness.

In anticipation of the arrival of the One through whom the nations would be blessed, God prepared history for his coming. For this purpose, he called the nation of Israel into a partnership with him.

Then Moses went up to God, and the LORD called him from the mountain and said, "Tell the house of Jacob, and the people of Israel, 'You yourselves have seen what I did to Egypt and how I bore you on eagles' wings and brought you to myself. Now then, if you will indeed obey my voice and keep my covenant, then you will be my treasured possession out of all the nations, for the whole earth is mine, and you will be to me a kingdom of priests and a holy nation.' These are the words that you will speak to the Israelites."

B.C. 2000   1850   1700   1550   1400   1250

2091 God calls Abraham?

Receiving the Law on Mount Sinai? 1446

1925 God calls Abraham?

Receiving the Law on Mount Sinai? 1260

194

God and Israel entered into a covenant whereby he would be their King and they his people. Israel was to live life under the rule of God according to his laws, sacrifices, and other observances. In doing so, Israel *advertised* to the world the blessing of the life of faith under the one true God in anticipation of God's fulfillment of the promise to Abraham. However, Israel rebelled in spite of repeated calls for repentance and obedience from the prophets. During this period mankind was to learn the extent of this lost condition and yearn for the promised One to come. God remained true to his Word. He clarified more and more on the details of his promise. Particularly, he revealed that the anticipated One would also be a son of David—a king to rule over an everlasting kingdom.

Moses receiving the Law
At Mount Sinai God created a nation out of a family of slaves.

Jean-Léon Gérôme, 1895—1900

> When your days are complete and you rest with your fathers, I will raise up your offspring to succeed you, who will come from your own body, and I will establish his kingdom. He shall build a house for my name, and I will establish the throne of his kingdom forever. I will be his father, and he will be my son. When he commits iniquity, I will discipline him with the rod of men, with floggings inflicted by men. But my steadfast love will never be taken away from him, as I took it away from Saul, whom I removed from before you. Your house and your kingdom will endure forever before me; your throne will be established forever.

2 Samuel 7:12–16

Paradise Regained
We live under the rule of the Spirit of God in anticipation of the hope of life with God in a re-created realm—life as God wanted it to be.

Jan Brueghel, 1620

At just the right time, God sent his own Son—a descendant of Eve *and* Abraham *and* David.

The arrival of Jesus Christ and his earthly ministry is the essential anticipated act that would fulfill God's promise to undo the intrusion of evil in his creation. The death and resurrection of Jesus is the basis upon which God's gift of eternal life with him is made possible without compromising God's justice. Though Satan has been defeated, he is yet to be destroyed. Believers in Jesus Christ today are the

1250	1100	950	800	650	500 B.C.

Saul becomes king 1050 | 930 The kingdom divides | 722 Northern kingdom falls to Assyria
David becomes king 1010 | Southern kingdom falls to
Solomon becomes king 971 | Babylon and the temple is destroyed 586

church. We live life under the rule of the Spirit of God in anticipation of the hope of life with God in a re-created realm—life as it should be. Until then, we proclaim God's offer to mankind in Jesus Christ—the gospel—displaying to the world the hope of life under the rule of God.

Ultimately, God's desire in creation will be fulfilled. The story is not yet fully developed in history, but the outcome is certain. God's plan continues to move to its culmination, when he will rule undisputed over creation once again.

Then I saw a new heaven and a new earth, for the first heaven and earth had passed away, and the sea existed no more. And I saw the holy city, the new Jerusalem, descending out of heaven from God, prepared as a bride adorned for her husband. And I heard a loud voice from the throne saying, "Behold, the dwelling of God is among human beings. He will dwell with them and they will be his people, and God himself will be with them. He will wipe away every tear from their eyes, and death will not exist anymore, nor mourning, nor crying, nor pain, for the former things have ceased to exist." And the one seated on the throne said, "Behold! I am making all things new!" Then he said, "Write these down for these words are faithful and true." And he said to me, "It is done. I am the Alpha and the Omega, the beginning and the end. To the one who is thirsty I will give water without cost from the spring of the water of life. The one who is victorious will inherit these things, and I will be his God, and he will be my son."

Revelation 21:1–7

The Contribution of Galatians

Galatians is one of Paul's key letters. Why is it so important? What role does it play in the story of history? Why did God preserve this letter for the church? Now that we have studied the biblical text carefully, we can affirm that Galatians makes several contributions to our *understanding* of God's eternal plan. Four major contributions come from the letter to the Galatians because they are addressed with *precision* and *detail*. These contributions are the subject matter in other letters such as Romans.

The first contribution Galatians makes is that *it clarifies the core terms of God's gospel*. The gospel presents God's offer of eternal life based on the work of Christ. This teaching is presented elsewhere in Scripture, but Galatians is distinctive in its precision while explaining what the gospel is *and* is not. Galatians focuses significant attention on the

Paul's Key Letters

Galatians, Romans, and 1 and 2 Corinthians are known among scholars as the *Hauptbriefe*. This is a German term for capital or principal letters in recognition of their importance among Paul's writings.

B.C.	1	A.D.		10		20		30		40		50

5? Birth of Jesus

4–6? Birth of Paul

John the Baptist begins his ministry 28–29?

Jesus begins his ministry 28–30?

Jesus is crucified and resurrected 30–33?

33–34? Paul encounters Christ on Damascus road

Paul writes Galatians 48?

46–47? First Missio Journey by

details of how one enters into a relationship with God. God's terms are spelled out. Galatians anchors the gospel of justification by faith in history, that is, within God's plan all along.

The second contribution of this book flows out of the first and is noticeable in the precision with which it is elaborated. *Galatians clarifies the logical implications of justification by faith, namely, sanctification by faith.* Sustained attention is granted to the operating principle of how one lives the Christian life in fellowship with God while awaiting the culmination of history. The letter reaches its climax in teaching about the daily Christian life. Freedom from the penalty of sin before God by faith should result in freedom to *live* before God by faith. No other letter declares as loud as Galatians that the Christian life is one of freedom—freedom to live by faith.

The third contribution of the book of Galatians emerges in the

Moses and the Decalogue
Moses brought down the Ten Commandments or *Decalogue* from Mount Sinai. It serves as an image of the law God called his people to obey. This was not to grant them justification before him but rather to guide them in life.

process of establishing the first two. It clarifies the issues surrounding the law. In order to spell out God's terms as they are laid out in the true gospel, *the letter must deal with the purpose of the law and its relationship to the gospel.* After all, we have a tendency to corrupt the gospel with our good works. In dealing with this issue, the apostle sheds light concerning the role of the Old Testament law in history and its relationship to the Christian life. No other book of the New Testament sounds as loud a warning as Galatians when it comes to the principle of how one lives life before God. It leaves no doubt that *God will not accept any trace of self-righteousness no matter how clothed in religious practices and biblical language it is.* Galatians helps us understand the proper function of the law in God's plan.

Galatians also makes an important statement concerning the apostle Paul. No other letter of Paul's presents such a passionate and sustained declaration of his authority as an apostle. He is presented as God's

Trumpet Call
"For freedom Christ has set us free. Stand firm, then, and do not submit again to a yoke of slavery."

Galatians as a Trumpet Call

"Martin Luther put [Galatians] to his lips as a trumpet to blow the reveillé of the Reformation. His famous Commentary summoned enslaved Christendom to recover the 'liberty wherewith Christ hath made us free.' Of all the great Reformer's writings this was the widest in its influence and the dearest to himself. For the spirit of Paul lived again in Luther, as in no other since the Apostle's day. The Epistle to the Galatians is the charter of Evangelical faith."

(The Epistle to the Galatians, George G. Findlay, 1888, p. 3)

50   60   70   80   90   100 A.D.

49? Jerusalem Council
50–52? Second Missionary Journey by Paul
60–62? Paul arrives in Rome under house arrest
64 Fire in Rome
70 Temple is destroyed
79 Pompeii and Herculaneum are destroyed by Vesuvius eruption
John writes Revelation 95–96?

197

Luther on Galatians

"The Epistle to the Galatians is my epistle, to which I am betrothed. It is my Katie von Bora." [Luther's wife]

(Martin Luther, *Lectures on Galatians*, 1535, ed. Jaroslav Pelikan, Hilton C. Oswald and Helmut Lehmann, 1999)

authoritative voice and what he declares is God's Word. Anchoring Paul's authority in God as Galatians does, establishes without doubt all his other writings in Scripture as authoritative for the church. Therefore, Galatians makes general and specific contributions to God's plan in history. It places the gospel of Jesus Christ on history's timeline. It looks *back* to what God promised and *forward* to the hope to come, which is assured by the Spirit. In the specifics, the gospel is placed under a microscope. Its key terms and implications are then closely observed.

How did it end?

We do not know what happened when the Galatian churches

Acts 15:1

Now some men came down from Judea and began teaching the brothers, "Unless you are circumcised according to the custom of Moses, you cannot be saved."

received this letter. There is no follow up correspondence that we know of. We can assume the letter was copied and circulated among the churches and read in public. Given Paul's passion for the gospel and love for the Galatians, it is hard to believe the issue remained unresolved.

In Acts 15:1, we read that a version of this same problem spreading among the Galatian churches infected Paul's home church of Antioch. If Galatians was written just after the first missionary journey, at around the same time as the events of Acts 15:1, then this issue was clearly spreading through the early church. Paul and Barnabas traveled to Jerusalem where the first Christian church council was held to deal with this very problem. Key leaders spoke at this meeting. The conclusion reached and proclaimed officially around the early churches echoed Paul's words in Galatians. As a result, circumcision ceased to be a problem in the early church for the most part. Before the decision of the Jerusalem Council, the

JERUSALEM COUNCIL

PROCLAMATION

From the apostles and elders, your brothers, to the Gentile believers in Antioch, Syria and Cilicia, greetings!

Since we have heard that some persons have gone out from among us without our authorization and have confused you, upsetting your mind by what they said, it seemed good to us, for we are of one mind, to choose men to send to you along with our dear friends Barnabas and Paul, men who have risked their lives for the name of our Lord Jesus Christ. Therefore, we are sending Judas and Silas who will tell you these things by word of mouth. For it seemed best to the Holy Spirit and to us not to place any greater burden on you than these requirements:

— that you abstain from meat that has been sacrificed to idols
— and from blood
— and from the meat of strangled animals
— and from sexual immorality.

If you keep yourself from doing these things you will be doing well. Farewell.

ACTS 15:23–29

B.C.	1 A.D.	10	20	30	40	50

5? Birth of Jesus

4–6? Birth of Paul

John the Baptist begins his ministry 28–29?

Jesus begins his ministry 28–30?

Jesus is crucified and resurrected 30–33?

33–34? Paul encounters Christ on Damascus road

Paul writes Galatians 48?

46–47? First Mission Journey by Pa

letter of Galatians may have achieved the same result in that particular area of the empire.

Acts 21:17–24

When we arrived in Jerusalem the brothers received us gladly. The next day, Paul went in with us to see James, and all the elders were there. After greeting them, he began to explain to them in detail what God had done among the Gentiles through his ministry. When they heard this, they praised God. Then they said to him, "You see, brother, how many thousands of Jews there are who have believed, and they are all zealous for the law, and they have been told about you, that you are teaching all the Jews that are among the Gentiles to forsake Moses, telling them not to circumcise their children or follow other Jewish customs. What should we do? They will no doubt hear that you have come. Therefore, do what we tell you: We have four men who have taken a vow, take them and purify yourself along with them and pay their expenses, so that they may have their heads shaved. Then everybody will know there is nothing in what they have been told about you, but that you yourself are living in conformity to the law.

In Acts 21:17–24, we learn that the Jerusalem Council did not completely solve the Judaizing problem in the early church. It remained a practical problem from time to time, which in this particular text, was resolved by taking the higher ground.

The history of Christianity in the Roman province of Galatia carries on well past the close of the New Testament era. What happened to these churches in Galatia? Through numerous inscriptions and traditions, we know that the area was a center of Christian activity. It even hosted a church council at Iconium in A.D. 235. When the Roman Empire split under Constantine, the eastern portion, in which the Galatian churches were found, became known as the Byzantine Empire. The Galatian cities where Paul and Barnabas had planted churches eventually fell to Islamic conquest beginning in the 8th century and were ultimately annihilated during the Seljuq wars of the 11th century.

Today the cities of ancient Galatia where Paul once preached are just

Acts 15:10

Now then, why are you putting God to the test by placing on the neck of the disciples a yoke that neither our ancestors nor we have been able to bear?

Jerusalem Council

The Jerusalem Council was a meeting of the main leaders of the church in A.D. 49/50 to address the issue of what was expected of Gentiles coming to faith in Jesus Christ

James Joseph Jacques Tissot, 1886–1894

Ebionites

In his *Dialogue with Trypho* (around A.D. 140), the early Christian writer Justin Martyr notes the existence of two types of Jewish Christians in the church of his day. There were those who observed the Jewish law by choice yet did not enforce it as a necessity on others; and there were those who desired all Christians live according to the law. The Ebionites, for example, were a Jewish Christian sect in the first few centuries of the Christian church. Our knowledge of them stems from the writings of early Church Fathers who wrote against them. Their existence indicates the ongoing struggle of some Jewish Christians to understand the role of the Jewish law in the era immediately after the death and resurrection of Jesus Christ. Many centuries later, an important factor behind the Protestant Reformation was its objection of the established understanding of the Roman Catholic Church concerning the role of man's works in salvation.

49? Jerusalem Council

50–52? Second Missionary Journey by Paul

60–62? Paul arrives in Rome under house arrest

64 Fire in Rome

70 Temple is destroyed

79 Pompeii and Herculaneum are destroyed by Vesuvius eruption

John writes Revelation 95–96?

The Writing of Galatians

Alongside the book of James, it is likely that Galatians is one of the first Christian works to be written—even earlier than the Gospels! If this is the case, the Holy Spirit starts the next phase of the New Testament compilation with a declaration *and* clarification of the gospel!

ancient ruins. Some have not even been excavated. However, the problems Paul addresses in the letter to the Galatian churches lives on. Misunderstanding the core of the gospel of Jesus Christ and its implications for Christian living abounds in church history and even today. The human heart still gravitates toward self-righteousness and works-based salvation. Even Christians who know better still find it hard to handle freedom in Christ in a Christ-honoring manner. They opt for restraint through ill-motivated rules of conduct. Because of the tendency to try to self-save, the timeless message of Galatians has long outlived the cities to which it was once written.

What does this have to do with Jesus?

Throughout our survey and excavation of the book of Galatians, we have repeatedly encountered lessons in the text that are utterly dependent on the person and work of Christ. By now, it should be very clear that the entirety of this book's message is Christ-centered. In this section, our purpose is to summarize and compile in a single place the many ways in which Galatians, like every other book of the Bible, ultimately lead us to our God and Savior Jesus Christ. Consider some of the affirmations that Galatians makes with respect to Jesus:

- The hope of history rests on the coming of Christ (4:4)
- The covenant with Abraham finds its fulfillment in Christ (3:6–18, 29)
- The Law of Moses fulfills its purpose in Christ (3:19–29)
- The Gospel of God is about faith in Christ alone (1:6–7; 2:15–17, 21; 3:13, 16–18)
- Redemption from the curse exposed in the law is through Christ (3:13)

Derbe

Derbe is another one of the Galatian cities Paul and Barnabas visited and planted a church in. Today, this *tel* or archaeological mound covers the ancient ruins of Derbe.

- The state of righteousness before God, which he offers in the gospel, is the very righteousness of Christ himself (2:15–16)
- Christian living is founded in Christ (2:20)
- The life of Christian freedom is only possible by the Spirit because of the work of Christ (2:4; 5:1)
- Daily Christian living in step with the Spirit produces a reflection of Christ (5:22–24)

Todd Bolen, www.BiblePlaces.com

As you can see, Christ is at the very core of the message of Galatians. God's redemptive promise in history is fulfilled only in him as the Savior. It is solely based upon Christ's death and resurrection that God's gift of life can be made

B.C.	1	A.D.		10		20		30		40		50

5? Birth of Jesus

4–6? Birth of Paul

John the Baptist begins his ministry 28–29?

Jesus begins his ministry 28–30?

Jesus is crucified and resurrected 30–33?

33–34? Paul encounters Christ on Damascus road

Paul writes Galatians 48?

46–47? First Missio Journey by

without compromising his justice. Galatians makes it clear that it is only by faith in Jesus Christ that God will be satisfied. And so, *the gospel is exclusive.* Salvation *unto* eternal life with God is only available *by* God.

Moreover, Jesus does not need nor does he seek help in saving mankind. He does not depend on the assistance of Jewish laws and practices. Man's good religious works are irrelevant for saving purposes. *Jesus is not looking for copartners in salvation.* To live like he needs help is to mock him like those who stood by the cross. It is another shameful scandal against the cross.

Finally, this letter makes evident that the Christian life is about becoming like Jesus. *The fruit of the Spirit is a portrait of him.* The Spirit desires to form Christ-likeness in every believer so that Christ might live through him or her.

Pisidian Antioch

In the distance are the remains of the Roman aqueduct which carried water to the city of Pisidian Antioch. At the time of Paul, the city was the most important of all of the southern cities in Galatia.

What does God want?

Our dig through Galatians now ends. In this exploration, God challenged us in many ways. Here is another opportunity to respond to God. Take time to consider these final areas of applicational truths to your life and your community.

Salvation is God's gracious gift to be received by faith in Jesus

In *Field Study 1,* as we prepared for our dig through Galatians, we asked you to consider your understanding of the gospel. We conclude now by declaring it in summary form: the gospel of Jesus Christ is God's gracious gift of salvation to be received by faith in Jesus Christ. God offers you life with him. How great is that? He wants you to receive eternal life with him and his offer is based on his divine terms alone through Jesus Christ. Salvation is by God's grace through faith. Nothing else can be added. You cannot improve on his work nor modify his terms. To do so is insulting to him. The question that remains is this: Have you received the gift of eternal life by faith in Jesus Christ? It is available to you. This is the good news of the gospel.

Live to express your love for God, not to be loved by God

Freedom from the law does not remove our responsibility to live in a godly manner. A certain lifestyle flows out of a relationship with Jesus

Paul's Writings

The Apostle Paul contributes to our understanding of the fulfilment of history in Jesus Christ. As an expert in the Old Testament Scriptures, he was the choice man to write a large part of the New Testament. Paul wrote the following letters. All are as authoritative to life as his work in Galatians:

- Galatians
- 1 and 2 Thessalonians
- 1 and 2 Corinthians
- Romans
- Ephesians
- Colossians
- Philippians
- Philemon
- 1 and 2 Timothy
- Titus

49? Jerusalem Council

50–52? Second Missionary Journey by Paul

60–62? Paul arrives in Rome under house arrest

64 Fire in Rome

70 Temple is destroyed

79 Pompeii and Herculaneum are destroyed by Vesuvius eruption

John writes Revelation 95–96?

Todd Bolen, www.BiblePlaces.com

Christ, and that lifestyle can only be called Christian if it is dependent on the Spirit by faith. God wants you to live an upright, responsible, and moral life because you love him, not because you think it will earn his favor. He cannot be bought because he's not for sale. In *Field Study 1*, we also asked you to consider the role that good, Christian works—lists of do's and don'ts—played in your life. We ask you now to consider this again. Church attendance, Christian service, tithing, Bible reading, baptism, and taking communion cannot sanctify you, only God can. However, engaging in these activities and many more in submission to his Spirit can express your devotion to God if motivated by faith. The slide toward legalism is all too common and subtle. Stand firm against it. God is not present in such a lifestyle. It is a life of bondage and sadness rather than freedom and joy. Live the Christian life of freedom God's way.

Jesus is not asking you to collaborate with him in salvation, but he wants you involved in its proclamation. Only Jesus saves. You receive and enjoy his salvation by faith. Aside from your responsibility to live well out of love for God, you are called to proclaim God's love in Christ to others by living a life of loving service.

Acts 1:8

But you will receive power when the Holy Spirit has come upon you, and you shall be my witnesses in Jerusalem, and in all Judea and Samaria, and to the end of the earth.

Then Jesus came and said to them, "All authority in heaven and on earth has been given to me. Therefore go and make disciples of all nations, baptizing them in the name of the Father and of the Son and of the Holy Spirit, teaching them to obey all that I have commanded you. And behold I am with you always, to the end of the age."

Matthew 28:18–20

This is the great privilege of every Christian. The gospel of Jesus Christ as defended and clarified by Paul in Galatians is now yours to proclaim.

Discoveries

Now that we have completed the analysis of the book of Galatians, it is time to examine carefully what we have learned and the difference it can make in our lives.

Connecting with the community

Here are some discussion questions to help you better understand the text. Do not merely reflect on them as an individual, but rather think each of each question, when applicable, in terms of your family, your community, your nation, and your church.

1. What is the contribution of Galatians to the story of the Bible?

2. What was the most critical issue that was disrupting the faith of the churches of Galatia? Could you identify the issue that is most disruptive to the faith of the members of your group or church? Is there something you can learn from this book regarding that issue?

3. Who were the Judaizers? How did their interpretation of the Old Testament and the law corrupt the message of the gospel? Are there any "Judaizers" in your community? What is it that they are seeking to add to the gospel?

4. Read the entire letter of Galatians one more time and look for the following concepts: law, grace, promise, justification, freedom, slavery, and salvation. What is the relationship that exists between these concepts?

5. On the basis of your study and analysis of the main concepts taught in this epistle, how would you summarize the true gospel? What are its essential components? Use several verses from the letter to the Galatians as the basis of your summary.

6. What does the book of Galatians teach us about the character of God? Think about this issue in the context of the importance that Galatians gives to the Word of God and to the content of the gospel.

Notes, Observations & Questions

7. How is the message of Galatians related to the person of Christ?

8. On the basis of what you have learned from the book of Galatians, what is the relationship of the Old Testament to the person and work of Christ? How does the law fit in the story of the Bible? Use texts and concepts from the book of Galatians as well as those you have learned from your study of these *Field Notes*.

9. Is the purpose of the gospel merely to justify sinners? That is, does God merely seek to grant justification to those who believe? Defend your answer from the teaching of Galatians.

10. Can a person truly believe the gospel and remain unchanged by it? Why or why not?

11. What image or artifact would best represent the book of Galatians? For example, we could say that Galatians is like a water filter, that is, a device that allows us to remove the impurities from the truly divine message of the gospel. You could also represent the book using a different image or creature. Which one would you pick?

12. On a scale of 1 to 10 with 1 representing a little and 10 representing a lot, rate again your knowledge of the book of Galatians. Did it improve over the course of this study? What will stand out in your mind one year from now when you think of the message of Galatians?

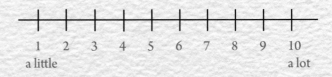

13. Learning how to summarize new information is a very important skill. Summarizing helps you to catch the essence of meaning from the text. Now that you have completed the study of the book of Galatians, enlarge the triangle chart that you see on the left. Fill it first with a summary paragraph of all of Galatians. Then narrow it into a summary sentence and finally narrow it into a phrase. Have you captured the intention of the apostle?

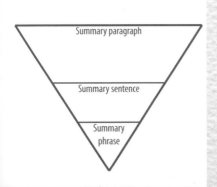

14. Now that you have summarized Galatians, it is important that you remember how this ancient letter fits in with the rest of Scripture. Create a large version of the chart on the right. The main topic is the message of Galatians. In the large box, fill in all the relevant information about the message of Galatians. Then in the largest box, tell how the message of Galatians fits into the story of Scripture. How does the book contribute to our understanding and proclamation of the gospel? In what sense is Christ the fulfillment of the message of this book? This will help you remember how Galatians contributes to the story of Scripture.

> What does Galatians teach us about the gospel of Jesus Christ?
>
> > What do I know about Galatians?
> >
> > > The message of Galatians

Probing deeper

These exercises are for your continued study of Scripture and go beyond the text of Galatians. They trace themes found in Galatians through other parts of Scripture.

1. Go back to page 14 of the *Discoveries* section of *Field Study 1* and complete your prediction chart by writing the actual problem in the Galatian churches. Was it what you expected? Does this teach you anything about how God works?

2. Why was it important for the apostle Paul to establish the validity of his apostleship? Discuss how the church in the present can validate the message of its leaders. What is our final source of authority? What is the standard of truth against which we can measure the truthfulness of our teachers and pastors?

3. Consider the attitude of the apostle Paul and the seriousness with which he addressed any alteration of the gospel. Compare this attitude to that of your church or denomination. Is the purity of the gospel the most pressing and relevant issue protected in your church or denomination? If not, what is the most pressing issue? Is that issue more important than the gospel?

4. Read and prayerfully meditate on Hebrews 10:1–24; 12:18–24. Can you describe in your own words the way in which the book of Galatians is an extended proclamation of the truths of these passages of the book of Hebrews? Write a prayer, poem, or song giving glory to God and expressing your gratitude to Jesus for his gracious and loving work on your behalf. Follow Galatians 1:24 giving glory to God because of the true gospel.

Notes, Observations & Questions

5. Write down five major lessons you have learned throughout the course of this study. For each thing that you have learned, describe at least one practical implication that such teaching will have in your daily life.

6. How would you start a conversation about the gospel with an unbeliever using the book of Galatians? Write down a paragraph that would show the beginning of your conversation. Start the paragraph with the message of Galatians and connect it to the person of Christ.

Bringing the story to life

Now that you have read through the entire book of Galatians, it is important to teach this book to someone else. This is one of the most effective forms of learning. It may be that you want to work through it with a friend or a family member, one on one. You may want to teach Galatians in your church or Bible study group. You may teach children at Sunday school or even your own kids at home. How could you creatively communicate God's message? Could you use a picture, a logo, a song, or a rhyme? Is there an object or illustration that would help to communicate the message? It is very important that you plan your lesson. What concepts do you want your students to understand? What themes in Galatians will you teach? Once you are ready, try it out!

Memorizing the key

Commit to memory the key phrase for the entire book of Galatians. The key phrase for Galatians is:

> Salvation is God's gift received and lived by faith

Go back and review all thirteen key phrases. The key phrases represent the basic message of the book in each section. They are meant to be a reminder of what the letter of Galatians is about. If you have taken the time to memorize the key phrases in order, then you will know the basic flow and message of the book of Galatians. If you do this with multiple books in the Bible, you will be able to recall quickly where the biblical authors address the various issues of Scripture.

Observation journaling

Developing a habit of writing what you have studied is a very helpful part of learning. Now, it is important for you to read Galatians in your own Bible and mark the key structures, terms, and meaning of each section. By transferring to your Bible what you have learned in this study, you will always be able to review what you have learned regarding the meaning of the text and its application. The process will also reinforce what you have learned. If you do not like to write in your Bible, create a piece of paper that you can insert and keep in your Bible. Consider the following practices anytime you read God's Word:

Before you read

Always work at linking information that you already know with what you are learning. Anytime you come to a passage, review the context, the author, and any other information you might already know to prepare you to learn more.

While you are reading

Every time you read the biblical text, mark the text with questions, key terms, notes, and structures. Keep in mind the guidelines on the art of active learning section, page xi at the beginning of your *Field Notes* to create a habit of active reading, learning and marking the text effectively.

After you have read

As soon as you have finished reading, write down any questions that you may have that were not answered in Galatians. Why do you think God left those questions unanswered? Are they answered in other parts of Scripture? Create a journal that records your thoughts about what you are learning. Be sure to continue to review and reread in order to master the material.

Pray

Write a prayer, psalm, or poem to God capturing his message in Galatians. What is the glorious gospel message that cannot be tampered with? Pray for the effect of the gospel on the worldwide Church, your church, nation, community, family, and yourself. We have provided a sample prayer on the following page. Use it as a guide for your prayer.

Notes, Observations & Questions

Heavenly Father

I thank you for the contribution the book of Galatians makes to the story of Scripture for it is so clear, instructive, and relevant to my life. I have heard your voice loud and clear. I realize you are not looking for copartners in salvation. That salvation is your gift to be received by faith. I also realize you desire that I live out my relationship with you in Christ also by faith. I now know that you want me to live the Christian life as an expression of my love for you not try to buy your love. Your love was never for sale. Forgive me for acting as if it were. I pray that you would help your church live out the gospel in a manner that represents you. Help us to proclaim your offer of life according to your terms. Also help me do it in how I live and participate within my family, my church, my community and my nation. I love you God. I come to you in prayer only by faith in the Lord Jesus Christ. Amen.

Glossary

Term	Definition
Abrahamic Covenant	A key covenant to understanding Scripture. Recorded in the story of Abraham in Genesis 12–22. This covenant speaks of God's promise of land, descendants, and blessing. It was made with Abraham and his seed, whom Christians believe to be Jesus Christ. The ultimate fulfillment of God's promises to Abraham are realized in and through Jesus Christ.
ad hominem	A type of argument which belittles the credibility of an individual in order to discredit his/her message.
Anathema	The word literally means, accursed. In the Bible, it is used of any person or thing that has been set aside for destruction as the result of divine punishment.
Antinomianism	It literally means, against the law. It refers to the idea that a Christian is under no obligation to live by any moral code since salvation is by grace alone through faith alone. It is often used in a derogatory fashion to proclaim that a Christian can live as he/she pleases (lawlessly) because he/she is under no obligation to keep God's law.
Antioch in Pisidia	A city in ancient Asia Minor territory (modern Turkey) to be distinguished from Antioch on the Orontes (Antioch in Syria).
Antioch on the Orontes	A large city in ancient Syria (modern Turkey) situated by the Orontes river. It was the apostle Paul's hometown after his conversion to Christianity. It was the departing city of all three missionary trips of the apostle Paul.
Apocrypha	Books written in the period between the Old and New Testaments and rejected by Protestant and Jewish traditions regarding their inspiration and canonicity. They were not officially included in any Christian canon until the Roman Catholic Church added them at the Council of Trent in 1546.
Aramaic	An ancient Semitic language in the same family as Hebrew.
Asia Minor	The ancient region of the Roman Empire roughly located in the same territory of modern day Turkey.
Augustine of Hippo	A philosopher and theologian who lived in the early fifth century A.D. in North Africa. He is an important theologian of the first two millennia of history of Christianity because his writings significantly shaped the development of Christendom, particularly in the West.
Badges (of Judaism)	An extrabiblical idea used to describe the emblems that were unofficially recognized as the marks of a good Jew.
Barnabas	Traveling companion and original mentor of the apostle Paul. According to the book of Acts, Barnabas and Paul made their first missionary journey together.
Byzantine Empire	The Byzantine Empire was the name of the eastern portion of the Roman Empire after the split from the western part early in the 4th century. It lasted in some form until the middle of the fifteenth century with its capital in Byzantium, later renamed Constantinople.
Christ	Title of the Anointed One who was to come and bring deliverance. The term is synonymous with Messiah. Christians believe that the Messiah/Christ is Jesus. The belief is reflected in the constant usage of the title Jesus Christ in the New Testament.
Christian	A name given to a person who believes in Jesus Christ, the Son of God is the redeemer of mankind. The term was first applied to the disciples in Antioch of Syria after Paul and Barnabas had taught there for about one year. See Acts 11:26.
Circumcision	The God-ordained act of cutting off the male foreskin as a sign of membership in the people of Israel. Given to Abraham in Genesis 17.

Term	Definition
Councils of Orange	The location of two important gatherings of church leaders in France (A.D. 441/529) discussing issues of church doctrine and practice, in particular the concepts of election, free will, sin, and grace.
Covenant	A formal agreement between two parties.
Day of Atonement	A special day in the Jewish annual calendar where the sins of the nation where atoned for through a sacrifice made by the High Priest on behalf of the nation. In order to accomplish the atonement the priest had to enter into the inner chamber of the tabernacle in the Temple of God.
Dietary prohibitions	The set of abstention rules imposed by some Jewish believers. Its purpose was to enforce the dietary rules regarding banned meals in the Old Testament law.
Doxology	A brief expression of praise to God, which became a traditional expression of Christian worship through the ages.
Essenes	A Jewish group dedicated to God through the rejection of worldly allurements and pleasures. They flourished from the second century B.C. to the first century A.D.
Feasts	God-ordained, Jewish national celebrations. The Jewish feasts are summarized in Leviticus 23.
Flesh	The capacity of every individual to live life independent of God and for one's self because of the corruption of sin. It is also described as man's sinful nature.
Galatia	A region in ancient Asia Minor (modern Turkey) referring either to a large Roman political province or to a smaller ancient geographical area. Scholars have proposed both interpretations with respect to the addressees of the biblical letter of Galatians.
Gamaliel	A leading first century A.D. Jewish scholar from the sect of the Pharisees.
Gentiles	Biblical term used to describe all peoples not of Jewish descent.
Glorification	The final consummation of Christian salvation. God´s promise of salvation in the Bible will reach its climax when a believer's transformation from sinfulness to righteousness is finally complete. It will only happen after the resurrection when the Christian is in the presence of God.
Gospel	The phrase literally means "good news." It can be used in several ways. In general, the gospel is that eternal life with God is available again. Specifically, the gospel refers to the basis upon which eternal life with God is made available, that is, the death and resurrection of Jesus Christ. At times the term is also used to refer to the New Testament books of Matthew, Mark, Luke, and John—the Gospels.
Grace	In simple terms, grace is an unmerited favor. In the Bible, grace is the foundation upon which God offers salvation to mankind. Salvation is therefore an undeserved gift, bestowed by God upon anyone who believes in the gospel of Christ.
Herodotus (484–425 B.C.)	An ancient Greek historian known as the father of history.
High Priest	The chief mediating priest between Israel and God under the covenant with Moses.
James the Just	One of the most prominent figures of the early Church. He was one of the leaders of the church in Jerusalem. He was also the half-brother of Jesus.
Jerusalem Council	The first important gathering of the church leaders in Jerusalem around A.D. 49.
Josephus	A first century A.D. Jewish historian. His writings constitute some of the most important extra biblical sources on ancient Jewish practices and beliefs.
Judaism	The religious system of belief and lifestyle for the Jewish people.

Term	Definition
Judaizers	A term used to describe those seeking to enforce upon Christians a Jewish lifestyle—particularly adherence to the Law of Moses and the rite of circumcision.
Justification	God's declaration of righteousness on an individual who has faith in Jesus Christ.
Law	A term widely used in the Bible to describe several important things: First, the term is used to describe the first five books of the Old Testament: Genesis, Exodus, Leviticus, and Deuteronomy. The law is also used to describe the covenant between God and Israel established through Moses at Mount Sinai. Finally, it is also used in reference to the actual laws that were part of the Mosaic covenant, that is, the Ten Commandments.
Legalism	A mindset in which one seeks to live the Christian life based on certain human standards of conduct in an attempt to gain salvation or favor from God.
Licentiousness	Licentiousness is living the Christian life indulging in sin with the presumption that this is permissible because God will forgive by his mercy anyway.
Love Feast	A Christian religious meal closely associated with the celebration of Communion, or Eucharist practiced by the early church.
Martin Luther	A German monk and biblical scholar who was the original leading figure of the Protestant Reformation of the 16th century.
Messiah	Term originally used to designate the king of Israel. Literally, means anointed. The king was anointed with oil at the moment of his accession to the throne, thus he was called messiah. In the New Testament, this title is assigned to Christ as the anointed Son of God.
Midrash	A Jewish approach to interpreting biblical stories, which seeks to fill in details and meanings in Scripture that the biblical stories do not explicitly teach. Many such interpretations have been codified in written form to become part of Jewish literature.
Mishnah	A written form of Jewish oral traditions.
Mosaic Covenant	A conditional covenant made between God and Israel by the mediation of Moses at Mount Sinai. It is also known as the Sinai Covenant. Obedience to the covenant brought God's blessing and disobedience brought his discipline. The covenant was God's gracious guidance for life for Israel under his rule so that they would represent him to the nations.
Nicaea	The location where an important council of Christian leaders gathered in 325 A.D. to discuss the doctrine of the divine nature of Jesus Christ and his relationship with God the Father.
Northern Galatian Theory	The position that affirms that the epistle to the Galatians was written to believers who lived in the smaller ancient geographical area called Galatia (modern Turkey) sometime after Paul's second missionary journey.
Paul/Saul	A Jewish Pharisee who lived in the first century after Christ. He was the most formidable persecutor of the Christian church before becoming a leading proclaimer of the gospel.
Pelagius	A Christian writer known for his debates with Augustine concerning the doctrine of original sin and free will. To this day, the doctrinal position that denies original sin and affirms the essential goodness of mankind is called Pelagianism and has been condemned as heresy.
Pharisee	One of the major sects of Judaism of the first century. The Pharisees were particularly zealous in the keeping of the traditions and observances of Israel, especially the application of the law.
Philo	A first century A.D. Jewish philosopher and historian.

Term	Definition
Primus inter pares	A Latin phrase used to describe the most senior member of a group of individuals sharing the same rank or office. It means first among equals. The concept describes the fact that in a group of equals there is usually one who by way of personality, age, giftedness, charisma, or group choice naturally rises as a leader of his peers.
Protestantism	The branch of Christianity that had its origins in the Reformation of the 16th century. The term is not related to any of the main tenants of the Reformation, which was a general call against the authority of the Roman Catholic Pope in favor of the sole authority of the Bible and its teaching on salvation by means of faith alone.
Redemption	A biblical concept used to describe the ransom paid to free something or someone for a price. With respect to salvation, it refers to the price paid by God to purchase and deliver mankind from its enslavement to sin.
Reformation	The Reformation refers to 16th century movement that led to the division of Western Christianity into Protestants and Roman Catholics. The movement of reform was led by individuals such as Martin Luther and John Calvin who protested against many of the doctrines and practices of the Church in the Late Middle Ages.
Sabbath	Jewish weekly day of rest mandated in the 10 commandments. Its celebration served as a constant reminder of God's work and rest patterned in his creation. The Sabbath was therefore the seventh day of the Jewish week and was the sign of the Mosaic Covenant.
Sacrificial system	The group of ceremonial sacrifices ordained by God to Israel as a gracious means to cover the guilt and punishment for sins. The sacrificial system included different types of offerings to God. They are described in detail primarily in Leviticus 1–7.
Sadducees	An aristocratic Jewish group of social, political, and religious influence who became responsible for maintaining the Jerusalem Temple during the times of the New Testament. This Jewish sect was characterized by their rationalism.
Salvation	Deliverance from the presence, power, and penalty of sin unto eternal life with God.
Sanctification	The process by which a Christian progresses in holiness by the operation of the Holy Spirit in his or her life. In this sense, sanctification is the work of God making a person righteous so that he or she can be in reality what he or she already is legally and positionally (justified). Sanctification is therefore the present, continuous aspect of Christian salvation.
Sin	Any action, thought or intention that departs from the will of God as expressed in the Bible. The word is also used to describe the general state of moral and physical corruption of all of mankind and creation in general as the result of Adam's disobedience.
Southern Galatian Theory	The position that affirms that the epistle to the Galatians was written to believers who gathered in churches in the southern region of the large Roman province of Galatia (modern Turkey) after Paul's first missionary journey.
Timothy	A half-Jewish convert, disciple, and the missionary traveling companion of the apostle Paul. He was originally from the city of Lystra in Asia Minor. The Bible includes two letters addressed to him by Paul.
Titus	A missionary traveling companion of the apostle Paul. He was a Gentile. The New Testament letter of Titus is addressed to him.
Trinity	The Christian doctrine of the Trinity teaches that the one true God exists in three distinct Persons—Father, Son, and Holy Spirit. Each distinct Person of the Godhead has distinct roles in the plan of salvation, but they are all co-equal.
Walk	Idiom used in the Bible for how an individual lives or behaves in life. A particular lifestyle is thus described as a walk of life.